EXPLOR ATIONS

British Sociological Association conference volume series

*Published by Macmillan

Methodological Imaginations

Edited by

E. Stina Lyon
Division of Sociology
South Bank University
London

and

Joan Busfield
Department of Sociology
University of Essex
Colchester

First published 1996 by
MACMILLAN PRESS LTD
Houndmills, Basingstoke, Hampshire RG21 6XS
and London
Companies and representatives
throughout the world

ISBN 0–333–63091–2 hardcover
ISBN 0–333–63092–0 paperback

A catalogue record for this book is available from the British Library.

10   9   8   7   6   5   4   3   2   1
05 04 03 02 01 00 99 98 97 96

Printed and bound in Great Britain by
Antony Rowe Ltd, Chippenham, Wiltshire

Contents

List of Plates

Notes on the Contributors

Joan Busfield is a Professor of Sociology at the University of Essex. She initially trained as a clinical psychologist; her main area of research is psychiatry and mental disorder. Her publications include *Managing Madness: Changing Ideas and Practice* (1986) and *Men, Women and Madness: Understanding Gender and Mental Disorder* (1996).

Paul Connolly is currently Lecturer in Sociology at Magee College, University of Ulster. His research interests lie in the area of culture, ethnicity and identity and especially in exploring the ways in which cultural identities are formed and reproduced within the articulation of discourses on 'race' and ethnicity, gender, class and age. He has published a number of articles in this area and is currently completing a book, *Growing Up in the Inner City: Racism, Cultural Identities and the Primary School*, to be published in 1996.

Geoff Cooper is a Lecturer in Sociology at the University of Surrey and was formerly a research fellow at CRICT (the Centre for Research into Innovation, Culture and Technology), Brunel University. His research interests, which lie within science and technology studies and social theory, include the rhetorical constitution of disciplinary identity, and the changing character of research culture.

Sheila Galloway is a Research Fellow in the Centre for Educational Development, Appraisal and Research (CEDAR) at the University of Warwick. She had conducted research on in-service training and professional development, curriculum evaluation, technology in training and supply teaching. She previously completed comparative research on sociological aspects of vocational education in England and France. A joint author of *Implementing In-service Education and Training* (1993), she co-edited *The Supply Story: Professional Substitutes in Education* (1994).

Barbara Harrison is a Reader in the Sociology of Health and Illness at NESCOT, Epsom's Higher and Further Education College, and has taught research methodology on undergraduate and postgraduate Master's courses for many years. She is particularly involved with developing qualitative research methodologies, especially visual and biographical approaches, and in ideas of practitioner research. Her other interests include historical aspects of health and welfare and the sociology of health and illness, particularly women's health. Her most recent research has been concerned with women and occupational ill-health in late-nineteenth- and early-twentieth-century Britain, published as *Not Only the Dangerous Trades: Women and Occupational Ill-Health, 1880–1914* (1995).

A. Mark Liddle is a Research Fellow at the Institute of Criminology, University of Cambridge, and Research and Policy Development Officer at the London Office of NACRO (National Association for the Care and Resettlement of Offenders), where he is conducting a three-year evaluation of community safety strategies in a large local authority area. He has published articles on crime prevention, multi-agency work, and child sexual abuse. His current research interests include masculinity and state-formation, and urban community safety and modernity.

E. Stina Lyon is Principal Lecturer in Sociology at the South Bank University. Her research and teaching expertise are in the areas of education and sociological research methodology. Her most recent research was on the relationship between higher education and the labour market, published as *Students, Courses and Jobs* with J. Brennan, P. McGeevor and K. Murphy.

Marlene Morrison is a Research Fellow in CEDAR at the University of Warwick. She is currently engaged in an ESRC-funded project on teaching and learning about food and nutrition in schools. Previous research has focused on in-service training, school development plans, supply teaching, and libraries in primary schools. Research interests span gender and time-focused issues in education. She contributes to postgraduate, INSET and research methods courses, and to development programmes for teachers. Articles and reports reflect her research interests. A joint author of *Implementing In-service Education and Training* (1993), she co-edited (with Sheila Galloway) *The Supply Story: Professional Substitutes in Education* (1994).

Geoff Payne is Dean of Human Sciences and Professor at the University of Plymouth. He has recently completed research in the Scottish Highlands. His latest book is *Sociology in Action* (edited with Malcolm Cross, 1993).

Anthony Pryce originally intended to be an art historian but surprised himself and others by becoming a nurse. He specialised in mental health, before taking his Masters in Sociology of Health at South Bank where he first realised how he could revisit art with a sociological gaze. He is now Director of Research at St Bartholomew and Princess Alexandra College (City University) and is undertaking his PhD in the Department of Sociology at the University of Essex. The research is concerned with the social construction of male sexualities in genito-urinary medicine.

Monder Ram is Senior Lecturer in the Management Department of the University of Central England in Birmingham. He has worked in, researched, and acted as a consultant to small firms, particularly ethnic minority businesses. He is also author of *Managing to Survive: Working Lives in the Small Firms* (1994).

Karen Ramsay is a Lecturer in Women's Studies at Bradford and Ilkley Community College. Her PhD, supervised through Staffordshire University, explores academic cultures and equality of opportunity for women academics and will be completed this year. Her interests include the study of sexuality and emotions in organisations and feminist methodologies.

Jenny Shaw is a sociologist in the School of Cultural and Community Studies at the University of Sussex. In addition to mass-observation, her research interests include shopping and the role of chain stores, time and the pace of life, gender and education, equal opportunities in the workplace and the application of psychoanalytic concepts to sociological issues.

Susan Smith is Senior Lecturer at NESCOT College of Higher and Further Education, where she teaches on research methods and teacher education courses. She completed her PhD on women's return to study experiences in 1993, and is currently developing her interest in the use of autobiography in teaching and research.

Steve Woolgar is Professor of Sociology and Director of CRICT (Centre for Research into Innovation, Culture and Technology) at Brunel University. He has published widely in social studies of science and technology including *Science: The Very Idea* (1988), *Knowledge and Reflexivity* (1988) and *Representation in Scientific Practice* (with M. Lynch, 1990). He is currently completing *Deus Ex Machina* (with K. Grint) and is researching the textual and reflexive dimensions of information technology.

Introduction

E. Stina Lyon and Joan Busfield

In putting together this volume of essays, selected from those submitted to the annual conference of the British Sociological Association in 1993, we have attempted to illustrate how changing conceptions of social research are finding an expression in the methodological consciousness of researchers and their research practices. The title of the conference, 'Research Imaginations', as several of the contributors note, in itself points to the inherent contradictions in academic work between the rule-bound, rational, rigorous and systematic activity called methods of inquiry, and the more personal, creative, critical and diverse leaps into the unknown afforded by the imagination. Although not always to immediate productive effect, it is through the combination of the two that disciplinary horizons are extended and path-breaking scholarship is generated. This was the view of C. Wright Mills, whose influential study *The Sociological Imagination* (1959) provided the inspiration both for the conference and this particular collection of papers.

Sociologists' methodological strategies have always varied considerably and have been shaped and structured both by their theoretical inclinations and their substantive concerns. In our view two developments have helped to emphasise once again the contribution of the imagination to the socio-logical endeavour. On the one hand, feminist theorising (see, for example, Ramazanoglu 1989; Smith 1988) has directed our attention to the significance of the realms of experience: to the private, the personal, the emotional, the subjective. On the other hand, post-modern theorising (Bauman 1992; Smart 1992), which emphasises the eclectic, pluralistic, situated and in essence *creative* nature of the social and cultural world, literary or scientific, has once more brought imaginative processes to atten-tion. Both have encouraged a new focus on ethnographic techniques (Hammersley and Atkinson 1983; Hammersley 1991) and new ideas about sources of data in sociological work that can provide more adequate inform-ation about experience, meaning and culture. There has, however, been little attempt to bring together essays that show how some of these methods and sources are now being used in sociological research and consider some of the key issues that are raised by the new theoretical sensitivities.

The important concept of 'reflexivity' (Steier 1991), the need continu-ously to examine one's own practices, has a long history within sociology.

Its implications for the interdependence of theoretical, methodological and substantive issues have recently generated much debate. Under the post-modernist gaze whether or not a research account is 'factually correct' has, in consequence, at times come to seem of less interest than how such an account comes to be read, understood and used. Yet recognition of the importance of reflexivity does not require this 'flight from reality'. The interpretation of research activities as social acts in their own right, which has brought the notion of the 'double hermeneutic' into the heart of the sociological research enterprise itself, requires a greater self-consciousness from those who engage in research. This awareness should not just be of the social nature of the research process itself, or the plurality of voices and experiences that post-modernists have emphasised, but also of the social and political context of research and of divisions of power which structural sociologies, including Marxism, have examined and analysed.

Far from stifling the research imagination in sociology, this reflexivity, when combined with new political, theoretical and substantive concerns about the research endeavour, has helped to open up new opportunities for fresh insight in several areas of the discipline. First, it has encouraged the exploration of new, previously uncharted and marginalised terrains of the private and often hidden areas of feelings, memories, emotions, and individual experiences, not only as substantive areas of enquiry, but also as dimensions of the research process itself. The socially structured and contested nature of this private domain vindicates its inclusion in the sociological enterprise. Second, it has encouraged the development of either new or under-utilised, almost forgotten, research techniques that can provide the means for exploring some of these new domains more effectively. These include the analysis of pictures, film and art, the collection of diaries and life histories, and 'exchange' interviews (Plummer 1983; Scott 1990). Third, it has led to reconsideration of the position of the sociological researcher *vis-à-vis* those who are being researched, as well as an awareness of their role as active participants in the generation of knowledge and the uses to which this can be put. This includes not only new assessments of the advantages and problems of insider status in doing research, but also a new concern about the legitimacy and possibility of adequately studying social groups to which one does not belong.

This volume is not intended to offer practical expositions of what to do in various research situations; there are up-to-date methodologically well-informed texts (for example, Gilbert 1993) that serve this purpose. The prime aim is, instead, to explore the critical and methodologically creative ideas and strategies that help us to answer questions about 'the social' and its many manifestations in the lives of individuals.

The research described in some of these chapters should caution against convenient but false dichotomies in the design and evaluation of research. There are many of these dichotomies, which when 'reified' into technical strictures, teaching practices, academic institutional boundaries and political jargon, undervalue the enterprise of sociology. Particular examples are: theory–data, quantitative–qualitative, researcher–researched, and pure–applied. Because they are so persistent, it is worth looking at them in more detail in relation to the changing culture of research expressed in these chapters.

The first such dichotomy these chapters call into question is that between *theory and data*. In all the chapters there is a strong emphasis on theoretical analysis, both epistemological and substantive, but it is an analysis which is strongly 'data' sensitive. The essays presented here are mostly the products of completed or still ongoing empirical research projects, the substantive results of which are being published elsewhere. The assumption that observations are the final arbiters of theoretical disputes has long been challenged within sociology. As can be seen in this collection, this is not because observations are held to be unreliable and unimportant in critically evaluating theoretical speculations, but because when it comes to human observations of social phenomena there can be no such thing as a 'final' arbiter, only a continuing evaluation and re-evaluation of different kinds of evidence of varying degrees of generality, depth and abstraction. For the post-modern theoretical purists, such an engagement with the 'real world' might belie the problematic of reflexivity and the social construction of sociological knowledge. For most theorists and researchers who wish to convey an argument of substance and meaning about the social world to an audience wishing to learn, such purism is of less value than new imaginative ways of accommodating these changing conceptions when describing that world. That may, as Geoff Cooper and Steve Woolgar point out, necessitate educating the users and the audiences into what the value of that research and its 'data' might be.

The debate over the relationship between *qualitative* and *quantitative* research paradigms is of long standing in sociological research (Bryman 1988). Greater methodological pluralism and openness towards alternative methodologies has led to a much greater acceptance of the use of overlapping and mutually complementary research approaches on any given topic. Often research relies on a range of methodologies, a point that is itself transformed into a methodological strategy through concepts such as 'triangulation'. This methodological pluralism is grounded, on the one hand, in the recognition that in quantitative approaches there is an irreducible interpretative element in the naming, ordering and numbering of categories and their use in classifying complex social phenomena. On the other hand, it is grounded in the greater acceptance of the ways in which the validity of interpretative and qualitative research approaches can be enhanced through techniques ensuring coverage and comprehension (Hammersley and Atkinson 1983). A dominant theme running through these chapters is a strong sense that whatever techniques are applied in the study of social phenomena, the outcome is an interpretative product that needs continuous and varied justification.

It would be a mistake, however, as some of these chapters show, to see this greater tolerance of variety of perspectives as a simple 'add on' factor in a more pluralistic model of sociological research. It is instead one where in-depth qualitative approaches can genuinely transform the standardised and systematised breadth offered by quantitative approaches, by providing motivational understandings and access to the hidden dimension of action, as well as occasionally showing quantification to be inappropriate. The discrepancy shown by Susan Smith between the qualitative interpretation of the concept of partner 'support' in self-completion questionnaires and in in-depth interviews conducted on an exchange basis, shows the critical caution with which assertions about the egalitarianism of modern marriage has to be met. The use of solicited diaries as an important and underused technique capable of offering both coverage and depth of information about the individual social activities and perceptions is discussed in Jenny Shaw's chapter on the use of dream accounts in Mass-Observation data, and in Marlene Morrison and Sheila Galloway's report on the practical and emotional complexity of daily life for supply teachers. Both chapters point to a general quest for a less fragmented and more holistic approach to the study of social relations. This quest for a stronger appreciation of contexts over both time and place is also reflected in many other chapters, ranging from Geoff Payne's critical overview of community studies, through Monder Ram's chapter on relations in the workplace, and the contributions on visual sociology.

It is, perhaps, in the two chapters by Barbara Harrison and Anthony Pryce on the uses of visual material that the complex interrelationship between quantitative and qualitative approaches is most clearly spelled out. Visual images of all kinds are more self-evidently seen to be 'produced' in particular social contexts and for particular audiences than the written or the spoken sociological word. The reproduction of culture through visual representations – photography, film, art – is so multifaceted and surrounded by traditions, styles and genres that it is not surprising to note that, in the use and study of visual documents, there is a clear recognition of the need for a multiplicity of research strategies. Issues of selection and coverage of material, as well as the need for authenticated interpretations of latent cultural meanings and contexts cut across the uses of visual data, whether used for 'illustrative' purposes or as investigative objects in their own right (Bell and Smith 1992).

For the reflexive researcher, the separation of objects of enquiry from the subjects experiencing them is a rule of investigation fraught with uncertainties. When even so-called 'unobtrusive methods' can be seen as 'obtrusive' in the way in which hidden researcher assumptions create imposed readings and interpretations of data, then an outsider is never an insider. If, in addition, the subjects of sociological research are themselves seen as permanently in the process of interpreting and theorising about the social circumstances in which they find themselves, then the distinction between 'insider' and 'outsider' in the research process disappears, leading to a series of epistemological, practical and ethical dilemmas.

There are several methodological consequences of such changing conceptions of the *relationship between researcher and researched*. First, if the researcher is not a privileged investigator, but an inquiring participant, then insider knowledge of, and acceptance in, the field becomes important to enhance rather than lessen voices, ideas and images and to reach the more intimate spheres of social life (Harvey 1990). How a researcher's own background and experiences can be put to good use is shown by Monder Ram's work on small, minority industries. The fact that researchers have multiple characteristics, not all of which at any one time reflect 'insider' status, brings problems in the field of the kind outlined in Mark Liddle's essay on doing feminist research as a white male. As Karen Ramsay shows in her chapter, the emotional labour involved in acting as a reflexive researcher is taxing.

Second, greater reciprocity between researcher and researched becomes epistemologically essential to enable continuing cross-validations of alternative interpretations. Third, the ethical and political responsibilities in doing research deepens with such reciprocity. The need for 'humility', to adopt Payne's term, when approaching communities in conflict and individuals in pain is echoed in many of the chapters, but also the need for self-awareness. Ram's self-description is an eloquent example of such awareness, and the good methodological use to which insider status can be put in exploring the more private, hidden aspects of relations at work. To this Woolgar and Cooper add the important observation that most research is group work, and their imaginative use of dialogue is an attempt to 'unpack' researcher roles and contexts in the production of the kinds of knowledge 'packages' that sociologists are at times required to deliver.

Finally, lest it be thought that this Reader is no more than yet another set of academic reflections of theorising sociologists, it is important to note that the chapters in this volume all have an *applied* focus despite the prevalence of a self-reflexive discourse. If, with Janet Finch we see 'applied knowledge' as 'useful and usable knowledge on topics which people outside the discipline would recognise as socially important, using perspectives and methods which are recognisably sociological in character' (1993: 141), then all the chapters are on research of an applied nature. In all instances they are concerned with the traditional sociological issues of how to describe a community, a workplace, a role, a cultural practice, an image in such a way that it enlightens and helps us understand daily social relations in policy and practice, and has relevance for a range of 'users' across the social spectrum, ranging from funding agencies to individuals on the margin of society.

The first essays in this volume 'revisit' and redefine some existing techniques of data collection familiar to sociologists. Jenny Shaw takes a fresh look at the study of everyday life as originally conceived in the Mass-Observation project of the 1930s. This project, based on self-observations, continues to be a unique source of evidence about the more intimate aspects of social life in contemporary Britain. Shaw's revaluation of the psychoanalytical and surrealist theoretical underpinnings of the project, and its inherent focus on various manifestations of subjectivity in dreams, emotions, artistic creativity and imagination, belies the charge of 'mindless empiricism' often levelled against it. It also opens it up to new and interesting questions about the role of 'inner states' in producing social life. In his chapter on the community study, Geoff Payne revisits a research tool of some standing in the history of sociology. He raises a series of questions about hidden assumptions in the community study as method, such as an exaggerated focus on kinship relations, an inherent inability to deal with animosity and conflict, and contradictions in researcher roles. But he points to its potentially more positive contribution to the study of social change over time, and to the role of localities in creating and forming social identity and social responses to the universal parameters of mass society.

Marlene Morrison and Sheila Galloway provide a discussion of the strengths and weaknesses in the use of diaries in exploring the complex ways in which individuals juggle the demands of professional and personal lives. Using time grids to study the changing nature of supply teaching, they highlight the need for research approaches capable of representing the complexities of working lives in their intersection with life beyond the factory gates. They also highlight the strategies teachers devise to cope with this intersection which, especially for women, is characterised by growing interconnectedness. From a feminist perspective, Susan Smith takes a fresh look at the role of in-depth interviews in not only complementing but also seriously questioning the use of survey data in providing valid information about personal relationships. Her detailed analysis of the concept of the 'support' provided by partners of women who return to education, shows the different responses achieved when alternative methodologies are used, and the different understandings of the idea of support expressed by women and men.

The next two chapters address important new developments in the use of visual material in sociological research. Barbara Harrison gives a comprehensive overview of the many ways in which visual evidence can be employed within different theoretical paradigms, and the new vistas of historical and contemporary social life such evidence opens up. Anthony Pryce gives a more detailed case study of the use of visual material in his analysis of the symbolic representation of death, sexuality and the body in nineteenth-century art. He also examines the contribution that the 'new' art history can make to sociological research and the growing recognition of the significance of the visual in understanding the links between codes of meaning and the structure of society.

The three papers by Monder Ram, Karen Ramsay, and Geoff Woolgar and Steve Cooper all share a strong concern with the need for reflexivity in the research process, be it personal or conceptual. Both Ram and Ramsay use their own experience of doing research in the workplace to raise fundamental questions about the nature of 'insider' research, and the costs and benefits for both researcher and the project itself of close personal proximity and interactions in the fieldwork situation. For Woolgar and Cooper, reflexivity is an inherently epistemological and conceptual issue which necessitates a new style of writing about the research progress capable of reflecting the multiplicity of meanings and discourses within which researchers operate. The lively dialogue they present is both thought-provoking and unsettling in the questions it raises about the claims to the validity of the sociological evidence made by sociological researchers who serve policy makers and other users.

In the last two chapters, Mark Liddle and Paul Connolly discuss key epistemological issues at the heart of the sociological enterprise itself. How can researching sociologists in their investigations and observations transgress the complex and shifting boundaries between groups of individuals of which they are themselves members, and the structured inequality which constitutes the very topics of their studies? In his paper based on issues encountered as a white male doing feminist and anti-racist research,

Connolly offers an important critique of over-simplistic approaches to so-called 'standpoint epistemology' (Harding 1991). Though certain research settings will remain more accessible to some researchers than others, the variability of individual experiences is such, he argues, that what a researcher is doing and why remain more important than the characteristics of who is doing it.

We hope this volume of essays will give a sense of the new directions in which some areas of sociological research are moving, and the imaginative way in which researchers have tried to come to terms with the changing epistemological and ethical dimensions of the discipline. In assembling it, we have attempted to present a series of examples of research ventures which we hope and feel will provide the reader with plenty of opportunities for gaining fresh conceptual insights and practical ideas of the kind likely to enrich the craft of doing sociology.

REFERENCES

Ball, M. S. and Smith, G. W. H. (1992) *Analysing Visual Data*. London: Sage.

Bauman, Z. (1992) *Intimations of Postmodernity*. London: Routledge.

Bryman, A. (1988) *Quality and Quantity in Social Research*. London: Routledge.

Finch, J. (1993) 'Applied Sociology in the Contemporary British Context', in G. Payne and M. Cross (eds), *Sociology in Action*. London: Macmillan.

Gilbert, N. (ed.) (1993) *Researching Social Life*. London: Sage.

Hammersley, M. (1991) *Reading Ethnographic Research*. London: Longman.

Hammersley, M. and Atkinson, P. (1983) *Ethnography*. London: Tavistock.

Harding, S. (1991) *Whose Science? Whose Knowledge?* Milton Keynes: Open University Press.

Harvey, L. (1990) *Critical Social Research*. London: Unwin Hyman.

Mills, C. W. (1959) *The Sociological Imagination*. New York: Open University Press.

Plummer, K. (1983) *Documents of Life*. London: Allen & Unwin.

Ramazanoglu, C. (1989) *Feminism and the Contradictions of Oppression*. London: Routledge.

Scott, J. (1990) *A Matter of Record: Documentary Sources in Social Research*. Cambridge: Polity.

Smart, B. (1992) *Modern Conditions, Post-modern Controversies*. London: Routledge.

Smith, D. E. (1988) *The Everyday World as Problematic: A Feminist Sociology*. Milton Keynes: Open University Press.

Steier, F. (1991) *Reflexivity*. London: Sage.

1 Surrealism, Mass-Observation and Researching Imagination

Jenny Shaw

INTRODUCTION

The title of the 1993 BSA conference, 'Research Imaginations', was both a tease and a challenge. Superficially it appeared to pull in different episte-mological directions, for *research* is defined in the Oxford English Dictionary as the close study of material phenomena and *imagination* as a mental representation of something that is not physically present. *Imaginations* implies even more diversity. However, leaving aside the vast philosophical literature that comments on the origins and implications of this dualism, the title usefully focused on a tension between the two words and opened up a space in which the place of imagination in research could be discussed. Moreover, it is a 'lost space' in which an embryonic sociol-ogy of the emotions was once located and could, if it wanted to, figure again.

While psychologists study creativity, affect and imagination, sociolo-gists tend to regard such phenomena as marginal. Of course, much research is 'imaginative' in the sense of being innovative or cleverly con-ceived, but in common sense terms there is an insecurity and volatility about 'imagination' and 'emotion' that seems at odds with the meticulous and cautious procedures that characterise well regarded 'research'. Wise men and women choose safer topics and leave the study of imagination well alone, or to literary critics. At least, they have done so for a long time, though it was not always the case. This paper will argue that a leaf could, and should, be taken out the book of Mass-Observation (M-O), as it was conceived in 1930s Britain, when imagination was allowed to play a central role in the process of sociological research.[1]

As a project centrally concerned with the study of everyday life M-O has been criticised for being atheoretical: the classic example, perhaps, of mindless empiricism. Yet there was, in fact, a very sophisticated model of

1

social life lying behind it, even if it was not always spelt out. This stemmed from the close association, in the early days, of M-O with Surrealism and, like Surrealism, with the central place it accorded to unconscious processes. Everyday life was not taken at face value, but was assumed to be the product of many complex forces, including unconscious ones. Like many intellectuals of the time, those associated with M-O fused an interest in the everyday with an interest in psychoanalysis and this led, directly, to some of the more exciting of the early M-O projects, such as those which collected dreams, day dreams and 'dominant images'. Though never finished, and later disavowed, many of these could well be revived and placed within a broader comparative, historical and cross-cultural study of changing patterns of subjectivity. For it is in the area of understanding feelings, emotion and how they affect everyday life that much of the research potential of M-O lies. Because of the particular, and peculiar, conditions under which people write for it, M-O offers a chance to harness imaginative capacities and explore the meanings of life in the modern world on a scale, and with a degree of detail and intimacy, that is impossible using more conventional research techniques.

Making imagination and unconscious processes central to its programme of social investigation was only one of many social science innovations that can be traced to M-O. These include starting what is now regarded as 'participatory research', applying an ethnographic approach to a Western industrialised society and inventing 'critical incident' analysis. The ethnographic contributions are generally attributed to Tom Harrisson, the best-known of the three founders, but the other two, the artist, poet and documentary film maker Humphrey Jennings, and the poet Charles Madge, put a spin on the project which, had it not been deflected by the Second World War, might have led M-O and British social science into a very different direction. Both Madge and Jennings were deeply involved in the Surrealist movement and saw M-O as a way of pursuing their Surrealist inspired aesthetic and political goals. If Surrealism and sociology appear to be light years apart from each other, this paper contends that they are not, and that M-O is the link.

In the person of Humphrey Jennings, the central thesis of Surrealism, that there is a 'hidden' reality just as important as any 'manifest' reality, was allied to a determination to study 'ordinary' everyday life sociologically. For a moment, the dominant, rationalist model of social life was almost toppled. A convergence of Surrealism and sociology on an understanding that life is largely determined by irrational and subconscious factors and that it can be studied empirically seems, with hindsight, a lost opportunity. Fifty years later, psychoanalytic ideas are no longer very radical or threatening and unconscious processes are accepted as playing a part in most social institutions (Rustin 1991). Although there are still many whose scepticism rests on the difficulty of testing psychoanalytical hypotheses empirically (Gellner 1985; Borger and Cioffi 1970), the positivist hold on sociology has loosened. Methods, such as M-O, that may once have seemed insufficiently rigorous, are re-evaluated for the very reason that they are flexible and can access aspects of the emotions that are unavailable through more conventional, predetermined and static methods.

Although Surrealism got going as an artistic movement before M-O, both came out of the same general social disquiet. As social movements they shared similar aims, namely, to overturn existing frames of reference and hierarchies (the art and sociology 'establishments' respectively). The desire to be subversive was not simply irresponsible or anarchic, it was because disruption and shock were valued as methods of perception. Both movements were interested in what surprised, in how unconscious processes intruded into conscious life, and in the boundaries and barriers between them. In other words, both were interested in the liminal, in repression and contradiction, or the 'underside' of life. This concern with boundaries led M-O to be particularly interested in escape, holidays and leisure and, again, to pre-date sociological work such as Cohen and Taylor's (1976) *Escape Attempts*. Jennings, especially, brought to M-O a concern with what 'moved' people, with rupture, breaks to routine, all that would now be called 'transgressive'; M-O allowed him to fuse his documentary and artistic interests and raised the question of the connection between 'art' and 'society'.

SOCIOLOGY AND ART

Jennings's belief that art and sociology were indivisible and mutually implicated underpinned the whole M-O project. It led, quite naturally, to a belief that artistic and sociological methods converged and, as Nick Stanley (1979) terms it, to 'artistic reportage'. Though critical of theories of 'proletarian art', M-O believed in the possibility of a workers' aesthetic; hence the Ashington experiment which set miners to paint (Feaver 1988) and sent photographers and artists into the community in the belief that, with a little encouragement, the artistic impulses of the population would emerge. What was probably only implicit in this scenario was the idea that artistic expression was an especially effective way of studying the emotional infrastructure of a society. Yet, as we learn more of the reasons why people write for M-O, and see it as one among a number of possible discursive practices, instead of worrying that the M-O writers are not 'representative' enough in categorical terms, we may come to see that the way in which they are unrepresentative (i.e. they write for M-O and are driven by some form of artistic impulse) is the reason that they, and their material, is so valuable.[2]

The idea of an affinity between art and sociology is not new. Robert Nisbet (1965) thought the roots of sociology actually lay in Romantic art and the revolt against the rationalist view of man and society, whilst Simmel's style of sociology has been classified as a form of Impressionism (Frisby 1991). Many more have stressed that there is no real difference in the creative process, whatever its product, art or science, though it is less usual to extend artistic methods to the social sciences. Yet there is a quality of attention and receptiveness to internal and external stimuli, a capacity to really 'observe', to suspend familiar frameworks, an openness to new views, and an opportunism that sees, and seizes, chance relationships which is characteristic of art work and needs recognising and valuing. In recent years, under the impact of post-modernism, confidence in the possibility of finding and holding to coherent accounts of society has diminished and, with this, notions of fragmentation and fracture have become more central; themselves a form of structure. Many of these insights were around fifty years or so ago and we may be only just returning to the point the Surrealists and M-O were at in 1937.

MASS-OBSERVATION AND THE SURREALISTS

The Surrealists' belief in a hidden reality, which had to be accessed through the unconscious, led them to be methodologically inventive. The methods they chose, self-analysis, dream work, free association were, of course, derived from psychoanalysis, which was sweeping through the intelligentsia at the time (see, for example, the autobiographical work of Marion Milner 1934, 1937), and depended on the hope that they could liberate repressed thoughts and reveal obscure connections. But the leap made by Jennings, Madge and Harrisson was to extend such enquiries beyond self-selected 'patients' or coteries of friends, such as those that clustered around André Breton and Paul Eluard to study sexuality (Pierret 1992), and collect and study a broader range of data.

They were first to take 'everyday life' and 'ordinary people' seriously, pre-dating later sociologists such as Goffman, Garfinkel, and de Certeau. They also pre-dated the structuralists of the seventies in being concerned with hidden meanings and structural relations. They regarded images and metaphors worthy of systematic study long before they became favoured tools of modern management consultants (Morgan 1993) or academic social science (Lakoff and Johnson 1980).

The relations between the part and the whole were not viewed as given, but as mutable. Out of a kaleidoscopic vision different patterns could be seen. If the viewer/researcher re-positioned themselves many more of the properties bound up in the object viewed could be seen. Bizarre juxtaposition and paradox were essential to setting off a trail of enquiry. For example, the first observers were invited to report on the following:

behaviour of people at war memorials
shouts and gestures of motorists
the aspidistra cult
anthropology of football people
bathroom behaviour
ears, armpits and eyebrows
anti-semitism
distribution, diffusion and significance of the dirty joke
funerals and undertakers
female taboos about eating
the private lives of midwives

This list, as has often been noted, reads like a Surrealist poem.

Jennings and Madge's book *May 12th* (1937), about the eve of the Coronation, was an ambitious project that sought to describe the mood of the nation, capture the collective unconscious and pin down the symbolic and emotional meaning of the Coronation. Assembled from detailed reports from observers, a mobile reporting squad and a questionnaire that was randomly leafleted and asked 'What did you do, see, think about?', 'What were "stirring" incidents?', 'What did your neighbours say about the Coronation?', it describes the events of the day, the public celebrations, the jokes, the ribaldry and the night-time goings-on that led up to it.

As a documentary film maker, Jennings depended on the notion of long-shots and close-ups, detail and ensemble and used this in his social interpretation though, as a text, it was left to speak for itself, with little in the way of gloss or interpretation. Jennings and Madge defended the early publication on the grounds that they had an obligation to give the observers, and potential observers, an opportunity to comment and contribute to the analysis. M-O was keen to be democratic, participatory and to break down the divide between the researcher and his/her subject. The organisers were uncomfortable about privileging the interpretations of the researcher over the subjects, although they did venture into interpretation as when Jennings and Madge discussed in Freudian terms the undertow of 'sinister' feelings around the Coronation in which they linked feelings about the King to a rash of horror/war stories (1937: 94). To a considerable degree M-O achieved the sense of common purpose it sought, as illustrated by one observer who, on visiting a Surrealist exhibition and being annoyed at the tone of the catalogue, notes with relief that Jennings was not part of it.

However, this sense of common purpose was not to last, as M-O was overtaken by the Second World War, its research objectives deflected and its organisation co-opted by the Home Office. The genuine interest in what lay on the borders of consciousness got misinterpreted and fed into fears about 'snooping'. Stung by criticisms that reflected the desire to make social science as 'scientific' as possible (Firth 1939), M-O dropped its artistic leanings and its most creative aspects. Madge and Harrisson grew embarrassed by the widely perceived link between M-O and Surrealism and turned away from the more imaginative side of the project. The Surrealist connection and visionary quality was lost (Stanley 1979), and what could have been a promising start to a grounded sociology of the emotions was also lost.

M-O AND THE SOCIOLOGY OF THE EMOTIONS

The dark ages in the sociology of the emotions is conventionally explained as the result of a long, dominant, Weberian stress on rationality that only cracked under the onslaught of post-modernism. Though now reinstated as a suitable subject (Hochschild 1983; Jackson 1993; Giddens 1991) there is a lot of methodological catching-up to do. Fortunately, the M-O is, once again, instructive. The writing produced for the M-O is an unusually good source of data on emotional, subjective and intimate matters and a place, or a space, in which imagination can be put to work.

M-O no longer collects observations of others, it concentrates wholly on self-observation through diaries (sometimes for just one nominated day, sometimes for longer) and responses to a 'directive' which is a theme, usually suggested by the Archivist, but occasionally by another researcher, which invites the correspondents to write fairly freely around the theme. Crucial to the quality and the production of the M-O data is the relation-ship that the writers have with the Archive and the imaginary relationship that they have with the Archivist or other staff. The whole project is con-ducted with a high degree of confidentiality, personal trust, reliability and continuity. People write in privacy, knowing that their writing will be read and acknowledged. The very absence of fact-to-face contact, for the most part, both 'frees up' the writing and encourages it to range widely around matters of personal importance and intimacy, a sort of 'free association' on paper. In all but name these conditions amount to the pre-conditions for basic psychotherapy and may facilitate a form of transference (Shaw 1994) which, in turn, generates the sort of material that comes up in psychotherapy.

However, very few sociologists are trained therapists or analysts and therefore do not have easy access to the inner states of the people they study; though few doubt that in many methods the researcher himself/herself is a key instrument. Still, it is one thing to be alert to 'interviewer effect' and quite another to take seriously the unconscious dimensions of research. There is little contemporary discussion of unconscious processes as method in themselves. Hunt (1989) discusses the psychoanalytic aspects of fieldwork and Levine (1981) considers dreams that informants have about the researcher as data, whilst Figlio (1988) argues that whenever a person is interviewed as a representative of a group, attention should be paid to the unconscious projections and idealisations which are a normal part of group processes. But in general this remains relatively uncharted territory for sociologists. Whilst the trust condition ensures a certain veracity, there are also aspects of writing for, and researching in, the M-O Archive that are anxiety-making and lead to defensive reactions (Devereux 1967). Such defences can affect the writer, the archivist and the researcher, and all are crucial to any interpretation of the data. In one sense this amounts to no more than recognising that any fieldworker must attend to their own responses (Wilkins 1993; Okely and Callaway 1992). What is new(ish) territory is the explicit study of the unconscious as data, both in terms of its effects on the researcher, and its products, e.g. dreams, metaphors, imagination.

DREAMS, METAPHORS AND THE IMAGINATION

The broad purpose of re-examining the contribution of M-O to sociology, in the light of its links with Surrealism, has been to explore how imagination can be researched and exploited for research purposes and to encourage readers to think creatively about how the M-O data might be used. When M-O collected dreams, day dreams and 'dominant images' in the 1930s it planned to compare war-time dreams with peace-time dreams. This analysis was never completed, but the idea of studying how people process frightening and traumatic events in different social contexts was an inspired one. By immense good fortune, Charlotte Beradt's (1966) *The Third Reich of Dreams* deals with dreams collected from German citizens over the same period and, in principle, allows a crucial cross-cultural comparison to be made. Assuming that dreams process social as well as individual experience it should be possible to see how people located in different social structures deal with, or internalise, crises of various sorts. Dreams collected in Germany in the 1930s could be compared to dreams collected by M-O in 1939–40 or, as the M-O writers were again asked to submit dreams in 1992, with dreams now, when everyone sees on their televisions the horrors of Sudan, Kurdistan, Somalia and Bosnia.

Dreams collected in this way cannot be 'interpreted' as they would in a conventional analytical setting, as the 'royal road to the unconscious' because the researcher cannot know the personal and idiosyncratic meanings of their content. But if particular images and themes are repeatedly described in certain ways it might be possible to detect patterns in response to major social threats. Connecting the public and the private, the mundane and the horrific, the global and the local at a personal level is a theme mentioned in most accounts of late modernity and a task that modern man and woman cannot avoid (Giddens 1990; Beck 1992). It clearly depends on the view that unconscious processes affect everyday life, though how this is to be studied empirically has never been clear. Although extreme caution is needed, and one of the first tasks must be consider what sorts of interpretation are possible, dream research, potentially, offers a way. Essentially, it relies on decoding the metaphors offered by a culture for general use among its members (Haug 1992; Lawrence 1991) and is a way that the normally repressed feelings, which nevertheless exert an influence on behaviour, can be researched. It may also be quite close, as Edgar (1993) argues, to the 'vignette' technique (Finch 1987).

Rather along these lines the pre-war M-O set the observers the task of recording their 'dominant images', that is, their recurring thoughts. Again, although no systematic analysis of these data was undertaken, even the briefest glance at them, and at the dreams reported in 1992, show the powerful influence of erotic thoughts, especially for men. One man recalls an image set off by reading a newspaper account of a boy who had crawled under a cart, which had then been driven from North London to Birmingham and back. The boy escaped unharmed, but the image plays on the observer and comes back in many forms throughout the day, including that of the cart and the boy as a set of male genitals. The same man recalls other erotic thoughts and is reprimanded by his wife for including them in his M-O report. He retorts that he is doing exactly what was asked of him. Which he was. Though day-dreams and dreams are not the same, the M-O material may, fortuitously, offer evidence of the gendered aspects of thinking and feeling in line with the work of Hudson and Jacot (1991) who argue that, typically, men's patterns of thought are more openly erotic as a consequence of their early emotional experiences and, especially, of separation.

Dreams and day-dreams are not the only way that M-O can be used to harness imagination to social research as another of Jennings's projects demonstrated. Popular imagery and metaphor are some sort of external evidence of internal subjective states. As society changes so must the inner world, although studying this is not easy. The posthumously published *Pandaemonium* (Jennings 1985) was an 'imaginative history of the Industrial Revolution' which traced how man's view of himself had been fundamentally altered. Jennings believed that: 'The machine is the link between man and his subconscious, for it reveals one to the other and bears witness to the deep organic impulse which makes the past present and vice versa' (Remy 1986). *Pandaemonium* offered the reader a collage of contemporary accounts and images which, Jennings argued, were: 'a record of mental events' which 'had passed through the feelings and the mind of an individual and forced him to write'. Such 'traces of Imagination' were: 'more delicate to handle than the facts and the events and ideas of which history is usually constructed', but just as crucial for understanding the period, for they revealed the conflicts of class, of animism and materialism, of expropriated labour and the means of production, of ideas and of religious, moral and political belief systems.

Again much of Jennings's approach pre-dates later work on the role of technology as *the* contemporary metaphor for social life (Leed 1980; Benston 1988; Romanshyn 1989; Zuboff 1988; Haug 1992). Whilst still ignorant of Jennings and the history of M-O, but engaged in a project on the pace of life and why it seemed to increase with modernity, I re-invented the metaphorical wheel. Anxious to find data on the subjective experience of a changing pace of life, I had set the M-O writers an imaginative task as part of a directive on the pace of life.[3] This was to think of themselves as a machine or object that expressed the way that they lived their lives. To my surprise most agreed and added explanations of why they chose their particular object as a metaphor. The request seemed to touch a chord and using a machine as a self-image was, for many, a chance to make a point about the loss of human values and autonomy. The range was wide and included cursors, shredders, Alessi coffee pots, ferrets, refrigerators, sewage plants, *The Guardian* newspaper, rose-bushes, racehorses, cars and old settees. Although the exercise was crude, it revealed a difference in imagery according to gender and employment status but not according to class. And it was in some of the most popular objects, clocks, computers and washing machines that social conditions were most apparent. Men, if they 'were' computers, were main-frame computers, whilst women were PCs, though they 'were' mostly washing machines. Interpreting this material in relation to the explanations given makes it very clear that gender is experienced primarily in terms of power, though, for both sexes, there was evidence of a widespread sense and resentment of loss of control. At its best metaphor-based research might get beneath the dominant discourses of self-presentation to more complex experiences of power and subordination.

WRITING, REPRESENTATION AND THE STRUCTURE OF FEELINGS

As important to M-O as the belief that everyday life, ordinary people and unconscious processes should be studied, was the related belief in the ubiquity or universality of artistic creativity or imagination in producing social life. In another context this would be understood as primarily religious but, because M-O was committed to empirical research, it laid the ground for a different and democratic view of the artistic impulse.

Representativeness is often raised as a problem for M-O and it is faulted for having too many women, over-sixties and middle class writers amongst its panel. Worse still, the writers are self-selected. However, not only can quota sampling deal with the 'over-representation' of some social groups, if 'representation' is understood in a political sense then the credibility of M-O takes on a different aspect. Self-appointed though the M-O writers are, in their sense of citizenship, of responsibility to posterity and of 'setting the record straight' they constitute a *political* rather than *technical* 'representativeness'. And one fired by a sense of dissatisfaction with contemporary and formal modes of representation. The Archivist of the M-O Archive, Dorothy Sheridan (1993), has suggested that what really marks out the writers is a pronounced concern that the truth be told about the times that they live through. While most people may not have quite such a well developed sense of public service, or need to write for posterity as the M-O writers, those who do may well be expressing a form of collective conscience. If so, the value of their testimony may depend more on an understanding of the conditions of its creation and rather less on a sampling frame.

Artistic expression can stem from exactly the same impulses as other forms of political action, but because it rests on a state of heightened perception, it can produce different reactions. Organisers of events such as the National Poetry Competition notice, annually, how often recent catastrophic events such as Zeebrugge, Hillsborough or Chernobyl feature in the poems submitted. Geoffrey Hosking (1990), writing about the recent history of the ex-Soviet Union, has a chapter entitled the 'Return of the Repressed', which refers to the avalanche of grateful letters received by Solzhenitsyn in response to his novels, especially *A Day in the Life of Ivan Denisovich*. It is often writers and painters, rather than social scientists, who are credited with expressing national sentiments. If we are interested in these sentiments and think that artistic endeavour may be inherently truth seeking, then the methods artists, including amateur ones, use have plenty to offer us.

Such a view underlies the work of Raymond Williams (1961, 1979, 1983) where he discusses what he calls a *structure of feelings*. Williams singles out the generation of thirty-something writers as being especially in tune with their times and able to crystallise the collective, social and emotional state of the nation. An exclusive focus on published writers may make the claim rather élitist, and certainly it rests on a somewhat fragile theory of the relationship between the reader, the writer and their society; but, if there is a grain of truth, it applies to the M-O data as much as to the canon of English literature. Many of the writers join M-O precisely for the opportunity it offers to write. For the non-professional writer, living a normal, varied life, the act of writing is sociologically valuable because of the social, creative impulse that lies behind it. The desire to observe and record is the same as that of a successful author and may render the product more representative of the efforts of any select list of key writers. Thus, if a way of analysing it accurately can be found, the M-O writing might be a rich source of the *structure of feelings*.

On occasion it has been said that M-O's finest achievement was the correct prediction of the 1945 British election result. In a similar way the material collected through day diaries in 1992 showed something of the emotions surrounding the impending election. Although it had only just been called, by 13 March 1992 a large number of people were heartily sick of the whole business and wrote vividly about it.[4] As one writer observed: 'Racism is bad, the law says so, so why isn't "politicianism" as

bad? I do not want to have to hate people of a certain political persuasion'. In the post mortem the exit polls were shown to be far from accurate
and many possible explanations advanced for the scale of the defeat of the
Labour Party. Though too late for another prediction, the emotional
manipulation of the electorate and its responses to it could be explored
further through the day diaries collected for M-O.

It is quite plain, from reading the day diaries, that across the land there
are, or were, some common factors that affected a wide variety of people
at an emotional level. The weather was important (it was very windy) and
so was what was shown on television. *Educating Rita* had been screened
that night and was mentioned extensively. In one case it triggered
extremely painful recollections from a woman who had been rejected as a
mature applicant for a university place, yet had later married a lecturer
and was now subjected to what she felt was a phoney form of social
admission.

METHODOLOGICAL STRENGTHS AND WEAKNESSES

There is obviously no reason to use the M-O Archive if a standard attitude survey will do: after all, why duplicate the British Social Attitude
Survey? Mark Abrams's (1950) criticisms of M-O have some point,
even if he was proselytising for his own brand of market research and
polling. The M-O Archive is best used to research the ephemeral, the
hidden, the paradoxical and the surprising. In fact it was Abrams who
raised, in the context of the M-O and the Second World War, the question of whether to take the mention, or the omission, of comment on the
War as the more significant? Inadvertently he pointed to the importance
of repression and to why it should be studied. Standard questionnaires
and surveys do not allow access to multiple meanings and contradiction.
They are designed to eliminate them. However, contradiction is central
to social life and ways of researching it need to be found. The fluid,
complex and interconnected M-O data, on almost a random number of
themes, is one such.

Many of the methodological problems that have to be considered are
common to most forms of qualitative research, but not all. When thinking
about M-O data it is clear that the more we understand about the 'writing
culture', the less any text can be read naively as a direct report of behaviour, thought or 'reality'. Writing, as with speech, is not 'natural'; it is
always constructed with some audience in mind, with some concern to
present a self. Yet there are some ways of using the M-O data that offer a

limited escape from these problems. Dreams are generated in the unconscious and, by definition, escape some of the censorship of conscious
thought, though their recording may not. The more M-O is used as an
adjunct to data normally collected in a therapeutic context, the more the
issues of how like or unlike that context M-O is, and which context should
be used to judge the other, are raised. One of the greatest strengths of M-O
is that the writers are not self-selected for therapy and there is a large
amount of social contextual information available about them (at no extra
cost of collection). Unlike dreams and free associations within a therapeutic context, that is critically detached from the everyday world, these data
are inseparable from it and appear constantly, whether asked for directly
or not. However, from a research perspective, the big difference between
writing for M-O and going to a therapist is that the numbers are much
larger than any therapist would ever encounter, even after a life time of
professional practice.

CONCLUSION

Perry Anderson's (1969) famous critique of British intellectual life
'Components of a National Culture' does not mention M-O, though it cas-
tigates the empiricism of British intellectual life and its failure to theorise
and/or be politically visionary. The omission is interesting because M-O
does not fit easily into a theory/empirical dichotomy precisely because it
combines imagination with research.

NOTES

1.   Mass-Observation started in 1937, the brainchild of Tom Harrisson, Charles
      Madge and Humphrey Jennings. It aimed to study the everyday life of ordi-
      nary Britons and depended on volunteer writers from all over Britain and a
      central staff to collate and interpret the material gathered. Much use has
      been made of the pre-war and war-time material, for example, Angus
      Calder's (1969) *The People's War*, Jonathan Cape; Dorothy Sheridan's
      (1990) *War Time Women*, Heinemann; and Harrisson's (1943) *The Pub and
      the People*, Gollancz. During the Second World War M-O was used by the
      Government as domestic intelligence and in the late forties the market
      research side split off. Aided by a grant from the Nuffield Foundation the
      project was re-started in 1981 by Prof. David Pocock, an anthropologist at
      the University of Sussex. It currently has a panel of around 500 writers who,

on average, respond to three 'directives' a year. It represents a unique source of data on everyday life in contemporary Britain.

2. The Mass-Observation Archivist, Dorothy Sheridan, and an anthropologist Brian Street, have recently completed a study of why people write for the MOA (ESRC No. R00233728).
3. The opportunity to work on the Mass-Observation material was made available by an ESRC grant No. LC14250027 for a project on 'Age, Pace of Life and Social Change'.
4. Fortuitously a day diary had been asked for in the Spring 1992 directive. The day was chosen almost at random to fall in the middle of the period in which most people could be expected to respond. Day diaries have no standard format and cannot easily be compared to Time Budget surveys, although some researchers have attempted to code up the pre-war day diaries in order to make them compatible with other data. In all 413 diaries were received, 301 from women, 112 from men.

REFERENCES

Abrams, M. (1951) *Social Surveys and Social Action*. London: Heinemann.
Anderson, P. (1969) 'Components of a National Culture', in R. Blackburn and T. Nairn (eds) *Student Power: Politics, diagnosis, action*. London: Penguin.
Beck, U. (1992) *Risk Society*. London: Sage.
Benston, M. L. (1988) 'Women's Voices/Men's Voices': Technology as Language', in Kramarae, C. (ed.) *Technology and Women's Voices: Keeping in touch*. London: Routledge.
Beradt, C. (1966) *The Third Reich of Dreams*, trans. A. Gottwald. Chicago: Quadrangle Books.
Borger, R. and Cioffi, F. (1970) *Explanation in the Behavioural Sciences*. Cambridge: Cambridge University Press.
Cohen, S. and Taylor, L. (1976) *Escape Attempts*. London: Allen Lane.
Devereux, G. (1967) *From Anxiety To Method in the Behavioural Sciences*. The Hague: Mouton.
Edgar, I. (1993) 'Using Non-Traditional Research Methodologies: The potential contribution of groupwork methods such as dreamwork and visualisation', British Sociological Association, Annual Conference, Colchester.
Feaver, W. (1988) *Pitmen Painters: The Ashington Group 1934–1984*. London: Chatto and Windus.
Figlio, K. (1988) 'Oral History and the Unconscious', *History Workshop Journal*, Autumn: 120–31.
Finch, J. (1986) *Research and Policy*. Lewes: Falmer Press.
Finch, J. (1987) 'Research Note: The Vignette Technique in Survey Research', *Sociology* 21: 105–14.
Firth, R. (1939) 'An Anthropologist's View of Mass-Observation', *Sociological Review* 31: 166–93.
Frisby, D. (1980) *Sociological Impressionism*. London: Routledge & Kegan Paul.
Gellner, E. (1985) *The Psychoanalytic Movement*. London: Paladin.
Giddens, A. (1990) *The Consequences of Modernity*. Cambridge: Polity Press.

Giddens, A. (1991) *Modernity and Self Identify: Self and Society in the Late Modern Age.* Cambridge: Polity Press.

Haug, F. (1992) *Beyond Masochism.* London: Verso.

Hoschild, A. (1983) *The Managed Heart: Commercialisation of Human Feeling.* Berkeley: University of California Press.

Hoskings, G. (1990) *The Awakening of the Soviet Union.* London: Heinemann.

Hudson, L. and Jacot, B. (1991) *How Men Think: Intellect, Intimacy and the Erotic Imagination.* New Haven: Yale University Press.

Hunt, J. (1989) *Psychoanalytic Aspects of Fieldwork.* London: Sage.

Jackson, S. (1993) 'Even Sociologists Fall in Love: An Exploration of the Sociology of the Emotions', *Sociology* 27: 201–20.

Jennings. H. and Madge (1937) *May 12th: Mass-Observation Day Surveys.* London: Faber & Faber.

Jennings, H. (1985) *Pandaemonium 1660–1886: The Coming of the Machine, as Seen by Contemporary Observers*, ed. M-L. Jennings and C. Madge. London: André Deutsch.

Lakoff and Johnson, M. (1980) *Metaphors We Live By.* Chicago: University of Chicago Press.

Lawrence, G. (1991) '"Won from the Void and Formless Infinite": Experiences in Social Dreaming', *Free Associations* 2.

Leed, E. (1980) '"Voice" and "Print": Master Symbols in the History of Communication', in Woodward, K. (ed.) *The Myths of Information: Technology and Postindustrial Culture.* London: Routledge.

Levine, S. (1981) 'Dreams of the Information about the Researcher', *Ethos* 9: 276–93.

Milner, M. (1934) *A Life Of One's Own.* London: Chatto & Windus.

Milner, M. (1937) *An Experiment in Leisure.* London: Chatto & Windus.

Morgan, G. (1993) *Imaginization. The Art of Creative Management.* London: Sage.

Nisbet, R. (1965) 'Sociology as an Art Form', in M. Stein and A. Vidich (eds) *Sociology on Trial.* Englewood Cliffs: Prentice-Hall.

Okely, J and Callaway, H. (1992) *Anthropology and Autobiography*, ASA Monograph 29. London: Routledge.

Pierret, J. (1992) *Investigating Sex, Surrealist Research 1928–1932.* London: Verso.

Remy, M. (1986) 'Surrealism's Vertiginous Descent on Britain 1930–1943', in A. Robertson, M. Remy, M. Gooding, and T. Friedman (eds) *Surrealism in Britain in the Thirties*, Leeds: Leeds City Art Galleries.

Romanshyn, R. D. (1989) *Technology as Symptom and Dream.* London: Routledge.

Rustin, M. (1991) *The Good Society and the Inner World: Psychoanalysis, Politics and Culture.* London: Verso.

Shaw, J. (1994) 'Transference and Countertransference in the Mass-Observation Archive: an Under-Exploited Research Resource', *Human Relations* 47: 1391–1408.

Sheridan, D. (1991) 'Ordinary Hard-Working Folk': Volunteer Writers for Mass-Observation 1937–50 and 1981–91', *Feminist Praxis*, Autumn, pp. 1–34.

Sheridan, D. (1993) 'Writing to the Archive. Mass-Observation as Auto-biography', *Sociology* 27: 27–40.

Stanley, N. (1979) 'Beyond Empiricism: Social Reportage via Artistic Means in the Mass-Observation Experiment 1937–40', paper given at University of Aston, 31.

Wilkins, R. (1993) 'Taking it Personally', *Sociology* 27: 93–7.
Williams, R. (1961) *The Long Revolution*. London: Chatto.
Williams, R. (1979) *Politics and Letters*. London: New Left Books.
Williams, R. (1983) 'The Tenses of the Imagination' in *Writing in Society*. London: Verso.
Zuboff, S. (1988) *In the Age of the Smart Machine*. Oxford: Heinemann.

2 Imagining the Community: Some Reflections on the Community Study as a Method

Geoff Payne

Our perception of 'community', and the local social systems that manifest this property, are shaped by 'community studies'. These range from the single researcher doing an ethnography of an isolated (rural) settlement – such as the contributors to Cohen (1982, 1986) – to teams using social surveys to explore the manifestation of economic restructuring in a given location or region (e.g. Roberts *et al.* 1985 or Gallie 1988). In between are a variety of studies which to a greater or lesser extent are issue-based (e.g. Moore, 1982), localised (Stacey *et al.* 1975), ethnographic (Gibbon and Steyne 1986), done by individuals or teams (Warwick and Littlejohn 1992), policy-oriented (Wengler 1984; Bulmer 1987; Willmott 1987) and explicitly related to the origins of the idea of community (Strathern 1981).

These studies did not depend on a single observational method, even though this was the more characteristic approach. Young and Willmott (1957) used a range of methods: indeed, the first edition made great play of the latest technology of the IBM card counter/sorter (Platt 1971; Payne *et al.* 1981). Brody's sensitive account of Inishkillane (1973) starts with a review based on historical and literary documents. Warwick and Littlejohn draw on both surveys and historical statistics and pull together medical researchers, archivists, adult education classes and SCELI support (1992: xiv–xv). It is not my intention to deny this richness of methodological styles or to denigrate them, even though my main concern in this paper is with the research carried out by individuals using qualitative methods: the single-handed ethnography that for most people typifies the community study.

In this brief re-exploration I shall be less interested in the perennial questions of the definition of community, or the sociological purpose of studying 'communities', as with five questions of research methodology and imagination. Why do we describe the social life of places in words without pictures? Why is it that, from most sociological accounts, communities seem so full of such *nice* people? Why are small settlements apparently so receptive of middle class sociologists and yet remain so hostile to other 'incomers'? How can sociologists know if their fieldwork is representative and comprehensive? And how can the sociologist evaluate whether a given finding is characteristic of 'communities' rather than of wider British society?

LOOKING IN ON COMMUNITY STUDIES

It may seem an obvious point, but any community study sets up mental images of a place and its people for the study's readers. These pictures are largely created by written descriptions. For example, a recent paper described a remote Scottish settlement in the following way:

> Fearnbeg is made up of nine linear and grouped townships spread over an area approximately twelve miles in length and five in breadth. There is a resident population of about 270, 200 of whom are adults. The settlement pattern is characteristic of such places throughout the northwest, as is the topography of the area. From a rugged coastline the land rises steeply to form a barren mountainous hinterland; scenically magnificent but almost totally unsuitable for intensive agriculture. Less than one per cent of the land surface can be classed as arable and this has restricted the settlement pattern to the lower-lying coastal margins. Here the traditional landholding pattern of crofting persists, interspersed with dwellings that have no agriculture connection. Typical of isolated settlements on the Atlantic margins, the area has limited services and facilities for recreation and leisure. Poor communication and transport networks leave it sufficiently cut-off from the outside world to make personal relations between its people crucial in everyday life. Key foci are the Post Office, two shops, two bars, the village hall and school, and to a markedly less extent, the one church (Payne and Macleod 1993: 2–3).

This kind of description is recognisable as a typical thumbnail sketch on which to ground more sociological observation. One can ask, however, whether one or two good pictures might add something to the description. Visual communication may have something to offer in addition to the written word to make it more powerful.

Few of the classic studies included much directly visual information. Frankenberg (1957) had a single very long-shot, scene-setting photograph, but his later book (1966) did not have any illustration. While sketch maps were sometimes included, no one would know precisely how Banbury or Gosforth or even Bethnal Green actually 'looked', except by visiting them as places and seeing for oneself. Later studies may have been unintentionally misleading: Holme's (1985) cover photograph is neither Bethnal Green nor Woodford but a library shot supplied courtesy of Shelter. Warwick and Littlejohn's (1992) photographs are either historically grainy shots from 1905, or contemporary symbolic compositions of pithead gear and little children sitting in the sunshine.

None of these studies confronts the central fact of human experience, namely that humans *see* as well as hear and think. If the locality is relevant, then it is even more important than in other walks of sociology to see what it looks like. The more we can recognise the places and the players, the better we comprehend what has been going on. Community studies without pictures are like reading Shakespeare's plays, but never experiencing them in the theatre.

Two objections can be made to this argument. The first is the problem of anonymity. Pictures of places, let alone of people, increase the probability that carefully disguised place names or local characters will become identifiable. There is some truth to this, but given the delays between fieldwork and publication, too much can be made of it. If care is taken over shots of faces, and normal ethical canons of informed consent are applied, much of the problem disappears, although the use of crowd scenes raises the interesting ethical dilemma of whether consent should be sought, and whether privacy has been significantly invaded.

The second objection is that the physical is not necessarily social nor sociologically interesting. Pictures of buildings and streets are superficial and concrete, whereas social relationships are fundamental and yet almost intangible. The photographer will take what is available to see, and what makes a 'good picture', rather than capturing the invisible or the less dramatic. Again, this is a valid complaint, but in turn it points to a general weakness. If photographs or videos can be so misleading, is not this itself evidence for the power and importance of the visual image? In a world which bombards us with images, why is it that most sociologists still think of the tape recorder as a pretty smart bit of new technology? Of course, the camera can lie, but the sociologist should not set out to lie with it. Of course, it concentrates on outward manifestations, but the sociologist need not stop at that level. Pictures are an *additional* resource which when sensibly used help the communication between writer and reader.

Indeed, one could go further; it is not just the pictures *per se* that add to our understanding but what we gain from *the process of collecting them*.

Thus, using a camcorder and then editing the results is a salutary experience that all sociologists should undergo. In editing, one is directly faced with choices of selection and omission: which sequences go into the final version, in what order? The 'pretty picture' because it is impressive, or the fuzzy one because it was not staged, or it contains a glimpsed clue to some crucial social process? Does the end product have to have all its clips in the same sequence they are recorded? Editing video is about the physical and social reconstruction of reality, and only by doing it does one fully confront the facticity of the experience. Having confronted it, the sociologist should then reflect on what he or she has been doing in *writing* about empirical data in all those previous years: one's casual acceptance of the written word is revealed to be just as physical and social a reconstruction of reality as the video!

One other methodological benefit of using the visual is that it is time-specific. A picture is likely to capture the style and feel of an era, and then to remind the viewer every time that the study took place in one specific historical setting. The survival of the Bethnal Green studies on undergraduate reading lists provides a good example: the work is now nearly 40 years old, and yet many undergraduates still learn about the survival of the extended family in urban areas. The era of post-war housing shortage has passed, the actual buildings have for the most part been demolished, and yet the mental image and inherited sociological wisdom continue to survive – at least in this writer's mind! But if we were presented with more visual images in the published documents, we would tell from the clothes, the consumer durables, the shop fronts, from the *style* that here were essentially historical documents. There is nothing wrong with such historical documents, as long as they are used as historical data. The visual helps to remind us of how society continues constantly to evolve, thus eroding our hard-won knowledge. If we can resist the temptations of nostalgia, we will learn yet again the need for empirical investigation in order to keep in touch with a changing society, let alone move our discipline ahead.

In trying to elaborate this idea, I took some video pictures in Glyn Ceiriog, Banbury and Bethnal Green during 1992. Replaying them prior to editing, one common theme leapt off the screen: the streets were full of 'For Sale' signs. In the middle of a depressed market in housing, an obvious issue for people living communal lives is their capacity to escape from a local milieu and the way their property ownership constrains them. In Banbury, a casual conversation about housing led on to complaints about how bad unemployment had become. The vacant shops, offices and factories, and the groups of young people on the streets, were the physical signs of Britain in the 1990s. Just as the 1984–85 miners' strike changed the definition of what were the issues of the day in coal communities for the 1980s, so the Heseltine plan to close down the British coal industry became the issue that any researcher in a coal community would have to confront in 1993.

Thus the 'community study' is not a project fixed for all time, or even one in slow evolution. It is blown this way and that by the concerns of the local people; the current community study issues are unemployment, housing, community care, race relations, and law and order. The sociologist may import a similar interest at the outset, either as citizen or as sociologically-informed researcher, or he/she may choose to tackle these issues with methods other than the community study, but in studying a community, local people will intrude their own agendas into his/her research programme.

WHY ARE PEOPLE SO NICE?

Although the community study literature reflects this capacity for actors to follow their own concerns, the main impression generated is one of a world populated with pleasant, likable people. Almost everybody seems to be so nice, and researchers have had no trouble in getting on with them. But is it really credible that sociologists have this ability to get on with everybody? One would have to believe so, because there has been little discussion in the studies or even in the methodological texts on ethnography, of how to overcome the researcher's own interpersonal hostility or dislikes, whereas our own common sense experience suggests that not all human beings are equally attractive to us (cf Whyte 1955).

The reader may like to imagine moving house to live in a small village of about 200 adults, plus their children (i.e. a domestic move, not a short stay purely for research purposes). Will the same relationships develop with *all* one's 200-odd new co-residents? Are one's feelings going to be the same towards the born-again evangelist, or the racially-prejudiced sexist, as towards the local Labour councillor with a degree in sociology?

The researcher faces a difficult task. Whereas the resident can, to a large extent, choose not to interact with other residents, the researcher is obliged by the canons of scientific method to treat all potential respondents in the same way. This means meeting and talking to them, evaluating their social behaviour, and reporting on their actions. It is bad enough to have to struggle with the more familiar obstacles to access, when other people decline to co-operate. Here we are talking about obstacles to access that lie within the researcher, and which raise the probability of bias in treatment.

In the course of fieldwork in several locations in the past half a dozen years, I have encountered people whom I did not like, and situations that felt most unpleasant. These include aggression, abuse, racist and sexist taunts, as well as simpler and less accountable 'clashes of personalities'. If one is uncomfortable dealing with someone, how much easier it is to leave them out of the data collection process and to concentrate on those with whom we are more at ease. Even if we do collect data on those we dislike, it is harder to evaluate and understand them. While it is not too difficult to protect sources and the identities of those we like, the application of the same ethical standards is more demanding when we write about those we dislike. Sociologists have not considered this inter-personal hostility, perhaps because we instinctively explain the phenomenon in sociological terms, as a cultural dissonance between the values of the researcher and the values of those being researched.

The people in community studies are too 'nice' in another sense. They seldom do unpleasant things or break the law. So, for example, one finds almost no index entries for 'crime', 'criminal', or even 'policeman' (Pryce 1986 excepted). And yet common sense tells us that crime is universal, and infractions of norms are likely to be more threatening in small, closed units than in looser urban settings. We are told about joking relationships and social control (e.g. Rees 1950: 83) but little about the public and private sorrows of people whom both local community and researcher perceive as seriously deviant.

To take some examples from recent fieldwork, what are we to make of an accusation of child abuse; an attempted suicide; the beating of a wife; or drug pushers? At a different level, should we discuss the elderly man who refused to leave his home, but whose incontinence was so severe that on his death major refurbishment was required to his house? How sociologically significant (in a village of 200 souls) are the pregnancy of a 14-year-old girl, family breakdowns, cases of senile dementia, the one in ten adults who drink more than a bottle of spirits every day, or drunken driving and almost weekly scuffles around 'closing time'? If we assume for the moment that these patterns are not wildly atypical (see below), then we need to consider why similar events do not loom larger in other community studies. There are good reasons for reporting them. Not only do we, as social scientists, need to know about communal life 'warts and all', but these 'deviations' are mostly regarded as deviations by the local culture and often help to illuminate both what is considered 'normal' and the limits of that normality.

There are three possible explanations for the apparent under-reporting of such cases. First, they are very visible in a small community so that any discussion of them, even under false names and similar disguises, cannot hide the identities of the people concerned. There would need to be the strongest reasons of public interest and sociological discovery before a breach of the principle of anonymity for respondents – and in particular such vulnerable respondents – could be justified. Second, such a breach is less likely in community studies because in these, even more than in most qualitative investigations, research involves closer personal relationships. It is not a nine-to-five mode of study; there is a greater sense of involvement with the people and to 'bad-mouth' them by reporting negative aspects becomes problematic. This can be seen as one specific variant of the 'going native' phenomenon which, together with the ethical dilemma, helps to produce a sometimes excessively sanitised version of social life.

The third reason for this outcome lies in the problems a researcher encounters in accessing this or that event. Local people may choose not to talk about something even if the researcher raises it (Macleod and Payne 1988). Although the researcher may be living in a village, he or she is not omnipresent. If the actors in a community are defensive, the quality of information available to the researcher declines. They may not even tell the researcher about it in the first place: it will depend on the stage of the investigation and the researcher's skills at tapping into local networks.

The upshot, for whatever good intentions, is a sociological portrait of communities that is a flattering one. Not only is there the nostalgia trap of romanticising working-class heroes (note the deliberate masculine term), but the added pitfall of selective reporting. Villages and villagers are simply not that *nice* (and this not just the voice of a misanthrope speaking). Sociologists have trapped themselves inside a research imagination that fails to present the actors concerned in all their shades of colour and circumstances. An enhanced fieldwork practice is required.

THE COMMUNITY RESPONDS TO THE PERSON

Just as sociological accounts of small settlements seem to the writer to be disproportionately full of nice people leading interesting – but not *too* interesting – lives, so, too, do these settlements seem remarkably willing to offer up their secrets to the researcher. It may be that I have little gift for ethnography or access: it certainly strikes me that community study is very hard work. Making contacts, building relationships and handling the wealth of necessary local information presents a substantial demand on the new *resident*. How much more demanding, then, is the task of the *researcher*, who in a few brief months must achieve all this *and* collect, analyse and understand matters of sociological significance?

A number of studies have drawn attention to the widely recognised problem of how incoming people adjust to life in a new location. Frequently referred to in terms of 'incomers' and 'locals', the interaction (or even non-interaction) between long-term residents and more recent arrivals is deeply problematic. This may revolve around manifest competition for jobs, housing, or control of local institutions (see Bryan 1987; Mosely 1982; Giarchi 1984; Musgrove 1974). Alternatively, it may be a subtle but all-pervasive distinction of identities, generated by culture contact and manipulated in the elaborate game of daily social negotiation (Frankenberg 1957; Cohen 1986; Macleod 1990). Either way, we are reminded in these and a number of other studies that local people mark themselves off from incomers and outsiders.

Despite this, most sociologists seem to have had relatively little difficulty in gaining initial access and acceptance in their chosen communities. To be fair, no article or book can go on for ever about problems of rapport etc., so that perhaps the conventions of publishing help to create an illusion of almost automatic access. Equally, to dwell excessively on problems undermines the credibility of the wider project. Despite arguments for reflexivity such as Bell's several collections (e.g. Bell and Roberts 1984), it is still not easy for (especially young) researchers to 'tell it like it is'. Even those reared to an ethnographic tradition tend ultimately to make the best they can out of any operational difficulties (e.g. Jenkins 1984).

In justification of scepticism about how fully the outsider sociologist is really accepted by local subjects, one can draw on a recent account of the local/incomer dichotomy that emerged from fieldwork: the test that the remarks occurred in conversation without prompting indicates their salience:

> In reviewing fieldwork notes from weeks in which there were no major social events or happenings (i.e. ordinary, uneventful weeks) it became apparent that there were a high number of references to locals and incomers in routine conservations. For example, in one randomly selected seven-day period (in June 1989) thirty-two explicit references to the local/incomer dichotomy were recorded. The following quotes were taken from that week's fieldnotes:
> 'I am a local because I've lived here all my life.'
> 'If you live and work in [Fearnbeg], even if you are an incomer, and if you have a family here, then surely you are a local?'

'I wouldn't think of them as real locals though. Maybe they are, but I don't think of them as locals.'

'The only people who can call themselves local are the ones who were born here and brought up here.'

These, and other quotes, bear testimony to a real social division that exists between locals and incomers. The two groups are often distinguished on the grounds that the latter were not born and bred in Fearnbeg. This criterion allows for locals to regard themselves as something akin to members of some sort of exclusive club to which incomers cannot gain entry (Payne and Macleod 1993: 3).

While the sociologist does not wish permanently to join the 'exclusive club', he or she does need to become a visiting member in order to gain access to information flowing within the club. This is not the point to enter the epistemological debates of cultural anthropology (see, for instance, Sharrock and Anderson 1980); rather a much simpler point is being made here. The first step for the researcher is to establish contact in order to be able to collect information. Unless there is this most basic access to the minds of local people, through conversations, interviews and observations, there is nothing available to be analysed sociologically.

The body of work demonstrating distrust, reserve and distance on the part of locals towards incomer residents must logically apply to the role of the outsider sociologist and so make this first step a difficult one. Unless the researcher has a privileged status (Macleod 1992; Jenkins 1984; Beynon 1983; Williamson 1982) the researcher is an incomer and is therefore struggling to overcome very deep-rooted attitudes of suspicion and possibly antagonism (and sometimes also barriers of language: MacKinnon 1977). Macleod writes about researching the settlement in which he was born and bred:

as well as being 'known' by the people living in Fearnbeg I was equally fortunate to know my 'cast of characters'. Furthermore, having learned the language in the same way as many of my research subjects did, and having experienced community life with the same rhythm, I was in a position where data were less likely to be distorted, taken out of context, or insufficiently qualified when reported (1992: 61; see also 62–81).

Access here means access to interaction, and also access by means of that interaction, to comprehension and a complete range of data. The researcher may not even realise how great the problem is: only the club members are in a position to know the answer to that, until the 'double gates' have been unlocked (Payne and Macleod 1993); by definition this takes more time than the typical sociologist can afford (see Wakeford's (1988) view that one-third of research time goes just in establishing rapport).

Writings about the general issue of the observer's role have made a greater virtue out of necessity than is necessarily justified. The strategy of keeping at the margins (a position which we are arguing is attributed by the locals, not selected by the sociologist) is held up as having unique value: the researcher generates 'creative insight' out of the marginal position of simultaneous insider-outsider (Lofland 1976: 97). Too close a sense of fitting in is seen as leading to a loss of critical perspective. Marginality is acknowledged to be uncomfortable but essential:

> The comfortable sense of being 'at home' is a danger signal. From the perspective of the 'marginal' reflexive ethnographer there can be no question of total commitment, 'surrender' or 'becoming'. There must always remain some part held back, some social and intellectual 'distance'. For it is in the 'space' created by that distance that the work of the ethnographer gets done (Hammersley and Atkinson 1983: 102).

While one has no trouble in accepting that the sociologist can derive an analytical perspective and a knowledge that is different from that of the actors, by virtue of being at an intellectual distance, the rest of this idea is far less plausible. Is there really any danger of the outsider becoming an insider, least of all in the community study? When residents can say 'I've lived here 20 years and I'm still an incomer', there can be no serious chance that the 'grab it and run' sociologist will be accepted into the exclusive club. Thus much of this talk of being a 'simultaneous insider-outsider' is self-delusion. The reification of 'social distance' is a dressing up of the inevitable into a methodological skill: the foxes with no tails would have us all proud to be outsiders.

This is not a simplistic plea for the Jules-Rossette model of total immersion in membership (1978). On the contrary, membership is for most of us normally an impossibility. It would have practical advantages, if only it were possible; only a few people in a limited number of settings are ever in a position to have these advantages. To quote Macleod again, being a local enabled him

> to cut through many of the characteristic problems faced by would-be ethnographers ... Even access to the subtleties of such phenomena as kinship and friendship was readily available ... All potential key informants were already known, as were where to go and who to ask in following up specific areas of enquiry. Any outside researcher seeking

information would have had to discover who to ask; who to ask first; whether permission was required and so forth ... My status as an insider meant I was afforded a great deal of trust by my informants, and I was allowed access to settings, detailed conversations and information that might not otherwise have been available (1992: 61–65).

Most of the time we do not have the opportunity to research ourselves or on our home territory. If we want to do better research under normal conditions, we need to confront our externality and acknowledge the limitations of our position with a little more humility.

Readers may recognise a parallel here with part of the argument for a feminist methodology, or for studies of ethnic groups to be carried out by black researchers. While sympathising with these arguments, it is still important to say that being a woman, or black, is not sufficient on its own. Other problems of access and understanding remain.

KNOWING THE COMMUNITY

Even if a person studying a community can cope with externality, there are three inter-related problems in completing fieldwork:

(a) is the coverage comprehensive?
(b) are the items highlighted in the analysis representative of that coverage?
(c) is some observed behaviour a characteristic of this one community, or all small communities, or typical of wider British society?

These questions with minor rephrasing could apply to any empirical study (say of a school or a workplace), but apply with particular force to the study of a locality.

The problem with coverage is that communities are in fact large geographical areas, consisting of places with four walls that hide what is going on, and containing more actors than can be comfortably observed or even identified. We can contrast this with the study of a school or workplace. Although the larger examples of such institutions present problems of their own, a community study is so much wider than either. It embraces the school, and all workplaces, and all leisure places, and all the other institutional systems as well. In as far as there is a characteristic of community studies, it is the potential for interconnection and intersection of all these elements.

However, communities are not homogeneous, nor do all of their component actors interact with each other in the same way. In the more anthropological work, perhaps most extensively shown by Arensberg and Kimball (1940), there is an underlying assumption that small settlements are cohesive and integrated systems. While, in contrast with some urban areas, this may be relatively so, it would be misleading to believe that partial coverage can be substituted for full coverage. A given area will contain a number of social subsystems, and not all these will overlap. An illustration of this from a 'Celtic fringe' study followed the greeting in the village store by a young local woman of an elderly woman who had lived in the village for over 30 years. As she paid for her groceries, the older woman asked:

> 'Who was that young girl I bumped into on the way in? I'm sure I should know her but I never seem to remember her name or who she is.'
> The shopkeeper, a recent incomer herself, explained who the young woman was and said:
> 'I'm sure you know her mother' (Cathy Ross).
> But, despite the fact that Cathy has lived in Fearnbeg for over sixty years, the reply was:
> 'No, my dear, I'm afraid I don't. I suppose I must have seen her around, but I wouldn't be able to tell you who she was if she walked in here just now' (Macleod 1992: 40).

Not everybody knows of, let alone interacts with, everyone else. Gender is a particular divide in this respect. To study only part of a community is to do just that: to see one part and to miss those others that are different. The logistics of fieldwork mitigate against comprehensive coverage of the breadth and complexity of the community. While this is in itself a problem, it is complicated by the inherent unknowability of how much has been omitted.

This in turn leads to the questions of whether what finally emerges in a report is representative, or distinctive of 'community'. For example, is the model of dense role relationships reported from rural settings characteristic of small settlements, or is it found in urban areas? If the former, should this be regarded as an aspect of 'community' *per se*, or a cause of communal feelings, or a product of 'community', or just as coincidence? Are the examples of deviancy listed above (p. 22) typical of small communities and/or urban areas?

This kind of question exercises Macleod: to what extent are the patterns of personal care for the elderly that he observed in some way distinctive?

> Including the niece/nephew cases, a total of six households out of the one hundred and twenty in Fearnbeg (i.e. five per cent) involve substan-

tial kin-based care support. It is not easy to say whether five per cent is high or not, because there is no systematic basis for national comparison. The work of Wenger (1984), Bulmer (1986), Finch (1989) and Giarchi (1990) would suggest that five per cent is not distinctive, but rather that Fearnbeg is similar to other places. In other words, the cultural values of Fearnbeg kinship are not special: the pattern of caregiving reflects the availability of key kin to give care (just possibly higher in rural than urban settings in which the latter is associated with high residential turnover), rather than the significance of kinship within the culture. In other words, whereas Cohen (1982), Fox (1982) and earlier researchers trained in social anthropology (e.g. see Frankenberg 1966) have treated kinship as the organising principle in rural life, this probably in part reflects their training rather than the unique features of rural settings per se.

Kinship in Fearnbeg certainly is an organising principle, but it is equally important to recognise that it is a contingent one, and one that has real limits (1992: 219–20).

The Fearnbeg study shows how both locals and incomers have similar patterns of kinship recognition and support; that there are many practical gaps in these 'systems' caused by an absence of people to fill the prescribed roles; that care is exchanged with, and also provided by, non-kin; and that kinship reckoning is not particularly extensive, widely considered important by actors, nor sociologically significant beyond inheritance of crofts and in legitimating 'local' status.

To generalise from this evidence, kinship in community studies has been given an exaggerated status because of the anthropological research imagination of the researchers, rather than because it was a characteristic of community *per se*. In turn, we can ask how the apparent significance of kinship relates to the equally reported significance of friendships, or neighbouring, or labour exchange, all of which have become part of the conventional wisdom of the community study. Not only should we revisit the old issue of how cultural systems relate to observable behaviour, but we need to set the local study in a wider context if we are to evaluate our findings.

SOME CONCLUDING OBSERVATIONS

The reader might be forgiven for thinking at times that the burden of this chapter is that community-based investigations are best avoided. Certainly the intention has been to inject a note of healthy scepticism into our view of research. In looking at the apparent ease with which sociologists are accepted into communities of such very nice people, or at the logistic difficulties of fieldworking a village and of interpreting the data collected, considerable play has been made of the limitations of the researcher confronted by a community as research object and field. Problems common to most sociological endeavours manifest themselves in a more extreme form when combined with the spatial and logistic peculiarities of communities. While it is generally true that all researchers struggle to gain full access and to collect sufficient data in the time available, the problem is exacerbated in a community study. For example, if one is concerned about the effect of the researcher's gender (or age, or class, etc.) on the subjects of the research, then one can often in other fields choose a sub-set of those subjects to minimise the problem: female sociologists can choose to study women, young sociologists to study youth crime, etc. However, in the community study, the nature of the beast is that the researcher has to deal with *all* community members; male and female, young and old, rich and poor.

The researcher's preconceptions and personality are also much more 'on the line' for the same reason. We cannot escape our personal likes and dislikes among the cast of social actors with whom we must interact (which is what 'participant observation' actually entails). There is no insulation between researcher and researched. The ethnographer has to be there with a wider range of people. The relative inattention in research methods writing to the sociologist's emotional biases in such settings is a curious gap.

It is tempting to over-psychologise this process, and suggest that, faced with a daunting task, the researcher unconsciously shifts his or her ground. The apparent 'niceness' of community dwellers reflects the incomer's need to seek social support. The concern about 'going native', or being accepted, is a product of the researcher's isolation and desire to be accepted. In an alien environment, the emphasis put on such institutions as kinship reflects a need to cling on to something which can connect raw fieldwork to the more familiar and comfortable conceptual systems of academic life, or possibly to identify something special and slightly quaint in order to justify the enterprise to oneself and one's colleagues. The over-emphasis on kinship (kinship is to anthropology what class is to sociology) makes more sense in such an explanatory framework than does its actual presence on the ground. It also goes some way towards explaining how the insider/outsider/social distance issue has been handled in the literature.

None the less, these difficulties should not blind us to the potential of community studies, nor become excuses for inaction. The community study remains a valuable and distinctive method, and despite all of this chapter's points to the contrary, one that still justifies its place in the sociological repertoire. It offers three key strengths:

First, as the comments about using visual images demonstrated, pictures are a reminder of how time passes, and the need to replenish our stock of contemporary materials. Empirical work decays into historical documentation 'even when we're standing still' – to re-run an old Spike Milligan joke. New 'issues of the day' constantly arise; rural survival, or the 'massification' of society transmogrifies into concerns for the environment, tourism, minority language maintenance, and local labour markets. Home ownership, unemployment, poverty, ill health, crime and racism re-emerge as public issues, and sociologists should not stand aloof (Payne and Cross 1993).

Second, community study justifies its place by bringing in locality as one component of a total explanation. While actors influence and are influenced by wider processes and institutions, they also influence and are influenced by local systems. We do not live in a uniform, mass society, and we lose sight of its subcultural variability at our peril. There is a constant need to balance the elegant simplification of sociological theory with empirical encounters with the complex messiness of human existence.

Finally, the community study reminds us to see more of such issues 'in the round'. Sociological fashions have led us to extract topics from their contexts and to disregard the fuller interplay of factors in human experience. The logistics of research tend to push us into researching narrow topics. A study of a factory cannot dwell too long on the familial roles of the workforce, or the workers' other roles in the church congregation, or as citizens coming to a decision on how to vote, or as neighbours, or part-time criminals. Electronic technology pushes us towards the exploration of variables and the association between small sets of variables. As a corrective to excessive narrowness the community study reminds us how the various parts of human life inter-penetrate.

The community study, in other words, represents a holistic type of sociology, with all the benefits of that, and all its attendant problems, too. It is not a corrective to the extraction of action from its physical location and its social context. If this dislocation goes unchecked, it produces a research imagination in sociology that is not grounded in social life, just as an absence of a sense of community in social life helps to produce the people lacking social identity that so concerned the original writers on the sociology of the community.

REFERENCES

Arensberg, C. and Kimball, S. (1940) *Family and Kinship in Ireland.* London: Peter Smith.

Bell, C. and Roberts, H. (eds) (1984) *Social Researching.* London: Routledge and Kegan Paul.

Beynon, J. (1983) 'Ways-In and Staying In', in M. Hammersley (ed.), *The Ethnography of Schooling.* London: Allen Lane.

Brody, H. (1973) *Inishkillane.* London: Allen Lane.

Bryan, G. (1987) 'White Settlers – a Red Herring', in *The Scots Magazine* Edinburgh, March: 290–2.

Bulmer, M. (1986) *Neighbours: The Work of Philip Abrams.* Cambridge: Cambridge University Press.

Bulmer, M. (1987) *The Social Basis of Community Care.* London: Allen and Unwin.

Cohen, A. (ed.) (1982) *Belonging.* Manchester: Manchester University Press.

Cohen, A. (ed.) (1986) *Symbolising Boundaries.* Manchester: Manchester University Press.

Finch, J. (1989) *Family Obligations and Social Change.* Oxford: Polity Press.

Fox, R. (1978) *The Tory Islanders: A People of the Celtic Fringe.* Cambridge: Cambridge University Press.

Frankenberg, R. (1957) *Village on the Border.* London: Cohen and West.

Frankenberg, R. (1966) *Communities in Britain.* Harmondsworth: Penguin.

Gallie, D. (ed.) (1988) *Employment in Britain.* Oxford: Blackwell.

Giarchi, G. (1984) *Between McAlpine and Polaris.* London: Routledge & Kegan Paul.

Giarchi, G. (1990) 'Distance, Decay and Information Deprivation: Health Implications for People in Rural Isolation', in P. Abbott and G. Payne (eds) *New Directions in the Sociology of Health.* Basingstoke: Falmer Press.

Gibbon, P. and Steyne, D. (eds) (1986) *Thurcroft: A Village and the Miners' Strike: An Oral History.* Nottingham: Spokesman.

Hammersley, M. and Atkinson, P. (1983) *Ethnography.* London: Tavistock.

Holme, A. (1985) *Housing and Young Families in East London.* London: Routledge and Kegan Paul.

Jenkins, R. (1984) 'Bringing it all back home', in C. Bell and H. Roberts, *op. cit.*

Jules-Rossette, B. (1978) 'Towards a Theory of Ethnography'. *Sociological Symposium* 24: 81–98.

Lofland, J. (1976) *Doing Social Life.* New York: Diley.

MacKinnon, K. (1977) *Language, Education and Social Processes in a Gaelic Community.* London: Routledge and Kegan Paul.

Macleod, A. (1990) 'Social Divisions in a Small Community'. Paper read at the BSA Annual Conference, University of Surrey, Guildford.

Macleod, A. (1992) *Social Identity, Social Change, and the Construction of Symbolic Boundaries in a West Highland Settlement.* PhD thesis, University of Plymouth.

Macleod, A. and Payne, G. (1988) 'Talkings about the Past'. Paper read at the BSA Annual Conference, University of Edinburgh.

Moore, R. (1982) *The Social Impact of Oil.* London: Routledge & Kegan Paul.

Mosely, M. (ed.) (1982) *Power, Planning and People in Rural East Anglia.* Norwich: University of East Anglia.

Musgrove, F. (1974) *The Migratory Elite.* London: Heinemann.

Payne, G., Dingwall, R., Payne, J. and Carter, M. (1981) *Sociology and Social Research.* London: Routledge & Kegan Paul.

Payne, G. and Cross, M. (1993) *Sociology in Action.* London: Macmillan.

Payne, G. and Macleod, A. (1993) 'The Double Gates: Culture, Interaction and Experience in Access to the "Exclusive Club"'. Paper read at the ESRC FASGNAG II Conference, Sabhal Mor Ostaig, Skye.

Platt, J. (1971) *Social Research in Bethnal Green.* London: Macmillan.

Pryce, K. (1979/1986) *Endless Pressure.* Hardmondsworth: Penguin; Bristol: Bristol Classical Press.

Rees, A. (1950) *Life in the Welsh Countryside.* Cardiff: University of Wales Press.

Roberts, B., Finnegan, R. and Gallie, D. (eds) (1985) *New Approaches to Economic Life.* Manchester: Manchester University Press.

Sharrock, W. and Anderson, R. (1980) *On the Demise of the Native.* Manchester: Occasional Paper No 5, Department of Sociology, University of Manchester.

Stacey, M., Batstone, E., Bell, C. and Murcott, A. (1975) *Power, Persistence and Change.* London: Routledge and Kegan Paul.

Strathern, M. (1981) *Kinship and the Core.* Cambridge: Cambridge University Press.

Wakeford, J. (1988) 'Review of G. Moyser and M. Wagstaffe (1987). Research Methods For Elite Studies', London, Allen & Unwin, *Sociology* 22: 158–60.

Warwick, D. and Littlejohn, G. (1992) *Coal, Capital and Culture.* London: Routledge & Kegan Paul.

Wenger, C. (1984) *The Supportive Network.* London: Allen and Unwin.

Whyte, W. F. (1955) *Street Corner Society.* Chicago: University of Chicago Press.

Williamson, W. (1982) *Class, Culture and Community.* London: Routledge and Kegan Paul.

Willmott, P. (1987) *Friendship Networks and Social Support.* London: Policy Studies Institute.

Young, M. and Willmott, P. (1957) *Family and Kinship in East London.* London: Routledge & Kegan Paul.

3 Researching Moving Targets: Using Diaries to Explore Supply Teachers' Lives

Marlene Morrison and Sheila Galloway

MAKING VISIBLE THE INVISIBLE

Imaginative leaps occur at many stages of research. This chapter exemplifies three quite distinct ways in which a creative approach can extend research horizons. First, we may choose themes, issues, phenomena, or groups which have previously been disregarded, perhaps because they appeared unworthy of attention, apparently peripheral to mainstream concerns. In articulating such themes we make visible what was invisible, and allow the reader to judge its importance or otherwise. Second, we can decide to study phenomena previously neglected because they presented particular logistical or methodological problems. In tackling what has been assumed to be 'undoable' we balance the risk of failure against the opportunity of breaking new ground. Third, we can adopt research methods that are familiar in other situations, but are now employed in a novel way, or in a new context. These were some of the substantive and methodological themes that preoccupied us in the research project from which this chapter draws.

During 1991–1992, a project entitled *Supply Teaching: An Investigation of Policy, Processes, and People in English Schools*, funded by the Leverhulme Trust, was conducted at the Centre for Educational Development, Appraisal and Research (CEDAR) at the University of Warwick. The study took an approach to teacher substitution, known mainly as 'supply cover' in the UK, which identified national and local policies, examined practice at institutional and classroom levels, and explored the impact and role of supply cover by drawing on the experiences of those most closely involved. The aim was to understand better the experiences of teachers, substitute teachers, and pupils when a regular teacher is unable to take a timetabled class and children are taught or supervised by another adult.

Much of the literature about teachers draws on research in which sustained relationships are developed between the researched, usually permanent teachers, and the researcher (as, for example, in life history approaches), or from detailed ethnographic studies grounded in a thorough understanding of one institution with which researchers have become familiar over lengthy periods of time. This is a key feature of studies by Lacey, Hargreaves, Burgess, and Ball. Here, the reader comes to 'know' teachers and institutions in which professional and personal beliefs are expounded, and practice described and analysed (Galloway 1992). In contrast, we 'know' relatively little about supply teachers or teaching. What is 'known' tends to be perceived as problematic rather than cause for pedagogic or professional celebration. Moreover, qualitative or quantitative methods require modification if they are to be successfully applied to research targets who move between schools, and into, and out of, differently organised employment situations.

Supply work is both ordinary (occurring frequently, if irregularly) and extraordinary (in that it sometimes brings into schools teachers who are total strangers to the pupils for whom they are fleetingly responsible) (Galloway 1992). Central to qualitative research is the combination of first-hand collection of data with documentary evidence. Diaries are one example of documentary evidence commissioned by the researcher, which have been used by teachers, by researchers, and by teacher researchers (Holly 1989, 1984). In our case, the use of supply teacher diaries provided opportunities to confront four major research challenges: first, the need to explore relationships between teacher substitutes, regular teachers, and pupils, which were often fleeting and transitory; second, to make connections between public and private aspects of supply teachers' lives which showed infinite variation; third, to capitalise on encounters between researchers and researched, which were sometimes (though not always) necessarily brief and opportunistic; and fourth, to resolve the logistical problems of research observation at multiple sites over relatively short and unpredictable time spans.

Fleeting Relationships

In very different contexts, Davis notes that 'most service relationships ... between professional[s] and ... clients[s] ... are characterised by certain constraints on too crass a rendering ... of the service' (1965: 336). 'Constraints' like reputations, status and practitioner skills tend to ensure that interactions between actors will 'exceed mere economic transactions' (1965: 336). In more binding relationships, the 'modicum' of visible 'continuity, stability, and homogeneity' helps to prevent relationships becoming 'reputationless, anonymous, and narrowly calculative' (1965: 346). Research into supply teaching relates to Davis's study of cab-drivers and clients in being characterised by two kinds of fleeting relationships: between researched and researchers, and between the researched and other institutional actors. Diary accounts provided one response to the methodological and conceptual challenges of researching areas of invisibility and anonymity. The diary's potential, therefore, was both as an approximation to observation 'for those situations where the problems of direct observation resist solution, or where further or more extended observation strains available resources' (Zimmerman and Wieder 1977: 481), and as an antidote to too 'crass' a rendering of the researched-researcher relationship.

The Public and Private

Diaries were also selected for their potential to reveal a complex and often rapid negotiation of time spent in public and private arenas. Most sociol-ogical studies of work concentrate on social relations in the workplace. Yet, a key feature of supply work is movement in and out of the work-place and of many workplaces. Diary accounts were, therefore, part of a holistic approach to tap into activities which might be variously described as work or employment, unpaid work, non-work or unemployment. In supply teaching, such concerns are made more complex by gender issues. Supply work has been viewed stereotypically as women's work. Beechey (1983) is among writers who have expressed unease about assertions of a distinctive women's experience of work which, it is argued, leads to a tendency to see men's working consciousness as dominated by the work-place and women's consciousness by the home. A key feature of the research was its attempt to reveal the interconnectedness of both male and female supply teachers' lives within and beyond schools. Diary accounts were important tools in this.

A focus on classroom practice adds a further dimension to assumptions about the workplace as 'public'. Teaching has been regarded as a private activity. Frequently, access into classrooms develops slowly and in accord with notions of rapport and trust between teachers and researchers. Reference has already been made to challenges in tracking and tracing moving targets. It was anticipated that diary accounts would provide illuminating self-report 'snapshots' of work in classrooms.

The Mechanics of Diary Use

Supply teacher diaries were used to explore what was becoming progressively, but only partially, visible to the researchers (cf Galloway 1993). Seventeen supply teachers completed diaries, allowing experience to be tracked in detail. The selection did not purport to be a representative sample; rather they exemplified a range of different situations pertaining to individuals doing supply work that went beyond what researchers could observe, given the practical constraints affecting the field work. In total, diaries provided data on eighty days to support that being obtained elsewhere. However, unlike interviewing (where self-report sometimes occurs over a lengthy recall span), daily accounts would add an immediate and alternative dimension to verbal accounts of experience.

In contrast to other formats (Bradley and Eggleston 1976; Campbell *et al.* 1991), stress was on qualitative features. The use of a time grid directed writers' attention to the day's events, and was not for the purpose of statistical analysis. Research interest also focused on the ways in which diarists sifted demanding features of daily activities from those considered more trivial. The critical incident approach (Oxtoby 1979) provided a framework for follow-up discussion, which was not restricted to work activities. Diary instructions were relatively open-ended, in line with the semi-structured interview schedules used elsewhere in the project. It was anticipated that diary accounts would deal with description rather than emotion. In the event, diaries did, in fact, use them as expressive instruments. Holly also notes that diary writing is frequently 'interpretative' and 'descriptive' on 'multiple dimensions' and thus it is not easy to separate 'thought from feelings from facts' (1984: 5). As the following sections indicate, such issues extended research opportunities and challenges.

The time-consuming aspects of the method previously identified by teachers and teacher researchers (Elliott 1982; Griffiths 1985) are more obvious than for some other research approaches. Preliminary consultation aimed to minimise the risk of reluctant diarists and useless information. This was complicated when research encounters were brief and occurred in schools where supply teachers' time is essentially class contact time. As Burgess (1981) notes, diaries are useful as preliminaries to in-depth interviewing. Whilst the method was less intensive and time-consuming than life or career history approaches (Woods 1990; Evetts 1990; Sikes *et al.* 1985), there were some similarities, especially where 'the observational log' (Zimmerman and Wieder 1977: 481) was used by diarists to move beyond a description of the day's events. Unlike regular teaching experience, it was rarely possible to schedule precisely times or days when supply work would take place. Instead, the research team set an overall time frame: diarists were invited to complete five-day schedules in which at least two days would be spent in schools as a methodological compromise between the immediacy of work situations and research project schedules.

Diary Accounts: Tales Out of School

Research paths are strewn with good intentions that end as time-sapping cul-de-sacs. Diary methods are especially vulnerable to diversionary pressures and unanticipated commitments (Morrison 1989, 1992). They share with other qualitative methods the opportunities and constraints of self-report. Diary writing is sometimes perceived as an intimate, personal act; in reality, research processes which include diary writing are *essentially* social. Despite the absence of researchers as observers (and unlike most secondary documents analysed by them), diaries are solicited evidence, written for readers other than the diarists. The implications are twofold. First, accounts can be written in ways which allow diarists to manipulate and control the image of self, either through a rationalisation of activities or a selectivity of data recorded. This leads, on occasion, to 'even-handed' descriptions of events, a case of the researched emulating actions for which researchers are frequently criticised. Second, the researchers become part of the act and context of diary writing. If, as Measor and Sikes suggest, there is 'a scaffolding of artifice and contrivance behind sociological accounts' (1991: 212), that construction may include actors' as well as researchers' written accounts. The following sections, therefore, focus on the various elements of that construction and consider its implications for data analysis. We begin with the processes of writing.

What to Write

Instructions to accompany diary schedules aimed to provide a basis for identifying themes across activities. However, multiple interpretations of the 'observational log' in terms of 'thickness' of description, made analysis complex. Along with post-diary interview opportunities to clarify and expand, these accounts alerted the authors to recurrent themes and emergent features at the private/public interface. Brief extracts (Figures 3.1 and 3.2) from two diarists highlight the issue and open up further explorations. The second set of comments (Figure 3.2) offer insights into aspects of preparing for 'a supply day' as well as an initial frame for focusing 'a life'. In the absence of follow-up interview, the first set of comments

Figure 3.1   Diary Extract (42.1)

Time	Main activities	Other
7.00		
8.00	Getting ready for work.	
8.30		

Figure 3.2   Diary Extract (46.2)

Time	Main activities	Other
7.00	Day 2 of Rosemary Conley's Inch Loss Exercise plan today. Shower, breakfast outside.	
8.00	Water tomatoes. Set off for school. Think it will be a reception class. Not absolutely sure.	School about 22 miles away so a much earlier start. Have covered at this school fairly recently.
8.30		

(Figure 3.1) would have little value for the research team. For the diarist, however, it may have provided a mechanism for indicating areas to which researchers would be unlikely to gain access.

The depth and breadth of diary accounts is also linked with interpretations of diary use by diarists; these included their value as reflective description or an expressive instruments. In Figures 3.3 and 3.4 the descriptive styles show marked differences. The first diarist works only in one secondary school; the second diarist in a variety of primary schools.

In Figure 3.3 description is brief, time-related and routinised. Minimal reference is made to issues of difficulty and guidance. In the follow-up interview one 'event' is discussed as a 'critical' moment in the school day, although its importance remains unclear from the written account. However, the brief reference provides an opening to discuss more general issues of female 'cover' for boys, girls and mixed ability PE groups. There is no initial reticence on the part of the second diarist who explains her diary entry subsequently as an opportunity to 'let off steam' about teaching 'difficult' pupils to a reader outside the immediate situation. Her written account goes

Figure 3.3   Diary Extract (43.1)

Time	Main activities	Other
9.00	Go to DH's office for cover slips. PE all day. PE Yr 9 mixed group – volley ball.	
10.00	Teaching game situation. Break. Yr 8 PE mixed group for dance.	Collected valuables. Locked them away.
11.00	Boys in particular needed a lot of guidance.	

Figure 3.4   Diary Extract (44.2)

Time	Main activities	Other
9.00	Fewer than one-third of children on time. Whole school assembly, infants and juniors, taken by a classteacher who is a fundamental Christian. School two-thirds Asian. Back in class, set children off on simple, algebra exercise. Had considerable difficulty with boy (D) who I'd been forewarned was 'dangerous'.	
10.00	He had spent most of Friday trying to wind me up and succeeded today. Different background, truculent, unmanageable personality. Doesn't work, moves around,	
11.00	argues, swears, picks fights, you name it. Typical Caribbean hard man. Not on playground duty so had chance to recharge batteries.	Able to swap tales with supply team member also doing cover here. One only has to mention the name of Y [another child/same school] and the floodgates open. Turned down 2 days work once when realised it was [Y's] class.

on to record an 'attempt not to be beaten … by a child who is totally untouched by authority and hasn't a consistent code to live by, either'.

Yet in the absence of methods to provide further context, both accounts remain free-floating. The second diarist provides detailed snapshots of each school because she believes these are 'unknown' to the reader (a correct assumption). The diary account is unconstrained by inhibitions, whether spatial, temporal or personal, which might feature in interview or observation situations. The method succeeds in giving access to events that the researcher was unable to observe. But the account is expressed very much in the teacher's own terms. In the former example, the researcher has observed in the school where the diarist works and is, therefore, invited to 'fill in the blanks', with detailed discussion confined to interviews. As is shown, diary accounts gave varied approximations to 'shadowing' supply teacher experiences, and our analysis challenges any simplistic interpretation of accounts as 'substitute' observation. Aspects of that challenge require further exploration.

'SUBSTITUTE' OBSERVATION

Diary accounts share with other ethnographic methods the aim of exploring vicarious experience. Earlier attention was drawn to whether the act of writing about experience adds an element of artificiality or superficiality to already complex features of data recording in 'natural' settings. The rationale for diary use was its potential to provide some form of substitute for observation. Assessments about validity in ethnographic research relate to whether accounts represent accurately the phenomena they describe or explain. The same event can be viewed from different perspectives, depending on the starting points and working assumptions of actors. Indeed, some writers point out the 'empirical phenomena are descriptively inexhaustible' (Hammersley 1992: 24). Among the implications for diary analysis, two are predominant. First, even if diary accounts are accepted as valid in terms of plausibility and credibility, 'how do we smooth out the contradictions in what people say [in this case, write] and do about their deeds?' (Hammersley 1992: 110). Second, in the absence of concurrent observations, to what extent do researchers and diarists share similar working assumptions in describing 'reality'? Where possible, opportunities were taken to observe activities which were also recorded by diarists. (Unlike many forms of qualitative research, negotiation of access was frequently speedy and fortuitous.) On occasion, diary accounts were at variance with observations recorded by the researcher. On days when researchers were absent, accounts sometimes showed a routinised even-handedness not apparent during research observations. Whilst the effects of the latter cannot be eliminated, the following examples point to some of the complexities.

Containment and Teaching

Research evidence suggested that the expectations and realities of supply work among regular and substitute teachers were complex and varied. Interview respondents focused on the multiple skills underpinning teaching in temporary situations, but the need for classroom control, order and containment were key concerns for senior management and permanent teachers. (For teachers contractually obliged to cover for absent colleagues, containment was frequently the sole criterion for judging internal cover.) The following extracts from a supply teacher diary (Figure 3.5) and an observer's record make visible the effects of these multiple perceptions for recording experience. Guy Symonds, supply teacher, completed a five-day schedule during part of a summer term spent in a boys' secondary school. On the third day he was observed by a researcher. One diary extract is shown in Figure 3.5.

Figure 3.5　　Diary Extract

Hours	Main activity	Other
14.15	Science lesson similar to previous one with Yr 10 but including more troublesome pupils with lower attention span. Pupils become pests at 15.15 approx.	
15.15		

Later:
'What was the most demanding task or situation with which you had to deal today?'
'Any additional comments . . . ?'
Dealing with (pupil) in last double, without telling him where to go. Today's activities were actually fairly straightforward.

The researcher's diary for the same period reads:

2.15 pm.　　Yr 10 dribble in over the next 10 minutes. GS [teacher] aims to repeat lesson given to another Yr 10 group in the morning. One pupil dribbles football up and down side of lab. Other boys at window observing fight below. Loud descriptions given. GS moves between lab. and back office. Returns from office with text books.
2.25　Pupil X enters. Informs GS he can be excused lesson to do English project in the library. No slip to confirm. Boys use loud expletives to deny truth of X's claim. GS moves to office again to

'phone English dept' re X's claim. Says 'there's no answer' and writes
X a slip to be excused. X exits.
2.30   Voice from the back: 'Are we going to get a lesson or aren't we?'
GS writes instructions on board and repeats them verbally. Gives titles
of book and author – writes: *You should have finished Qs 1–5 on
p. 37 and Qs 1–3 on p. 35. If not, then finish. If you have then copy
Fig. 1 on p. 32. Answer Qs 1–3 on p. 33.* Boys who are standing or
moving are told to sit. One boy distributes books by throwing them to
individual pupils. Noisy. Difficult to record everything. One pupil runs
tap at bench, soaks his companion's file. He'll 'get the bastard later'.
GS moves round class – answers queries – some genuine, some
spurious? One pupil drinking from Coke can loudly. Told to remove to
bin. Continues drinking – once finished, throws can into bin. Boys are
then told not to touch equipment or run water.
2.46   X returns. Has been 'thrown out' of the library. GS issues him
with paper. Sits down at lab. bench with 4 pupils.
3.00   Ducks fly past window. One boy shouts 'Ducks'. Except for 2
pupils at front bench, all rush to the window. 2 pupils at front work
quietly; finish exercises. When finished, 1 goes to the toilet. On his
return, both put their heads down on the bench till the end of the lesson.
3.10   6 boys (half class) put their coats on, and sit by window. GS
hopes they have finished work, will be examining exercise books.
Football dribbling recommences.
3.20   All boys close books of own volition. General talk.
3.25   GS switches lights off.
3.30   Bell. 6 boys kept behind. Not X. GS informs them of his dis-
appointment at behaviour. Expects it of X, he says, but not of them.
Future visit to D/Head is threatened sanction. Boys exit. GS talks to me
briefly about pupil 'backgrounds'.

Guy Symonds' diary schedule describes a 'fairly straightforward' day
marred by a few 'troublesome pests', especially pupil X. In the absence of
observation the researcher would be obliged to assess notions of 'straight-
forwardness' in relation to other research findings about supply *and*
regular teaching experiences. This teacher's language is linked to what he
views as success, in containing classes without outside interference/help;
avoiding a major confrontation with one pupil, and keeping a group on
task till 15.15 hours. Threats to classroom order and judgements about
quality of work are also related to pupils' socio-economic and ethnic backgrounds; their achievement potential; regular teachers' confirmation of
X as troublesome (with two previous school expulsions); the temporal

constraints of afternoon double lessons in midsummer; and pupils' immi-
nent transfer to another school. The 'arena of struggle' (Woods 1990) is
implicit rather than explicit.

In what ways does the observer's record contribute to our understanding
of supply teaching experience? Except for two boys, the group has
avoided the tedium of textbook exercises and outside interference. The
library escapade seems likely to have enhanced the peer group status of
one pupil whilst diverting teacher's attention from other classroom events.
Combining the accounts contributes evidence for assessing what formal
learning took place. Given Woods's summary of research evidence that
most pupils see 'ideal teachers' as those 'who are human [and] ... make
you work' (1990: 17), these accounts would suggest that future relations
with the group will involve contestation over the meanings of learning.
Whether this is viewed as 'straightforward' will depend as much on
previous experiences as a regular and a supply teacher, as to the attention
given to self-image and definitions of supply work.

The low-key assessment of difficulties faced and strategies used to cope
with them, is complemented by the researcher's account documenting
several high-risk features of the classroom situation that afternoon. Bridget
Jones', another supply teacher, however, exemplifies over a longer time-
scale the 'even-handedness' that diarists can adopt to smooth out the image
they wish us to have. At Mrs Jones's invitation, the researcher observed her
working in a first school which invited her one Tuesday to do supply work
for three days starting the next day. Access was negotiated for the Thursday.
Bridget had previously worked once at an adjacent school, so she knew this
school's location and had some sense of the intake. At 8.30 a.m. on the
Thursday she explained that the class of thirty-three six and seven year-olds
had made the previous day demanding: 'They pinch rubbers. They poke
each other with rulers. They throw things. It's just horrendous'.

Her description was confirmed by Thursday's observation, at the end of
which she ruefully wondered how to ensure a more satisfactory experience on Friday both for the pupils and herself. Her candid reflections did
not minimise the problems. However, the next Friday, Bridget Jones
worked at another school, when her diary entries demonstrated a style of
even-handedness different from that of Guy Symonds. They provide a
positive counterpoint to the day observed by the researcher. With a class
of thirty-five Year 3 and 4 pupils, the start of her day contrasts with the
previous Thursday: 'Children arrived, sat beautifully on floor. Chat about
[local area] (topic). Registers.' Though the regular teacher had been away
all week and this class had been taught 'by others, including part-time and
deputy', the day unfolds without problem:

Deputy told me what to do and produced paper with complete plan of day one. I wrote this on board and the children just went and *worked*!!! Very well organised! ... I spent most of the day checking work and helping where needed and teaching maths skills.

Her final thoughts emphasise the organisation required for a large mixed-age group.

Guy Symonds and Bridget Jones construct their own images of teachers at work, placing their chosen data alongside observation. Substitute teachers were often vulnerable in that they worked in unfamiliar contexts where they did not know pupils, and might feel particularly exposed because their professional skills were very much on trial. For them *in particular*, the degree of choice offered by the diary method gave a chance to present their own version of themselves as professional teachers. The teacher selected whether to write, when to complete a diary sheet, and what to report. The end result often gave the research team a record of uplifting as well as dispiriting experiences. It is tempting to repeat the comment of one supply teacher, echoed by many others, that 'There's no typical day on supply'. If this is so, this semi-structured diary method at least offers the researched the chance to represent this varied experience. To the researcher, in place of statistically representative information, it offers glimpses of the infinite variety of life as a 'stop-gap teacher'.

Diary accounts also focused on activities beyond school, and on links between activities. Such inter-connections are now highlighted in relation to gendered experience.

GENDERED ACCOUNTS

With exceptions (for example, Acker 1983), writing on teachers' careers draws heavily on male-oriented life cycles (Levinson *et al.* 1978) and careers which are hierarchical, continuous, and individualised (Sikes *et al.* 1985; Evetts 1990). Feminist writers (Gilligan 1982) focus on the public/private interface, and contrast the dynamics of female life cycles. The use of diaries provided opportunities to make visible some of these connections for substitute teachers (mostly women) whose careers were following alternative trajectories to those of permanent colleagues. In mining a rich ethnographic vein, the aim was to focus on gender as a first-order construct without analysis being totally absorbed by it. Diary accounts confirmed the predominance, but not exclusivity, of women in supply work for a multiplicity of reasons. This research drew upon, and added to, the contribution of gender studies in making women's work visible. In educational settings where professional work is shared among men and women, the implications of gender relations are already complex and contradictory, and are cross-cut by class, ethnicity and institutional contexts. However, the research team were reluctant to view supply teaching only in relation to gender. Following Morgan (1986: 30–58), it was considered that a 'catch-all' concept would reduce the extent to which supply teachers could be studied as 'fully fledged sociological actors' (Fildes 1989: 124). We were also unwilling to eliminate the contribution of unusual cases to the understanding of experience. Set alongside other methods, then, diary accounts were central to a research balance between public and private, men and women, and understandings at institutional as well as individual levels.

Two examples (Figures 3.6 and 3.7) offer gendered insights. Each combines elements of 'objective notetaking' and 'discursive writing' which Holly (1984) separates analytically as journals and diaries. Dee Knight, a supply team member, makes visible the skills and adaptability daily required by substitute teachers. Figure 3.6 also reveals these public/private connections: in relation to bodily functions, caring, dieting, and social contacts. In Sue Daniels's day (Figure 3.7) work activities repeatedly intersect with the demands of multiple roles as mother, daughter, housewife and custodian of the family pets. Such records contrast with dairy accounts which focus only on critical 'work' incidents, and with life histories which tend to present longer term, ironed-out career accounts. How should ethnographic research sift the minutiae of vicarious experience from the central themes? Evidence from the diary accounts suggested that it was through these kinds of combinations and connections that such minutiae structured gendered experience. Their implications for women teachers in particular have been largely assumed.

ETHICAL BOUNDARIES

Ethnography generally recognises the importance of relationships between researchers and researched. Sustained aspects of friendship and reciprocity feature frequently in ethnographic accounts like life histories and case studies. The authors' relationships with diarists were usually more transitory, yet these diaries gave access to experience which crossed boundaries between the personal and public, the social and the professional. At first sight, the research bargain appears strange and one-sided. Yet we did not underestimate these relationships. Observing a supply teacher at work

Figure 3.6   Diary Extract (46.4)

Time	Main activities	Other
7.00	Day 4 of exercises – shower Breakfast inside today. Up later not feeling totally together. Watered garden. Nursed rabbit for 1/2 hr trying to get her to drink or eat.	Nowhere yet to go so can set off to base at 8.15 and still be there before time.
8.00 8.23 8.45	Feeling a bit down (PMT and rabbit referred to in previous day's schedule) Set off to base. Arrive base. Chat to fellow supply – see how things are going.	
9.00 9.05 9.25	Just getting breath when message comes to go – but no age range given I & J school. Set off. Arrive school. Look for entrance and park. School deserted – no sec. in office even.	Had to follow A–Z quite carefully. Hadn't been to this school for 2 yrs and then only for part of a day.
10.00	Eventually find hall – children in Assembly. Teacher near door beckoned me in. When ready to go out same teacher pointed out the class – Yr 2 class.Tells me they are worst in school – messed about. 10.00 go to class. Chat about self. Set them picture and writing to tell me about self. A lot of disruption. One or two quite difficult.	Listened to end of Assembly. Introduced by the Dep. as Mrs A. at end of Ass. 10.40 Play. Went to staffroom for a coffee and put lunch away.
11.00	Collect children from playground. Took ages to get order– so much fuss. Back to class – for milk. Lunch had been taken out. Carried on writing – if finished did their maths. Following Peak which I know. Heard some readers but difficult as children needed disciplining a lot.11.30 Singing.	Got told at play that my class goes swimming after dinner. Singing – I was left with the 2 Yr classes and a peripatetic pianist. Wow, what a hard session.

(*Fig. 3.6 cont'd overleaf*)

Figure 3.6   Continued

Time	Main activities	Other
12.00	Dismiss children. Quite a lot went home – unusual. Mark work up to date and change any books. Get changed for swimming. Fill in a form for my mum. Ring Vet to book rabbit in. Ring bank – slight cash flow problem. Eat lunch in staffroom. Staff not particularly chatty but glad of the rest!	Ringing up took ages. Office locked – no idea where key was till found someone to tell me.
13.00 13.10 13.20	Children in. Did register. Didn't tally. Incorrect from morning! Took ages to sort out; some children's names difficult to pronounce. Reg. not very clear. Needed to be accurate for swimming. Eventually set off. Took a while to get there as kept starting and stopping. Worn out when I arrived!	A mum came with me – an older lady – very nice but not very effective. Very noisy in changing areas. I was dotting from one to the other.
14.00	Eventually we got there down to the pool instructor. He took the more able group – leaving me alone with 20 children in small pool. We worked hard but they didn't tire. Changing took ages. Walked back better after a great lecture from me. Got back 14.40. Too late for play.	I have never felt so worn after swimming. Only I had to get out of water for a short while. Miracles never cease.
15.00 15.30 16.00	I kept them out for 10 mins play whilst I had a drink. An EMS teacher took a group for reading. I let rest finish off any work then get an activity whilst I heard readers. Behaviour improving. Dismiss children. Write note for teacher.	Didn't think they'd settle to a story and they hadn't read all week. Dep. wished I was going back as I'd controlled class!!

Figure 3.6 Continued

Time	Main activities	Other
16.50 17.00	Arrive home. 10 mins walk for Ben. Rang Bill to tell him about rabbit. Collect rabbits. Go to vet's. Ben came for company. Female rabbit had to be put down. I brought her home.	Not feeling wonderful!
17.30	Called at friend's for our weigh-in. I had *not* lost any weight from last Thursday!! Told friend about rabbit!	I stayed for longer than I'd planned.
18.00 18.30 18.45	We had a chat over a red wine and tonic – much needed! Call at friend's with a book I'd picked up for her. Got home. Played with rabbit. Had a bath. Soak! Soak!	
19.00	Ate nothing as no time! Rang my sister to tell her about rabbit. Mum rang. Rang Bill to tell him. Got dressed.	My nieces had given me the rabbits at Christmas
20.00	Went round to friend's house from my base school to a Pippa Dee. Very expensive for what it was. Resisted all the lovely cakes – just had a bit to taste as they were homemade (from a friend's piece). Listened to the demonstrator telling us what a stressful day-time job she had.	Only bought some orange foam bath Tried on some clothes with rest of base school – just for fun.
21.00	She wasn't a teacher!! Offered a coffee by hostess's daughter and gratefully accepted. Just a few left – all base school staff. Had a chat and laugh. Put the world to rights.	I needed that!

(*Fig. 3.6 cont'd overleaf*)

Figure 3.6   Continued

Time	Main activities	Other
22.00		
22.30	Set off home.	
22.50	Arrive home.	

Anything before 07.00 hrs?	Anything after 22.00 hrs?
6.45 Got up later! Quickly walked dog – short walk.	
Fed fish and checked rabbits.	Female very ill. Cover rabbit. Walk dog. Have a bite to eat – literally.
Pack for Wales.	Flop to bed.

What was the most demanding task or situation with which you had to deal today? Any additional comments on today's activities?
Singing – not really fair to be landed after only 1 hr in a school with 2 difficult classes.
Coped, but throat sore.
Swimming – very dangerous situation – particularly at the baths. 1:20 ridiculous.

Figure 3.7   *Diary Extract (43.3)*

Time	Main activities	Other
7.00	Got up, washed, dressed etc. Fed dogs and cats. Gave dogs a run. Prepared breakfast etc.	
7.45	Woke kids – got them washed and dressed. Made beds.	
8.00	Ate breakfast – washed up. Checked kids were prepared for school. Left house at 8.30 – took kids to schools then travelled to Dartmouth.	

Figure 3.7   Continued

Time	Main activities	Other
9.00	Picked up cover slip. Yr 9 PSE Tutor Group. Lesson on 'Problems they find at this stage in their Lives'. Not seen work before. Last minute cover.	
10.00	Break followed by Yr 10 GCSE Dance group. Supervision of theory work. Messy because of room changes.	
11.00	Yr 7 History cover. Work set.	
12.00	Returned home. Washed and set mother's hair. Cup of coffee then back to school.	
13.00	Yr 7 PE Mixed group for dance. Followed up previous week's work. (Kids informed me). 'Directions'. Did a lot of work on warm up first – why etc.	Collect valuables before lesson – keep, then return at end.
14.00	Yr 11 PE. Aerobics – girls only. Gave ideas, supplied music. They worked in groups routine.	
15.00		
15.15	Return to changing room – supervise and return valuables.	
15.30	Left school to fetch kids. Returned home. Combed mother's hair out.	
16.00	Fed dogs, gave them a run. Prepared tea. Got kids' swimming kit ready.	
17.00	Ate tea. Sorted clean washing from yesterday ready for ironing sometime!!	

(*Fig. 3.7 cont'd overleaf*)

Figure 3.7   Continued

Time	Main activities	Other
18.00		
18.15	Left to take Petra to swimming lesson (6.30–7.00). Went to Asda to do some shopping – returned in time to dry and dress her at 7.00.	
19.00		
19.15	Took Petra and shopping home. Picked John up and took him for his lesson (7.30–8.00). Went to Slimming Club for 'weigh-in'. Returned for John at 7.50 pm (i.e. saw last 10 mins of lesson)	
20.00	Sorted out swimming stuff. Did a load of washing – put it to dry. Got kids to bed after washing and drying their hair.	
21.00	Cup of coffee	
21.30	Until 22.30 fell asleep on the settee!! (Didn't want to watch tele anyway)	

Anything before 07.00 hrs?	Anything after 22.00 hrs?
No.	No – only bed!

What was the most demanding task or situation with which you had to deal today?
Any additional comments on today's activities?
1. Doing aerobics with Yr 11 for 1 hr 15 mins, with my knee hurting too much to take a full active part.
2. Finding my 'lightest' clothes for Slimming Club weigh in!!

provided a fairly sound basis for developing rapport, especially when time together was spent in demanding, and, on occasion, fairly intimate (home) circumstances. There were other safeguards. Initial encounters were usually in schools. Here, an interest in supply teaching issues, addressed *to* supply teachers, was generally welcomed *by* them as overdue and relevant.

This moved relationships beyond the importance of being listened to; 'making visible' was a reciprocal point of contact for researchers and researched. Diary accounts were also set alongside other methods and some preferred to give interviews rather than write diaries. Post-diary interviews provided opportunities for formative, verbal respondent validation and advanced the diary analysis in important ways. Finally, diaries offered some emancipation from the one-sided constraints of other methods, for example interviewing. They gave participants explicit opportunities to control the selection of data and the mode of description.

Other aspects raise more contentious issues. At a general level, there was agreement among researchers and diarists about the purpose of the accounts. Diarists knew that these were important bases for recording and analysing lives at and beyond school, and that work would be presented using pseudonyms. For several, the act of writing raised consciousness about complexities at the private/public interface, yet mechanisms to support that consciousness remained beyond the research agenda. There was no format for networking, and diarists did not know each other, so this activity left them as much in isolation as they normally were (Trotter and Wragg 1990). The contribution of diaries for future writing was not fully formulated. Indeed, at this stage of the work the research team could not reliably predict the nature of the data or how it might be appropriate to use such information.

Linked to recent commentaries (for example, Burgess 1989), the ethical boundaries of diary research are comforting or assuaging, depending on whose perspectives are taken. Moreover:

> In research relationships there is no natural bargain that would be recognised as fair by all. Respondents are not fearful victims who open up their lives and souls because they are asked or told to. People have boundaries and strategies to protect themselves in research situations (Measor and Sikes 1991: 230).

As diarists decide whether, what, and when to write, their freedom is greater than that afforded in interviews: once the decision is made of *whether* to agree to be interviewed, the *when*, that is, the timing, is negotiated. *What* may be more problematic. The interviewee can resist, sidestep, or ignore questions put by an interviewer, but the face-to-face call for a response has an immediacy that creates pressure, and evasion is rarely complete. Interviewees do present images of themselves, but diaries offer greater freedom to manipulate inform-ation, whether consciously or unconsciously, without the immediate presence of 'the listening ear'. Manipulation can also extend to the interpretation of guidance given to diarists as recent work by Morrison and Burgess on the completion of food and drink diaries suggests (Burgess 1994).

CONCLUSIONS

This chapter has considered some strengths and weaknesses of the diary in enabling researchers to make sense of, and make visible, the realities of teaching in the context of supply teachers' lives. Where targets were constantly moving for both the researchers and the researched, diaries provided valuable data. In doing so, they raise important questions about ways of representing professional and personal lives when teacher professionalism is itself being reappraised, and there is persistent resistance to recognising the role of teacher substitution in mass education systems.

The authors had always foreseen that this research would be methodologically challenging. The core of the work was the study of phenomena that are discontinuous and unpredictable (both in schools and in the lives of supply teachers), whilst the scarcity of information at national and local levels provided only a patchy framework for the fieldwork. Diaries were, therefore, part of an exploratory study which set diverse qualitative perspectives alongside each other. Throughout the project the research team sought to:

> steer a path between, on the one hand, those views of ethnographic research that are based on naive realism whereby the goal is simply to represent social phenomena 'in their own terms', and on the other hand, those that abandon realism in favour of a direct, practical payoff and/or the creativity of ethnographic analysis and writing (Hammersley 1990: 127).

Judgements about the effectiveness of diary accounts as a research strategy have been linked to research definitions and focus, and to conceptual frameworks of work, invisibility, and transitory relations among key actors (including researchers) at the public/private interface. We have sought to make links with validity, in terms of plausibility and credibility, and with relevance in evidence from diary accounts, exploring writing in relation to action, process, circumstance and interpretation. Relevance has been considered in terms of contributions to knowledge about teacher absence *and* substitution. This does not exhaust the relevant issues;

research knowledge can provide both a rhetorical argument and a coherent basis for more effective developments in substitute teaching at national, local, institutional, and individual levels.

Diary accounts were part of a trade-off, in resource and contingency terms, against interviews and observation. Neither were ethical issues ignored in efforts to make supply teachers' lives visible. What is public and/or private, either in school or domestic settings, is not always clear-cut. What supply teachers said, wrote, or did, could make the invisible visible. Their omissions were also important. The authors' intention was to minimise negative consequences for the researched, and maximise opportunities for follow-up.

This research reveals the differing importance of teacher substitution for sociologists and educationalists. While social scientists are primarily interested in explanation and educationalists in solutions or improvements, researchers working with dual aims need to be explicit about the methods used to record and analyse experience. Against the theme of this volume this exploration into the use of supply teacher diaries provides one contribution.

Acknowledgements

The authors wish to thank The Leverhulme Trust for the funding of the project on which this chapter is based and all those who contributed to the research but remain anonymous. Thanks also go to Professor Bob Burgess, project director, and to those who contributed to the discussion of this chapter at the 1993 BSA Annual Conference.

REFERENCES

Acker, S. (1983) 'Women and Teaching: A Semi-detached Sociology of a Semi-Profession', in S. Walker, and L. Barton (eds) *Gender, Class and Education*. Lewes: Falmer.

Beechey, V. (1983), 'What's So Special about Women's Employment?' *Feminist Review* 14: 23–45.

Bradley, R. and Eggleston, J. (1976) *An Induction Year Experiment*. Report of an experiment carried out in Derbyshire, Lincolnshire and Nottinghamshire LEAs and the University of Nottingham School of Education, Nottingham University School of Education.

Burgess, R. G. (1981) 'Keeping a Research Diary', *Cambridge Journal of Education* 11: 75–83.

Burgess, R. G. (ed.) (1989) *The Ethics of Educational Research*. Lewes: Falmer Press.

Burgess, R. G. (1994) 'On Diaries and Diary Keeping', in N. Bennett, K. Glatter and R. Levacic (eds) *Improving Educational Management*. London: Paul Chapman.

Campbell, R. J., Evans, L., Packwood, A. and Neill, S. R. St. J. (1991) *Workloads, Achievement and Stress*. London: AMMA.

Davis, F. (1965) 'The Cab-driver and his Fare: Facets of a Fleeting Relationship', in D. Potter and P. Sarre (eds) (1974) *Dimensions of Society: a Reader*. Milton Keynes: Open University Press.

Elliott, J. (1982) 'Action Research into Action Research', *Classroom Action Research Network*, Bulletin No. 5, Cambridge Institute of Education.

Evetts, J. (1990) *Women in Primary Teaching: Career Contexts and Strategies*. London: Allen & Unwin.

Fildes, S. (1989) 'Gender', in M. Haralambos (ed.) *Developments in Sociology*, 4. England: Causeway Press.

Galloway, S. (1992) 'Investigating the Irregular and the Unpredictable: Reflections on Research on Supply Teaching'. Paper presented at St. Hilda's Ethnography Conference, University of Warwick, September.

Galloway, S. (1993) '"Out of Sight, Out of Mind": A Response to the Literature on Supply Teaching', *Educational Research* 35: 159–69.

Gilligan, C. (1982) *In a Different Voice*. Cambridge, Mass.: Harvard University Press.

Griffiths, G. (1985) 'Doubts, Dilemmas and Diary Keeping' in R. G. Burgess (ed.) *Issues In Educational Research: Qualitative Methods*. Lewes: Falmer.

Hammersley, M. (1990) *Reading Ethnographic Research: A Critical Guide*. London: Longman.

Hammersley, M. (1992) *What's Wrong with Ethnography?* London: Routledge.

Holly, M. L. (1984) *Keeping a Personal Professional Journal*. Deakin: Deakin University Press.

Holly, M. L. (1989) *Writing to Grow*. Portsmouth, New Hampshire: Heinemann.

Levinson, D. J. *et al.* (1978) *The Seasons of a Man's Life*. New York: Knopf.

Measor, L. and Sikes, P. (1991) 'Visiting Lives: Ethics and Methodology in Life History', in I. Goodson (ed.) *Studying Teachers' Lives*. London: Routledge.

Morgan, D. (1986) 'Gender', in R. G. Burgess (ed.) *Key Variables in Social Investigation*. London: Routledge & Kegan Paul.

Morrison, M. (1989) 'An Exploration of the Meanings of Part-time for Those Who Experience it in a College of Further Education.' Unpublished M.Ed. thesis: University of Warwick.

Morrison, M. (1992) 'Part-time: Whose Time? Women's Lives and Adult Learning', in M. Morrison (ed.) *Managing Time for Education*, CEDAR papers 3, University of Warwick.

Oxtoby, R. (1979) 'Problems Facing Heads of Departments', *Journal of Further and Higher Education* 3: 46–59.

Sikes, P., Measor, L. and Woods, P. (1985) *Teachers: Careers, Crises and Continuities*. Lewes: Falmer Press.

Trotter, A. and Wragg, T. (1991) 'A Study of Supply Teachers', *Research Papers in Education* 5: 251–76.

Woods, P. (1990) *The Happiest Days? How Pupils Cope with School*. Lewes: Falmer Press.

Zimmerman, D. H. and Wieder, D. L. (1977) 'The Diary-interview Method', *Urban Life*, January: 479–99.

4 Uncovering Key Aspects of Experience: The Use of In-depth Interviews in a Study of Women Returners to Education

Susan Smith

INTRODUCTION

This chapter is derived from a qualitative study of the experiences of a group of women studying in further and adult education. It presents a case for the contribution that in-depth interviews can make to an understanding of these experiences, and specifically, how they are shaped by women's lives in the private sphere.

A key issue which arose was the amount of support given by husbands/partners and I will outline how the adoption of a 'feminist paradigm for interviewing' (Cook and Fonow 1990: 76) led to the women sharing with me what Pat O'Connor calls 'the backstage areas of self' (1991: 243). In the context of this research, these 'backstage areas' relate to their relationships with the men to whom they were married or with whom they were living, and the effect that these relationships had upon their academic success. In producing a sociology 'for' women (Duelli-Klein 1983; Smith 1987; Harding 1987; Cook and Fonow 1990) I argue for the importance of viewing interviewing as a reciprocal process where 'the interviewer is prepared to invest her own personal identity in the relationship' (Oakley 1981: 41). Also, we must ask the kinds of questions which will enable us to explore the personal and lead to greater understanding and knowledge of women's lives and experiences when they return to education.

RESEARCH INTO SUPPORT

The importance of the kinds of questions asked and what the resulting data reveal about women students' experiences can be seen from previous research. The studies which have demonstrated that husbands/partners are supportive tend to be based upon self-completion questionnaires. The word 'support' is not used explicitly; instead questions are asked about 'encouragement' or 'approval' from family members. Woodley *et al.*'s (1987) study of five thousand mature students, for example, included one question which can be linked to the issue of support. The question was 'How do the following people feel about you taking this course? Are they a source of encouragement or discouragement?' In response to this question, Woodley reports that 16 per cent said only their spouse/partner was 'neutral' and three per cent that they were 'generally discouraging'. It would be interesting to know how many of these were women, but he does not give any breakdown of the data by sex. Equally there is no explanation of what 'neutral' or 'generally discouraging' actually means. He concludes that:

> The great majority of people have positive or at most neutral attitudes towards the idea of older men and women going back to study, so discouragement is rarely met by a person who decides to become a mature student (1987: 141).

Similarly, the research by Burwood and Brady (1980) of women studying on two courses in one college details the finding that 80 per cent of the women on one of the courses (GCE) and 60 per cent on the other (TOPS) said their husbands gave 'unconditional approval' and none that they 'unconditionally disapproved'. A small percentage on each said their husbands gave 'conditional approval', but there is no analysis of what this meant.

A study which explicitly used the word 'support' is that of Katz (1976) into the support given by men to the educational and occupational aspirations of their wives. He found that 62 per cent were 'very supportive', 20 per cent 'somewhat', ten per cent 'neutral' and five per cent 'not'. He concludes from this that 'husbands were overwhelmingly supportive', yet his statistics show 35 per cent of women experienced lack of support to varying degrees. This, however, is not explored and significantly there is no analysis of what exactly is meant by 'support'. He also reports that nearly half the men said they had taken on more chores around the house, and one is left with the impression from this study, and the others previously mentioned, that women who return to study receive 'help' and encouragement from their husbands/partners. There are perhaps a minority who do not, but their experiences are not regarded as significant. In addition, there is no analysis of what 'support', 'encouragement', 'approval' actually mean in practical terms; they are presented as unproblematic notions. As a result, very little insight is gained into this aspect of the lives of women students. In fairness, a number of the studies do acknowledge the importance of support for women returners. Oglesby, for example, says, 'Support of the husband is crucial to survival let alone success' (1976: 14), but the issue seems to have received very little analysis.

In contrast, the studies which have utilised interviews provide rather different insights into the notion of support. Swarbrick, for example, in her study of women Open University students found a discrepancy between the general claim of family support and enthusiasm, particularly from husbands, and the actual range of support provided; she notes that: 'For some this meant a passive acceptance, a mere lack of opposition, for others it could mean a generally approving, reassuring attitude with any practical help as a bonus' (1978: 177). Kirk, who also studied Open University students, reveals that husbands' support was conditional on not having their lives disrupted, and concludes from her data that: 'Domestic problems for married students are an important cause of student withdrawal and academic difficulty' (1977: 9).

The research into support, particularly the quantitative studies, raises, I would argue, some questions about the epistemological assumptions upon which it is founded. Why is the lack of support which evidently exists in the data not explored? One possible explanation can be linked to feminist critiques of mainstream social science and the theme of the invisibility and distortion of female experience (Acker 1981; Duelli-Klein 1983; Stanley and Wise 1983a; Oakley 1985; Westcott 1990; Cook and Fonow 1990). In addition, Harding argues that traditional social science has grounded its analysis only in men's experiences and has asked only those questions about social life which men want answered. This leads to '... partial and even perverse understandings of social life' (1987: 6).

In the light of the data from qualitative studies, the findings based upon quantitative techniques do seem partial and one explanation for this relates to the actual questions which were asked. In fact Lovell (1980a), whose research used both questionnaires and interviews, comments that her findings seemed contradictory. Whilst a number said they received encouragement, she found that some were blocked from achieving their objectives by what she calls 'domestic sabotage'. If the findings from feminist research are included the discrepancies become even more acute. For example, the work of the Taking Liberties Collective suggests that:

> The reality of most women's lives under the present system handicaps us before we start. We have to bear the main responsibility of domestic and child care labour, regardless of whether we are studying or not. We can't automatically rely on the kind of ... support for own studies that we would expect if we were men (1989: 68).

Important insights can also be found in the work of Edwards (1991) who, in her conclusion to her research into mature mother students studying in higher education, says that little had changed with regard to their responsibilities in the private sphere.

A FEMINIST PARADIGM FOR INTERVIEWING

A starting point for a feminist approach to the use of interviews, according to Nielsen (1990), can be found in Oakley's study of the transition to motherhood. Oakley compares textbook 'recipes' for interviewing (1981: 30) with her experience of interviewing women and suggests that in the light of her experience these 'recipes' are 'morally indefensible' (ibid: 41). Within these 'recipes' much emphasis is placed upon the 'researcher-researched' relationship and the importance of objectivity and detachment on the part of the researcher. The image projected is that of a hierarchical relationship, where the researcher has the power to control the conduct of the interview with a respondent who is essentially passive. Moser and Kalton's definition of interviewing would seem to exemplify this: 'A conversation between the interviewer and respondent with the purpose of eliciting certain information from the respondent' (1971: 271). The interview, therefore, becomes a specialised form of conversation, a one-way process in which one person asks the questions and the other gives the answers. This one-way process, where one gives and the other takes, can also be seen in Bogdan and Biklen's (1982) definition of interviewing as, 'a purposeful conversation ... that is directed by one in order to get information' (quoted in Ely 1991: 135).

The power in this type of interview lies firmly with the interviewer who must remain detached from those providing the answers. The call for detachment is made strongly and, I would argue, sometimes rather worryingly, as in the following:

> But the interview is still more than a tool and object of study. It is the art of sociological sociability, the game we play for the pleasure of savouring its subtleties. It is our flirtation with life, our eternal affair,

played hard to win, but played with that detachment and amusement which gives us, win or lose, the spirit to rise up and interview again and again (Benney and Hughes 1977: 234).

This account portrays the interview almost as if it were some fleeting, non-involved sexual encounter, where the interviewer exploits the respondent in order to satisfy an almost voyeuristic desire for information. There also seems to be the implication of a lack of care or concern: the interview is a game not to be taken too seriously, good for the ego of the interviewer who takes but gives nothing. I find this approach ethically suspect. Oakley sums up the textbook approach succinctly when she says, 'The paradigm of the "proper" interview appeals to such values as objectivity, hierarchy and science' (1981: 38).

Oakley found that advice about maintaining distance between interviewer and interviewee limited her ability to communicate with her respondents in a way that would generate meaningful information. Nielsen comments: 'In short, she got involved. The ... consequences of her involvement directly challenges the subject-object separation' (1990: 6). Rejection of the subject-object separation is a key feminist methodological principle, and it has been argued by Duelli-Klein that the polarisation of the subjective and objective falsifies experience and reality:

> The challenge for feminist science will be to see, name, describe and explain without recreating these dichotomies, without falling into the old pattern of objectifying experience ... by withdrawing from it ourselves to a position of assumed neutrality (1983: 112)

This issue is central to much of the discourse on feminist methodology; Stanley and Wise, for example, argue that traditional relationships which involve: 'Treating people as objects – sex objects or research objects is morally unjustifiable' (1983a: 170).

The rejection of the subject/object separation as a guiding principle and viewing the interview as an 'interactional exchange' (Cook and Fonow 1990), had important implications for the rapport I was able to establish with my respondents. The issue is explored further later in the discussion.

INTERVIEWING WOMEN STUDENTS

The twenty women who participated in the research were studying on a range of courses in further and adult education. Their ages ranged from thirty-four to fifty-two, nine were working class and eleven middle class, all were married or living with a male partner and had children under the age of sixteen.

Each of the women was interviewed twice during one academic year. The first exploratory interview utilised a life history approach; its purpose was to enable the 'telling of experiences in the biographical context in which they occur' (Graham 1984: 110). The interviews lasted from one to four hours with two hours the average. The second interview was conducted three to six months later and focused primarily upon the experience of being a student. These interviews were shorter and lasted on average one hour. For this I used an 'interview guide' which contained themes that I explored with the women; but equally a number of issues were raised that I had not even conceptualised. All interviews were tape-recorded which is imperative if full attention is to be given to the interviewee), and later transcribed.

Building Rapport

I discussed with the women where they would like the interviews to take place as I was aware of the demands on their time and I also felt it important to indicate my willingness to meet them on their own terms. This approach was underpinned by my view that they were doing me a favour rather than the other way round. Ely (1991) suggests, in fact, that a vital characteristic of qualitative research is the researcher being responsive to participants' schedules. A key issue was that they were able to talk to me without being interrupted by children or partner. This resulted in the majority of the interviews being conducted in the women's homes, either during the day when children were at school or in the evening when they were dispatched either to bed or to another room with instructions not to interrupt. It was interesting, but perhaps not surprising, that none of the women wanted their partners present. I suspect that the outcome of this study would have have been very different had they been present.

An issue well documented in the literature (Oakley 1981; Finch 1984; Corbin 1971) is the warmth and hospitality shown by women respondents. My experience was no exception, I was made to feel welcome, introduced to other members of their families and invited to share meals with them. Some were a little nervous initially but I sensed a commitment to the goals of the project and a willingness to take part. The connection between showing hospitality and a commitment to the research relationship as documented by Oakley (1981) has, however, been criticised by Ribbens who says: 'I find this evidence singularly unconvincing as there is a strong norm that you offer refreshment to anyone visiting your house for any period of time, including workmen' (1989: 583). This point is certainly valid, but I would argue that the warmth with which I was received extended beyond what could be described as polite or customary. Like both Oakley (1981) and Finch (1984), I was expecting to have to work at 'something called rapport' and was both surprised and pleased to find this was not the case. Finch suggests a reason for this which is based upon the idea of a shared identity and understanding: 'When the interviewer is also a woman, both parties share a subordinate structural position by virtue of their gender. This creates the possibility that a particular kind of identification will develop' (1984b: 76).

In addition to this, I would add another dimension which facilitated rapport and which could be termed the 'perceived relevance' of the study to the women's lives. During my initial discussions with the women I had attempted to explain in detail the purpose of the project and to answer any questions of which there were many. It became clear that the women wanted assurances about what I was going to do with the information they provided. Was I just another 'academic' who wanted to encroach upon their lives, take all that I could and use it to further my career? This scepticism is understandable and, whilst I could give no assurances that this work would change the course of women's education, I did stress my intention that it should be used in the promotion of 'equal opportunities'. Whilst I was prepared to answer any questions, I was not prepared for a response I got which touched me considerably. A number of the women said that they thought this was a worthwhile project making comments like: 'It's probably too late for us but it might help women in the future' (comment from field notes).

Another factor which I think helped to establish rapport is what Finch (1984) and Edwards (1990) refer to as 'placing the interviewer'. During the discussions I have just described I talked about my background and indicated that the origins of the project lay in my own experience of being a mature student and also a teacher of mature students. The fact that I had experienced and understood some of the problems they faced meant that we had a 'shared universe of meaning'. It is certainly the case that the interviews in which I shared more of myself yielded some of the 'richest' data I received. This would seem to corroborate Finch's (1984) point regarding the richness of data that can be obtained when:

A female researcher interviewing another women abandons the mystified role of researcher and instead presents herself as an ordinary woman with many of the same concerns as the woman she is interviewing (quoted by Riddell 1989: 84).

The issue of the 'richness' of data equates with establishing a relationship where the women felt they could trust me with some of the more intimate details of their lives, where they were prepared to reveal the 'backstage areas of self' referred to in the introduction to this chapter. One particularly poignant example occurred in my interview with Julie. The life-history interview had to be conducted in two phases as she had a great deal she wanted to tell me, and I was invited to supper on an evening when her husband was working and her children had gone to stay with friends. On that day I was particularly anxious because a member of my family was very ill, and when Julie asked if I was all right I did share my concerns with her; this led to her revealing some very intimate details about her own family. These details are not directly relevant to this discussion but what she did go on to tell me which proved to be extremely important to the issue of support, was the following, said in a voice which was almost a whisper:

> 'My husband has always made the major decisions, various arguments are put forward as to why his are the best decisions and I don't always agree with them. It's nice to have a partnership but there isn't such a thing... I don't know how much he earns. He gives me housekeeping, if I need more I have to ask for it.'

I would argue that sharing my concerns and revealing details of my own life led to Julie sharing with me a 'private' account and is testimony to Oakley's statement that there is 'no intimacy without reciprocity' (1981: 49).

A further aspect of reciprocity in the interviews was the response I gave to the many questions I was asked. These questions were about the research and I was also asked for advice on courses, grants and study techniques, which I answered as fully as I could, seeing this as something I could offer back to the women. A number of the questions were directed at seeking reassurance (which I gave) about what they were doing, particularly as a number had experienced guilt feelings about their studies.

> 'I just want education for the sake of it really, it doesn't seem like a good motive does it?' (Mary).
> 'Is it really important though? Sometimes I just don't know' (Julie).

They were keen to find out what I thought and to defer to what they saw as my greater knowledge and experience. My response was to be encouraging, to outline the positive aspects of their return to study, although I am aware that my attempts to give positive encouragement could be seen as double-edged. On the one hand, it was a genuine attempt to boost confidence; on the other, it could be seen as manipulative, i.e. telling them what I thought they wanted to hear in the hope of developing rapport so that they would give me the 'private' rather than the 'public' account. This does raise an interesting issue about interviewer involvement and whether it is possible to attain 'genuine reprocity' (Ribbens 1989: 583). I can offer no solutions as to how an interviewer might determine whether the reciprocity within the research relationship is 'genuine'; indeed, this does seem to equate with another equally problematic question as to the 'truth' of the accounts given by respondents. Clearly, this is an issue faced by all researchers irrespective of the research method employed. I can only restate that the interviews in which I gave more of myself yielded the greatest disclosure of the more personal details of my respondent's lives.

The guilt feelings referred to above were linked to the women's perceived neglect of their families and the amount of support which they received from their husbands/partners. The exploration of the issue of support further exemplifies the value of adopting a feminist paradigm for interviewing.

USING IN-DEPTH INTERVIEWS TO 'UNPACK' THE NOTION OF SUPPORT

I approached the issue of husband's/partner's support by asking the women to tell me how they met their husbands/partners and this often initiated a detailed story of time, place and the subsequent development of the relationship. By this stage in the interview we had already discussed such issues as family background, schooling and the jobs they had done. On the basis of the information I was given I was able to initiate a discussion about how their husband/partner felt about them returning to study. I asked specifically whether they felt they had support (I made no attempt to define the term at this stage) and in 80 per cent of cases the answer was an unequivocal 'yes'. The following comments were typical:

'He's a very supportive husband' (Amy).
'Oh yes, he supports me' (Emma).
'He's been very encouraging' (Katherine).

Had I not probed further my conclusions would have been very different. However, Anderson suggests in her discussion of the use of interviews in feminist research that we have a 'unique opportunity to ask directly, how did it feel, what did it mean?' (1990: 98). Interestingly, in a later article with Dana Jack (1991) they talk of 'support' as a word which needs to be explored and that women '... should have an opportunity to explain what they mean in their own terms' (1991: 17).

Having received the comments cited above later in the interview I returned to the issue of support and asked if they could tell me more about how their husbands/partners felt. Amy, Katherine and Emma said the following:

> He's been very supportive ... I think he found it a bit difficult when I went to do the course last year in that for the first time he was asked to help, there were things I wanted to do because I wanted to do a bit of work. He found that a bit much really because basically he didn't really want me out of the house, he wanted me here for himself and the children. He couldn't quite understand why I wasn't content to be in the house pottering around. So to a certain extent there was a sort of conflict (Amy).
>
> One thing that's come up was, um, that I might possibly go to Birkbeck to do art there but it's a couple of evenings a week and he was absolutely against that straight away. I'd have to leave here at about 5.30 p.m. and he said that wasn't acceptable. I think he was worried that I wouldn't be able to cook his meals ... he likes me to be here and also that the boys' lives won't be affected. He thinks that I should be here for them. I mean he never wanted me to work full-time (Katherine).
>
> Um, one of the stipulations was that it mustn't interfere with his workload ... If I was to say that you've got to stay at home to look after the children because I'm going to college, that wouldn't be acceptable because he has got to be available for meetings. He definitely does look upon my role as housewife and mother, as long as it doesn't prevent me from being a housewife it's not going to worry him too much (Emma).

These comments provide very different insights into the notion of support and are rooted within the 'private' accounts which emerged once rapport had developed and the women felt able to trust me with some of the more intimate details of their lives. These 'private' accounts revealed the reality of the preconditions of their husbands'/partners' support. These were:

(1) There is no change in the division of labour in the home, i.e. the husband/partner is not asked to take on any aspect of the role he has designated as hers.

(2) His time is not encroached upon either for his work or leisure.

(3) The lives of the children are not disrupted.

The message these men were giving was clear; it was a message imbued with patriarchal values towards women's role in the family. Her primary consideration must be her responsibilities as wife and mother and anything else taken on, i.e. the student role, must be accommodated without making changes to his life.

By exploring the notion of support with the women I was able to identify three elements: practical, financial and emotional support.

Practical Support

I explored this by asking how much help the women received with domestic work and child care so that they had some time to study, and discovered a commonality of experience across class divisions, for example:

'He doesn't help me at all I'm afraid' (Emma–M/C).
'He doesn't help me at all if he can possibly avoid it' (Marie–M/C).
'He thinks a woman's place is to do what there is to do in the home ... sometimes I ask him to make a cup of tea but he won't do anything like that. He still can't make a bed' (Julie–W/C).

It is clear from these comments that men are regarded as wishing to avoid domestic labour and having the power to do so. Roles within both the middle class and working class relationships took a traditional form with areas of responsibility clearly defined. Male as breadwinner, female as homemaker existed right across the spectrum of social class and I would argue that the data support the feminist questioning of assertions of egalitarianism in modern marriage, particularly amongst the middle class, made by writers such as Young and Willmott (1975).

Scant evidence does exist in the data that husbands did help occasionally with household chores and child care but this was placed in the context of doing their wives/partners a favour and led to a time of self-congratulation.

'... if I say, could you hoover a room he will do it but I have to ask, he doesn't do it off his own back' (Marie).
'... if he helps me he tells me he's helped me and makes a big thing of it, aren't I wonderful, I've just cleaned the bathroom' (Helen).

Responsibility, however, ultimately lies with her and this finding corroborates a point made by Oakley and Rajan that 'Women continue to assume the major responsibility for housework and child care' (1991: 47).

Financial Support

The issue of money was another example where the women revealed some quite intimate details and is in fact an area that O'Connor (1991) cites with reference to 'the backstage areas of self'. The women needed money for course fees, equipment and buying the services of other women (labour substitution). The data provide examples of the extent to which this support was forthcoming and also corroborates the proposition that money is the source of power that supports male dominance in the family (Pahl 1989). It was within relationships where the man was in a professional occupation that the most profound role segregation occurred and these men were the most vociferous in articulating their demands. Due to the power they wielded economically, they placed heavy demands on their wives/partners to fulfil their traditional roles:

'He said ... I earn far more than you do. I think he feels as he has a higher earning capacity that what I do is secondary' (Helen).
'... he wants somebody to look after his children and the home ... he earns so much more than I ever will' (Penny).

The middle-class women were able to utilise the financial resources available to buy in the services of other women for child care and domestic work thus freeing them from some of their responsibilities for some of the time. To the extent that money was provided for the women to buy in some of the practical support their husbands/partners would not or could not give, they were providing financial support. However, one of the men was giving financial support unwittingly. Emma told me towards the end of the second interview that:

'I certainly cannot tell my husband how much the course cost, if I was to tell him he wouldn't want me to do it ... it's quite naughty really. I shall start saving up now out of the money I take out of the bank and putting it on one side, it won't notice. As far as my husband is concerned he doesn't really want to know about the financial side of things so I can quite easily get hold of the money ... .'

The working-class women, in contrast, struggled to meet the financial demands of their return to study and expressed feelings of guilt about taking from the family income:

'I felt really bad about spending money on myself, it seems so extravagant but I really want to do the course' (Shirley).

'One course I would have liked to have taken costs £150; well there's no way I'm going to pay that one, me, you know. I struggle at buying a skirt, I'm certainly not going to just for my benefit' (Julie).

The most vivid example of the problems of the lack of financial support came from a comment made by Sandra:

'He won't support me financially and I've been trying to work out if I was offered a place at the college next year how I could afford to do it. I've been thinking I should cancel the interview and then I thought it would be wonderful to learn ... I still have to pay my way here, he won't keep me at all ... he might put me out on the road.'

Emotional Support

What the data reveal about emotional support could be summed up in a quotation from Oakley and Ragan:

So far as emotional support goes, though this is often what women provide for men in marriage, it does not appear to be what men by and large offer women (1991: 47).

The data yield little in the way of examples of emotional support apart from the women initially saying that their husbands were encouraging, but as discussed earlier this was conditional. The lack of emotional support can be seen in the ways in which the women had to judge their husbands'/partners' moods before broaching the subject of returning to study:

'I had to do it gradually and not talk about it too much to start with' (Katherine).

'I got a prospectus and put my name down. I thought about it for a week before I mentioned it to my husband. I explained it wouldn't interfere with anything' (Julie).

These comments reveal that the women expected to receive little emotional support and, indeed, after the battles to actually do the course, Julie had then to contend with the comments and criticisms made by her husband about her work:

'I'd enjoy being able to express myself without somebody saying that's terrible, you haven't said the right word or you've spelt something wrong ... he always liked to read what I've written and he says 'comma there', 'punctuation', 'I wouldn't say it like this'. He's a bit of a perfectionist, it annoys him to see that something isn't written properly ... .'

Penny's situation provides another example of the lack of emotional support. Just as she started her college course her husband had to go to the USA to work, she decided to stay behind and I asked her how he felt about her decision:

'Angry, very angry. We discussed and discussed it ... the practicalities are his job comes first. If things fitted around his job he would be delighted.'

She did eventually tell me in the second interview that she would have to go if she wanted to remain married. Four of the women did tell me that they were having serious problems in their relationships but all were still with their partners when they finished their courses. It would be interesting to know whether this is still the case or whether they have followed in the footsteps of 'Rita' from Russell's play. If they are still with their partners I would argue that it is because of the strategies of appeasement and compromise the women adopted, perhaps at the expense of their academic ambitions.

CONCLUSIONS

When women speak for themselves they reveal hidden realities, new experiences and new perspectives emerge that challenge the 'truths' of official accounts and cast doubt on established theories. Interviews with women can explore private realms to tell us what women actually did instead of what experts thought they did or should have done. (Anderson *et al.* 1990: 96)

The adoption of a feminist paradigm for interviewing has facilitated the discovery of some important insights into the private worlds of women returners. By enabling the women to tell their own stories and creating a context in which they felt comfortable exploring their feelings and experiences, I was able to learn more about those aspects of their lives which crucially affect their chances of success when they return to study.

Through the stories they told in response to my questions and the rapport which developed, I was able to discover details of what Ettoré calls experiences of 'patriarchal pain' (1991: 60). These experiences were located within the 'backstage areas' (O'Connor 1991) of the women's lives. I would argue that the data substantiate a point made by Lovell that

While women may wish to expand their horizons beyond the domestic field, men do not exhibit a similar desire to scrub floors and wash their own shirts, let alone anyone else's. Unless men can accept a change of lifestyle, the most women will achieve is the right to do two jobs (1980b: 224).

The data reveal that the lives of women returners, irrespective of class, symbolise a perpetual 'juggling act' between the demands of family and education. Lack of husbands'/partners' support constitutes a major obstacle women have either to overcome or accommodate into their lives if they are to take on the student role.

Oakley highlights the vital role that the interviewer has to play as a '... tool for making possible the articulated and recorded commentary of women on the very personal business of being female in a patriarchal society' (1981: 48). It is precisely this type of knowledge which is required in the production of a sociology 'for' women and, thus, exemplifies the contribution that a feminist paradigm for interviewing can make to the exploration of new ways of knowing and seeking 'truths' (Ramazanoglu 1992).

REFERENCES

Acker, J. (1983) 'Objectivity and Truth: Problems in Doing Feminist Research', *Women's Studies International Forum*, 6: 423–35.
Anderson, K. *et al.* (1990) 'Beginning Where We Are: Feminist Methodology in Oral History', in J. M. Nielsen (ed.) *Feminist Research Methods.* USA: Westview Press.
Anderson, K. and Jack, D. (1991) 'Learning to Listen. Interview Techniques and Analyses', in S. B. Gluck and D. Patai (eds) *Women's Words: The Feminist Practice of Oral History.* London: Routledge.
Bell, C. and Newby, H. (eds) (1977) *Doing Sociological Research.* London: Allen & Unwin.
Bell, C. and Roberts, H. (eds) (1984) *Social Researching: Politics, Problems, Practice.* London: Routledge & Kegan Paul.
Benney, M. and Hughes, E. C. (1977) 'Of Sociology and the Interview', in M. Bulmer (ed.) *Sociological Research Methods.* London: Macmillan.
Bogdan, R. C. and Biklen, S. K. (1982) *Qualitative Research For Education: An Introduction to Theory and Methods.* USA: Allyn & Bacon.
Bowles, G. and Duelli-Klein, R. (eds) (1983) *Theories of Women's Studies.* London: Routledge & Kegan Paul.
Burwood, R. V. and Brady, C. (1980) 'The Meaning of Coming to College'. *Journal of Further and Higher Education,* (2) Summer.
Cook, J. and Fonow, M. (1990) 'Knowledge and Women's Interests: Issues of Epistemology and Methodology', in J. Nielsen (ed.) *Feminist Research Methods.* London: Westview Press.

Corbin, M. (1971) 'Problems and Procedures of Interviewing', in J. M. and R. E. Pahl (eds) *Managers and Their Wives*. London: Allen Lane.

Cotterill, P. (1992) 'Interviewing Women: Issues of Friendship, Vulnerability, and Power'. *Women's Studies International Forum*. 15: 593–606.

Crowley, H. and Himmelweit, S. (1992) *Knowing Women: Feminism and Knowledge*. Cambridge: Polity Press.

Dubois, B. (1983) 'Passionate Scholarship: Notes on Values, Knowing and Method in Feminist Social Science', in G. Bowles and R. Duelli-Klein (eds) *Theories of Women's Studies*. London: Routledge & Kegan Paul.

Duelli-Klein, R. (1983) 'How to Do What We Want to Do: Thoughts about Feminist Methodology', in G. Bowles and Duelli-Klein (eds) op. cit.

Edwards, R. (1991) *Degrees of Difference: Family and Education in the Lives of Mature Mother-Students*. Unpublished PhD. South Bank Polytechnic.

Edwards, R. (1990) 'Access and Assets: The Experiences of mature mother-students in higher education', *Journal of Access Studies* 5: 188–201.

Ely, M. *et al*. (1991) *Doing Qualitative Research: Circles within Circles*. Lewes: Falmer Press.

Ettoré, B. (1991) 'Renewing Our Politics of Resistance: Unearthing "Old" Strategies in a "New" Climate', in British Sociological Association, *Women and Social Research*.

Finch, J. (1984) 'It's great to have someone to talk to: The Ethics and Politics of Interviewing Women', in C. Bell and H. Roberts (eds) op. cit.

Gamarnikow, E. *et al*. (eds) (1983) *The Public and The Private*. London: Heinemann.

Gelsthorpe, L. (1992) 'Response to Martyn Hammersley's Paper "On Feminist Methodology"', *Sociology* 26: 213–18.

Graham, H. (1983) 'Do Her Answers Fit His Questions? Women and the Survey Method', in E. Gamarnikow (eds) op. cit.

Graham, H. (1984) 'Surveying through stories'. C. Bell and H. Roberts (eds) op. cit.

Harding, S. (ed.) (1987) *Feminism and Methodology*. Milton Keynes: Open University Press.

Katz, J. (1976) 'Homelife of Women in Continuing Education', in H. Astin (ed.) *Some Action of Her Own*. Massachusetts: D. C. Heath and Co.

Kirk, P. (1977) 'The Tip of the Iceberg: Some Effects of Open University Study on married students'. *Teaching at a Distance* 10: 19–27.

Lovell, A. (1980a) 'Fresh Horizons: The Aspirations and Problems of Intending Mature Students'. *Feminist Review* 6.

Lovell, A. (1980b) 'Fresh Horizons for Some'. *Adult Education* 53: 219–24.

Mies, M. (1983) 'Towards a Methodology for Feminist Research', in G. Bowles and R. Duelli-Klein (eds) op. cit.

Moser, C. A. and Kalton, G. (1971) *Survey Methods in Social Investigation*. 2nd edn. London: Heinemann.

Nielsen, J. M. (ed.) (1990) *Feminist Research Methods: Exemplary Readings in the Social Sciences*. London: Westview Press.

Oakley, A. (1981) 'Interviewing Women: A Contradiction in Terms', in H. Roberts (ed.) *Doing Feminist Research*. London: Routledge & Kegan Paul.

Oakley, A. (1992) *Social Support and Motherhood*. Oxford: Blackwell.

Oakley, A. and Rajan, L. (1991) 'Social Class and Social Support: The Same or Different?' *Sociology* 25: 31–59.

O'Connor, P. (1991) 'Women's Confidants outside Marriage: Shared or Competing Sources of Intimacy?' *Sociology* 25: 241–54.

Oglesby, K. (1976) 'General Education Courses for Adults', *Adult Education* 49: 11–17.

Pahl, J. (1989) *Money and Marriage*. London: Macmillan.

Personal Narratives Group (eds) (1989) *Interpreting Women's Lives: Feminist Theory and Personal Narratives*. Indianapolis: Indiana University Press.

Ramazanoglu, C. (1992) 'Male Reason versus Female Empowerment', *Sociology* 26: 207–12.

Ribbens, J. (1989) 'Interviewing: An Unnatural Situation?' *Women's Studies International Forum*, 12: 579–92.

Riddell, S. (1989) 'Exploiting the exploited? The ethics of feminist educational research', in R. Burgess (ed.) *The Ethics of Educational Research*. Lewes: Falmer Press.

Roberts, H. (ed.) (1981) *Doing Feminist Research*. London: Routledge & Kegan Paul.

Scott, S. (1985) 'Feminist Research and Qualitative Methods', in R. Burgess (ed.) op. cit.

Smith, D. E. (1987) *The Everyday World as Problematic*. Milton Keynes: Open University Press.

Stanley, L. and Wise, S. (1983a) *Breaking Out: Feminist Consciousness and Feminist Research*. London: Routledge & Kegan Paul.

Stanley, L. and Wise, S. (1983b) 'Back into the Personal or Our Attempt to Conduct Feminist Research', G. Bowles and R. Duelli-Klein (eds) op. cit.

Stanley, L. (ed.) (1990) *Feminist Praxis*. London: Routledge.

Swarbrick, A. (1978) 'Backgrounds, Developments, Futures: A Study of Twelve Open University Women Graduates', *Studies in Adult Education* 10, October.

Taking Liberties Collective (1989) *Learning the Hard Way*. London: Macmillan.

Walby, S. (1990) *Theorizing Patriarchy*. Oxford: Basil Blackwell.

Westkott, M. (1990) 'Feminist Criticism of the Social Sciences', in J. M. Nielsen (ed.) op. cit.

Woodley, A. *et al.* (1987) *Choosing to Learn: Adults in Education*. Milton Keynes: Open University Press.

Young, M. and Willmott, P. (1975) *The Symmetrical Family*. Harmondsworth: Penguin.

5 Every Picture 'Tells a Story': Uses of the Visual in Sociological Research

Barbara Harrison

Visual social science isn't new... but it might as well be
(Becker 1974: 7)

INTRODUCTION

The last two decades have witnessed a revival of interest in sociology's broad heritage of research methodologies and in the use of techniques and data sources which have, for too long, been on the margins of research practice in the discipline. The cause of the life history method was taken up by Ken Plummer (1983) in the early 1980s, and we are now witnessing the growth of a range of auto/biographical approaches. It now seems timely to consider a neglected history within the social sciences of using visual methods and data, building on important recent texts (notably, Fyfe and Law 1988; Ball and Smith 1992). It is my contention that the value of visual imagery and visual methods to the sociological enterprise is such as to warrant a more central location in research training and research practice. In doing so we will inevitably draw on, and benefit from, an increasing multidisciplinarity in research methodologies available for our use.

The purpose of this chapter is to present the case for the potential of the visual in sociological research closer to the mainstream of enquiry. First, I outline our visual heritage and its place on the margins of the discipline. The chapter then presents an overview of what might be called the field of visual sociology, focusing on visual techniques within sociological methods and methodological approaches to the analysis of the visual, drawing on examples from published research. In developing my analysis I focus on the role of photography – still and moving. This is not only because I consider them to offer greater theoretical and practical potential

75

for the researcher, but because the literature seemingly accords photography a privileged role as visual data, imagery and technique (see, for example, Wagner 1979; Collier and Collier 1986).

A VISUAL HERITAGE?

The marginality of visual materials and technologies in sociological research has been accounted for by two main features in the heritage of social science disciplines, which have continued to some degree into the present.

It was Margaret Mead, herself a pioneer of ethnographic film and photography, who noted the problematic status of visual data in 'disciplines of words' (1963). Sociology has also given symbolic power to language and the written text as the means of communicating observations of researchers, and in constructing what we treat as knowledge. Where visual material has been used it is in a subservient role as illustration, more or less informing or documenting the written or spoken text. In fact this 'decorative role' was often to be criticised (Stasz 1979) in the context of early American sociology for both its poor technical quality and also for its lack of, or arbitrary, relationship to the written text. Since then the sociologist's use of the visual has remained primarily as an aid to the communication and presentation of written text.

The second major factor which seems to have been important in marginalising visual material and methods in sociology has been the dominance, for a major part of this century, of positivistically oriented methodologies as a basis for sociological knowledge. With the primacy of observation, and the necessity that these be value-free, as epistemological priorities within the positivist paradigm, it is perhaps surprising that the possible benefits of photographic technologies were not explored. Whereas other bodies of knowledge or disciplines did claim some objectivity for 'camera' observations, sociology distrusted the camera record, viewing it as subject to the fallibility of human selectivity (Collier 1967). Clarice Stasz (1979) suggests that the loss of visual images from the *American Journal of Sociology* accompanied the change in control of the editorship to the behaviourists around 1916. However, this rejection of photographic images for their lack of 'objectivity' was also compromised by other sociological uses of the photograph which were also perceived to be problematic.

In this respect it was difficult to separate the work of the early sociological photographers, Lewis Hine and Jacob Riis in particular, and the writings they helped to illustrate, from the muck-raking tradition of written and photographic journalism. In this country the photograph was also used in a social reform context. At the end of the nineteenth century, for example, Cameron, a physician, documented the Quarry Hill 'slum' in Leeds (Tagg 1988). In the USA the photograph continued to occupy a key role in relation to social policy. It was the deliberate creation of the photographic record as a policy tool that gave us many of the best-known images of the impact of the 1930s depression on America and of 'New Deal' policy responses. There was an ideological project for these images: to engineer consent for the reforms through the documentation of conditions and need, and to demonstrate how programmes of intervention were working to improve life. We might define such work as propaganda, although Stryker, Head of the Farm Security Administration Photographic Department, preferred to see their role as education and persuasion (Stoeckle and White 1985). Certainly, we can now appreciate their functions in an apparatus of control and power, mobilising a discourse of 'truth' about poverty and deprivation (Tagg 1982). Thus, there were two dimensions to a lack of 'objectivity' which discredited visual methodologies as not worthy of a discipline that aspired to 'scientific' status.

While the claims made for these factors as inhibiting visual sociology seem valid, it is, nonetheless, surprising that they should have had such long term negative consequences, especially as challenges to positivistic knowledge claims have expanded. More fundamentally, I would suggest it is surprising because the visual is a central dimension of social life and social being. We are surrounded by visual phenomena and images which display culture and particular aspects of it; visual features and visual skills are used to communicate, and perform an integral role in formulating the understanding on which social action rests. As with language, visual phenomena and images perform social work. As participants in social life visual abilities play a major role in ethnomethods (in the accomplishing sense), and it is competence in observing a seen world that forms the foundation of social science investigation. If observation is a principal tool in sociological research why have we failed to supplement or complement the ability of the human eye by using available visual technologies?

Earlier I alluded to a different status for visual technologies in other disciplines. In the physical and biomedical sciences, for example, such technologies have been viewed as important to advances in scientific knowledge, and it was rendering the unseen world as seeable that gave them such a powerful role in knowledge production and professional politics (see, for example, Petschesky 1987; Pasveer 1989). Their attraction lay not only in their power of observation, but also because the observations were seen to be untainted by human observers; as having some claim to objectivity:

> The value of the camera was extolled because the optical and chemical processes of photography were taken to designate a scientifically exploited but 'natural' mechanism producing 'natural' images whose truth was guaranteed (Green 1985: 294).

Foucault (1977) drew our attention to the important status which photography acquired as a tool of disciplinary power in late nineteenth-century Britain. Techniques of control rested on opportunities for surveillance, and by providing a means of observation, classification and organisation, photography contributed to new knowledge of individuals that permeated and sustained disciplinary power. This knowledge/power nexus was important in the institutionalisation of health and welfare and law and order (Tagg 1982). However, it would be a digression to discuss the role of photographic observation in disciplinary institutions here in any more detail. What is important for my purpose is that this particular analysis demonstrates how the use of visual methods in these contexts was underpinned by assumptions about the reality of the photograph and the real in the photograph which sociology, perhaps rightly, seemed to reject from the outset. I return to this issue later in the chapter.

The visual as a topic of investigation has had a more recognised place in sociological work, not least because a number of sub-fields of sociology have interests in aspects of visual culture, such as art, style and the mass media. Zolberg argues, however, that despite the 'ubiquity and omnipresence of the arts in all known human societies' (1990: 6) a sociology of the arts has not been a central concern of the discipline. As I have implied in the case of visual methods, Zolberg also suggests this was in part because the progress of the discipline was linked to science, while art was seen as qualitative, humanistic and aesthetic in character.

So are we now to witness new possibilities for a visual sociology? Essentially it is my argument that for sociology it was not the value of visual methodologies, either to a 'scientific' enterprise or to the achievement of more faithful recordings of 'naturally occurring situations', that gave some impetus to reconsidering the role of the visual. By the 1970s there was a limited return to using the photographic document in relation to policy issues, and some interest in the technical possibilities of more efficient and accurate measurement or recording. Rather, it has been the changing interests of sociology in, for example, forms of representation and discourse, with seeing as social action and, as with auto/biography, a

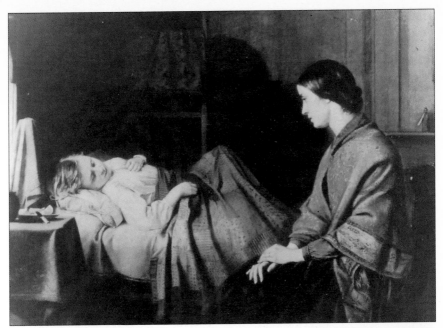

1. Mrs Alexander Farmer. *An Anxious Hour* (1865). London: Victoria and Albert Museum

2. Édouard Manet. *Le Déjeuner sur l'Herbe* (1861–3). London: Courtauld Institute of Art

3. Augustus Leopold Egg. *Past and Present I* (1857–8). London: Tate Gallery

4. Augustus Leopold Egg. *Past and Present II* (1857–8). London: Tate Gallery

5. Augustus Leopold Egg. *Past and Present III* (1857–8). London: Tate Gallery

6. William Holman Hunt. *The Awakening Conscience* (1853). London: Tate
   Gallery

reassertion of the importance of subjectivity in social life. Technical issues as well as the methodological warrant for the visual within different epistemological concerns will, however, remain important considerations in the evaluation of visual methods and the kinds of research questions for which they may be relevant.

THE VISUAL AS TOPIC AND RESOURCE

In my discussion of what might constitute visual methodologies, I consider it useful to utilise a distinction first made in the context of ethnomethodological approaches to language: that between topic and resource (Zimmerman and Pollner 1971). Thus language was a resource used in everyday life and in research to derive meanings: a tool of communication in which the worlds of others could be accessed and made available. In this context language provides us with data about social life. Ethnomethodology, however, suggested that this approach to language led to assumptions about language data that required problematising – for example, the correspondence between subjects' and researchers' understandings of phenomena. Rather, understanding through language required investigation in its own right. The use of language and communication would then be the topic of sociological interest: to investigate how it is that meaning or 'sense' are achieved. Further, it was stressed that such an approach revealed how language performed social work, and the means by which it did so was to become an important research topic. Visual material similarly lends itself to resource and topic-led research questions and, as such, will serve a number of different theoretical interests in sociology.

The early use of visual data in sociology was, in the main, as a resource – that is, as a medium through which description and understanding of other topics of interest could be accessed, understood and presented. I have suggested that it was not even fully exploited in this sense, being used mainly as illustration of the topic(s) under investigation. The text remained the principal source of understanding. It is suggested here that the development of visual methodologies which utilise the resource approach has occurred mainly alongside an interest in the visual as topic.

The growing body of work on representations has, of necessity, considered visual as well as written texts, and this has once again opened up the visual as topic with different concerns to the wider sociology of art or arts. Following on from a body of structuralist-informed work on advertisements, and feminist approaches to the analysis of visual media, there has been an increasing focus on what social work is done by visual phenomena and how that work is done. In their introduction to their edited collection, Fyfe and Law summarise such a topic approach to the visual:

> A depiction is never just an illustration. It is a material representation, the apparently stabilised product of a process of work. And it is the site for the construction and depiction of social difference. To understand a visualisation is thus to inquire into its provenance and into the social work it does. It is to note its principles of exclusion and inclusion, to detect the roles it makes available, to understand the way in which they are distributed, and to decode the hierarchies and differences that it naturalises. And it is also to analyse the ways in which authorship is constructed or concealed and the sense of audience realised (1988: 1).

Thus those visual images which surround us in everyday life must be viewed as actively at work in constructing the world how it has to be, and not just reflecting how it is. In taking representations as topic, the analyst can then move on to those areas such representations work on and with. Furthermore, we can now take our project beyond the decoding of visual messages or representations, to questions of visual skills and cognition – an understanding how the work of seeing is done.

Having summarised this resource/topic distinction, I now turn to some specific methodological approaches and techniques which allow us to utilise visual techniques, images and other visual phenomena as topic and/or resource in sociology.

USING VISUAL IMAGERY AS AN ELICITATION TECHNIQUE

As a resource visual imagery can be effective as an integral part of other data collection methods in which visual material acts as a stimulus. Most commonly this will be within types of qualitative interviews, but may also form part of ethnographic fieldwork in which visual phenomena form part of the observational record and key informant interviews. There are two different approaches evident in the use of visual material as an eliciting technique, although in both cases I suggest that such stimuli essentially enable an exploration of subjectively constructed social life, and tap cultural and personal meaning.

In the first approach, the researcher makes use of visual material that the subjects have themselves produced or are asked to produce during the research process. These are used to construct a personally oriented interview. The visual material can be constituted as personal documents.

Photographs, drawings, paintings and other visual media can be regarded as personal displays of self, self and others, and aspects of everyday life. The assumption is that, if the production of visual imagery embodies subjective meanings of self and experience, then we can also use these images to elicit these meanings. Early research by Musello (1979) used family photographs in this way and a more recent collection focusing on a similar theme (Spence and Holland 1990) demonstrate the variety of ways in which such domestic photography can be used to explore meaning in context.

In the second approach, the use of visual imagery or documents is not necessarily viewed as a personal document. The elicitation is in response to a particular image or set of images. The purpose of gaining insight into personal orientations and subjective meanings may still be paramount, but removing the subject from their own personal productions may serve to highlight different aspects of subjectivity. Furthermore, this use of visual material may reveal important dimensions of wider cultural and social values. Bendelow has suggested that visual imagery may serve a similar desensitising function to the vignette in qualitative research (see Finch 1987). Reactivity in interviews may be reduced in situations where topics are either particularly difficult to access because of their very personal and subjective nature, and/or where normative expectations enter into subjective experience and the management of self-presentation in the interview. Bendelow (1993) used a variety of visual images (paintings, etchings, drawings, and photographs) in order to explore gendered notions of pain. Pain is an example of a difficult concept, theoretically and experientially, for people to verbalise, and here the mode of enquiry proceeded by seeking interviewees' responses to the images in terms of the presence or absence of pain and what kind of pain. Only later were they asked about their own identification with the images.

In contrast, Harper (1986) used 'snapshots' which he had taken as part of his field work as a focus for his interviews with his subject on the meaning of work. The subject, Harper suggests, was encouraged to take on the role of teacher about the reality presented in the images. Although the images were not personal documents in the sense discussed above, they were essential to the researcher's understanding of his own observations and field notes, and also accessed the subject's personal construction of his work: that is, a reality behind manifest appearances. Harper does suggest there are difficulties here in integrating the voices of researcher/subject with the visual in the final text, and in general how we 'write' in the visual as a sociological text requires further consideration if we are to move beyond an illustrative documentary role.

In a teaching workshop I recently used participants' holiday snaps to explore the meaning of holidays, not only by utilising the large sample formed to conduct both traditional and structuralist oriented forms of content analysis, but also to construct an interview around a subject's own holiday pictures. Further interviews were then constructed around sets of holiday photographs that were not the subject's own. What both these exercises demonstrated was how powerful images can be in sparking off narratives, revealing experience and meaning, and enabling a construction of the personal and social significance not just of holidays and travel but other topics as well. The exercise suggested that visual stimuli may also operate very effectively in the context of focused group interviews.

In addition, it is possible to use any images in an interview in order to explore how it is that images may be read/interpreted – to ask how meaning is derived and constructed – in the same way that we may ask how any textual understanding is reached. Existing images or the construction of new ones can be used as an eliciting technique for both resource and topic projects.

OTHER APPROACHES TO USING EXISTING VISUAL IMAGES

As the example above on holidays demonstrated, the existence of visual materials provides numerous opportunities for research projects with images acting as resource or topic by utilising quantitative and qualitatively oriented forms of content analysis. Traditionally content analysis has been seen as a method for systematically analysing all forms of communication content and especially mass communication materials (Holsti 1969; Krippendorf 1980; Weber 1990). With a focus on the development of classifications of manifest content, this form of content analysis essentially remains a descriptive method, although certain inferences might be made on the basis of these descriptions. This approach to the analysis of communication content has been criticised for its tendency to fragment content and divorce it from its context, thus losing the symbolic meaning that is embedded in texts or visual representations as wholes.

Interest in forms of holistic analysis has also served different theoretical purposes some of which are resource rather than topic oriented. Even given the different epistemological relevancy for visual data or methods, these more qualitative approaches share assumptions that visual phenomena stand for, or represent, wider social and cultural arrangements. It is features outside of the manifest content or visual appearance that are important. Meanings are held to be latent and are interpretable by reference to the wider social world which provides the resources allowing meaning to be constituted. Our understanding and use of visual phenomena thus utilise and incorporate conventions that display and decode meaning in everyday social life. A considerable amount of anthropological work, for example, has analysed dress, facial and other forms of decoration in terms of how these code hierarchies of social relations. Visual phenomena are viewed as systems of symbols which form socially ordered and socially recognised codes.

Following anthropological concerns with symbolic codes, and European philosophical interests in how representations and forms of communication, including visual images, could embody and reproduce powerful ideological myths, methodological approaches which decoded manifest content developed into deconstructing the forms of grammar which connect image/object and its meaning (see Barthes 1973; Williamson 1978). This approach is exemplified by some of the work on advertisements. The choice of advertisements is apt, since we understand that such visual images are produced with an expressed purpose. They have work to do in selling things. As Williamson points out, 'we can only understand what advertisements mean by finding out how they mean and analysing the way in which they work' (1978: 17). Earlier Goffman (1976) used advertisements to elucidate the various ways in which body posture, facial expressions, poses and arrangements of people and groups display cultural ideas about women and men. He argued that, despite the 'distorting' or contrived nature of advertisements, they draw on everyday behavioural vocabularies, trading on our competencies in recognising the familiar, and his large sample of advertisements shows the degree to which there is some homogeneity in the conventions which encode meaning. Reading advertisements is but another occasion in which we orient to, and draw on, visual resources in social life. To this end Goffman suggests:

> the job the advertiser has of dramatising the role of his (sic) product is not unlike the job a society has of infusing its social situations with ceremonial and with ritual signs facilitating the orientations of participants to one another. Both must use the limited 'visual' resources available in social situations to tell a story; both must transform otherwise opaque goings-on into easily readable form (1976: 27).

Williamson also stressed that the knowledge produced by advertisements is knowledge produced from what is already known; advertising trades on culturally specific systems of meanings which the images invoke. Her work demonstrates particular devices that perform the work of conveying meaning. One device is correlative sign-work, where products are juxtaposed with 'personalities' who stand for particular characteristics, so the product becomes identified with the characteristics because it is endorsed by the 'personality'. To do the work of selling we must see ourselves as having or desiring such characteristics, so that the advertisement will signify us and we will see the product as for us. Outside of advertising we can follow such an approach with other kinds of visual images and phenomena. Newspaper and magazine photographs, the domestic photograph, paintings and drawings, to name some, can be utilised for both structuralist and phenomenologically oriented projects.

One such example is Denise Farran's (1990) study based on a photograph of Marilyn Monroe. Her interest is in 'how a photograph of Marilyn works', how the 'sexuality of the photograph is achieved or not achieved'. The photograph is not taken as a statement of fact, and whether the image is taken to be a sexual image, she suggests, will rest on what we take as signifiers of sexuality. The particular reading of the photograph will thus depend on ideas brought to it about Marilyn's biography and about sexuality, the readers' own biographies, social knowledge and experiences. Thus, like an advertisement the photograph utilises signifiers so that the sexual can be seen, but it will only be seen if they are recognised by viewers and given this meaning. Farran suggests, then, that it is particulars outside the frame of the image that influence the interpretation that is made, particularly our knowledge of Marilyn's biography; there will thus be many versions of what this particular photograph is of and about. In this way photographs are also readings of biography and not just a resource we use to make sense of them.

WAYS OF SEEING

While structuralist and semiotic approaches to the analysis of visual images and visual display provide insight into processes of encoding and decoding meaning, there are still further questions which can be asked about such processes. I have already indicated that signs use conventions to perform work in the sense of directing us to what is seen. How people read images can also inform us about what is involved in the process and experience of seeing. Cognitive skills and experience are, thus, also socially constituted and not just constitutive of the social, and there are researchers who direct their projects more specifically to questions of visual cognition as an everyday activity. This concern with the visual dimension of experience is an extension of interest in all forms of cognitive activity that perform the ongoing tasks of organising, in ways that are to be viewed as social, people's everyday worlds. Cognitive anthropologists share such interests with ethnomethodologists and direct their methodologies toward actual human conduct as opposed to extant images; to how members practically accomplish understanding in which seeing and the seen provide methods for that accomplishment. Heath (1984) has demonstrated how clinical encounters rely as much on seeing work, on non-verbal actions, as they do verbal ones.

The recognition of the socially constituted nature of visual competencies has consequences which impinge on the use of visual methodologies also, and in teaching these to students. Curry and Clark (1979) have stressed the need to develop the ability to 'read' photographic observations, and that skills required to interpret imagery are distinct from those required to produce it. And, despite the ubiquity of photographic images in everyday social environments, the intelligibility of the photograph, as Burgin (1982) reminds us, 'is no simple thing'. This then raises questions about the influence of different ways of seeing on images constructed for research purposes.

CREATING VISUAL IMAGES AS INVESTIGATIVE TOOLS

Thus far I have discussed the use of existing visual materials as data within a variety of research methodologies. In this section the deliberate creation of visual data is considered. The purpose to which these methodologies can be put are often similar to those above, but they also offer new opportunities for research.

Earlier in this chapter I suggested that the use of the camera had given it a privileged position in relation to the development of scientific knowledge, through its assumed ability to offer more complete and objective observational data. In the social sciences the attitude to the use of photography and film in relation to 'scientific' observation has been one of scepticism. At the same time, there have been a number of researchers who regard visual technologies as offering opportunities for more complete observational records, which can also preserve 'naturally occurring' social action for future scrutiny. Moreover, the visual record has been essential to those researcher/observers with interests in non-verbal as well as verbal data. The development of video technologies has proved to be particularly useful in this regard, and there are now a number of examples of how video may be used (see, for example, Dowrick and Biggs 1983).

An interesting example of how video cameras were used in conjunction with traditional field work roles is provided by a study of market 'pitchers', where 'patter merchanting' – buying and selling as a form of local economic exchange – was viewed as a set of accomplishments based on social conventions and requiring interactional skills (Pinch and Clark 1986). It should also be mentioned that the analysis and the use of the camera as part of ethnographic field work subsequently gave rise to some debate (Cherrington *et al.* 1987; Pinch and Clark 1987). Such debates alert us to issues of both reactivity and ethical concern that the camera does not preclude, although they do not necessarily invalidate their use. Heath (1984) videotaped recordings of naturally occurring medical consultations in order to explore the relationship of verbal (speech) and non-verbal (body movement) as aspects of the occupational activity of medical consultation. Body movements and gaze, he demonstrates, are important components of involvement in the interaction, and the maintenance of involvement is essential to getting the work of the consultation done. The video record can be used also to provide a detailed record of other kinds of interactions that may be occasional and fleeting in nature. Brooker (1993) used the video camera in her research into nurses' interactions with visitors and relatives. The camera was set up above the door of the ward office. The observer presence (which in this case would have been more intrusive than the camera) was not required, and complete interactions were available for later analysis of both verbal and non-verbal action, revealing the importance of 'ownership' of space to interactions. As interests in how people relate to and use spatial environments have emerged, the visual may become important as both topic and resource for such studies. In addition, as psychologists have realised, the video camera accesses some human behaviours which can only be partially understood through retrospective accounts that we so typically use as data. Anders *et al.* (1983) is an example of a study that opted for the visual record rather than retrospective accounting – in this instance, to record sleeping and waking patterns in children at night, not something that readily lends itself to more traditional forms of data collection. Finally, an added advantage of video, film or other visual records is that they provide the opportunity to 'see' the same phenomenon several times, or for different observers to view the same events, a factor that might be considered to enhance validity.

Film or photographic projects can be initiated as part of explicit research objectives. For example, rather than use existing records as personal documents within auto/biographical approaches, such documents may be created at the researcher's behest. We may use these materials for narrative purposes, or they can function in the traditional documentary usage as illustration to support verbal and written texts. These techniques also provide a means to render actors' perspectives visible. Psychologists have been at the forefront of developing photograpic methods to study the self systematically. Photo-observation (Zillier 1990) and photo-analysis (Akeret 1973)) developed in part alongside therapeutic concerns. In these approaches the research subject as photographer is directed toward providing an answer to a specific question: Who are you? or Who am I? The objective is to obtain personal constructs and orientations, and it is suggested these products of consciousness may be (best?) communicated to others through a visual medium. The rationale for photo-observation in this sense draws on symbolic interactionist conceptions of the links between self, others and environment in the social nature of personhood. The link with biographical approaches is evident in Zillier's (1990) description of his work in this tradition as being autophotography. Photographers also have become interested in the idea that photography may be used autobiographically and therapeutically (see, for example, Spence 1986; Spence and Martin 1988). Such approaches draw on the idea of the naive photographer (although as professionals they are not), especially through challenges to both the conventions and practices of photography (that is, technical and aesthetic criteria and its power relations) and the topics or subjects that may be photographed.

Photo-observation as part of ethnographic field work has used the naive photographer as a biographer in addition to the more traditional researcher/observer role. Still and film photography have been used as documents in this context, but also to develop subjects' perspectives on what is 'important'. Worth and Adlair (1972), for example, described his work, with the Navaho as the film makers, as biodocumentary.

In addition to subject generated photographic or film data, the researcher may also direct research subjects to produce other kinds of visual data. This may be a useful approach with research subjects where there may be difficulties in relying entirely on traditional verbal or written skills. One example is children. In a project on primary school children, the Health Education Authority developed 'The Draw and Write Investigative Technique' (1986). The technique still rests on spoken instructions and requires thinking and writing about a particular topic, but central to the exercise is the use of drawing. In one project children were asked to draw pictures of themselves doing things which make and keep them healthy; in another are told a story in which children find a bag of drugs and are then asked to draw what was in the bag, who they think lost it, what the person was going to do with it, and what the children did with the bag (Wetton 1992). The advantages of a technique like this is that it is likely to be a less intimidating and reactive mode of data collection, and it can access areas of knowledge, perception and experience that might otherwise be difficult to obtain.

A brief final comment is required in concluding this section on creating new visual data. Such an emphasis may result in a neglect of the possibility of constructing or using archives for forms of secondary analysis. The case for recycling old photographs has been made in the context of the environmental consequences of 'mass snapshots', but equally Johan Schmid's recent exhibition of German amateur photographs since 1900 has shown that archival records can be reconstituted for contemporary documentary (and research?) purposes (*Independent*, 15 March 1994). It will, however, require some conscientious archival work to realise historical and sociological research possibilities.

PHOTOGRAPHY AND FILM: A PRIVILEGED VISUAL METHODOLOGY?

I have suggested that the camera has acquired a privileged position as a methodological tool for research in a number of disciplines within the social sciences and outside. The validity of this claim requires brief examination here before summarising some of the methodological issues which arise in the context of visual methods and data.

Still photographs and moving film have a powerful claim to realism and this undoubtedly underpins their status as documentary and observational records. Underlying such claims to realism are two important characteristics of the photographic process: first, the mechanical, instantaneous depictions of the subject; and second, the fact that cameras essentially operate to produce a mirror image of how things appear. It is assumed that it is cameras which take pictures and cameras never lie. Such assumptions and the claims they support require questioning.

There are a number of relevant points which can be raised, albeit briefly, in this regard. We must first question the idea that it is cameras alone which take pictures. Even if the camera is left to perform its task independently, as some observational video uses may do, the decision about where and what will be taken will have been the researcher's. More often it is people not cameras who take pictures. Thus what constitutes a photograph or photographic/film record is determined by processes outside of the image the camera captures. As Berger (1972: 10) argued, photographs are not mechanical records in that the photographer selects 'that sight from an infinity of other possible sights'; the subject reflects the photographer's way of seeing. The mechanical process of depiction cannot be considered as independent of a wider context. The researcher, like the documentary film maker or photographer, may also utilise aesthetic conventions. Indeed, it has been argued that realism itself is a contrived aesthetic (Sontag 1978). The naive subject producer of visual images does not escape from these influences either. To return to my holiday snap example, I would argue it is possible to discern aesthetic and cultural conventions of holiday photography which domestic and commercial sectors share: witness the similarity in holiday brochure photographs, travel journalism, postcards and personal collections of photographs. These conventions enter into what is taken to be a photographic subject, reproducing the social and cultural values of holidays and travel.

In addition to these kinds of aesthetic manipulations of the photographic image it seems researchers will accept, as photographers already do, that photographs represent often small and certainly selected samples of the 'real' world. The issue, then, becomes: if the photograph does not have a reality warrant, can we still claim for it an ability to report on some portion or aspect of it? Becker suggests that the question is not, do photographs tell the truth? but 'is this photograph telling the truth about *what*?' (1979: 101, his emphasis). However, even if we can establish what the topic(s) might be, we are still left with establishing what is being said about it. For the researcher the questions are not necessarily those the photograph suggests or the photographer was addressing. So why is this such a particular problem for the visual methodologist? As Becker further points out, all data is in some sense a product of processes which interfere with their evidential quality:

> every form of verbal material poses the same problems, for writing and oral testimony are likewise shaped with some audience in mind and must be interpreted and understood accordingly (1979: 111).

We do have to recognise that photographs have conventions, a language which we may need to understand in order to utilise them for our research purposes, but so do language texts, field notes of observed social contexts and research interviews.

That people not cameras take pictures in the sense discussed above, may raise doubts about the claims to realism of photographic methodologies, but need not invalidate other uses for these techniques. Indeed, it may be that it is the capacity these techniques have for revealing subjective 'bias' that gives them their value for research purposes. In many of the contexts I have described as fruitful for visual sociology, it has been the selective, contrived and highly personal production and interpretation of images which needs to be emphasised. Candid and contrived pictures are different kinds of pictures, and may serve different knowledge purposes, but they are, as Goffman (1976) pointed out, still pictures. For the researcher the contrived picture can be useful because it represents a subjective reality, and because we should be interested in the way contrived images perform important work and how any image may be interpreted. As the example of structuralist analyses of advertising demonstrates, contrived images utilise conventions which will lead the viewer to understand their message in terms of deeply entrenched cultural rules (Williamson 1978) or myths (Barthes 1973).

The interest of the sociological researcher is not just with what data we may obtain by the production of visual images and observational records, but in how visual images may be understood and interpreted. The fact that images are contrived or bounded by aesthetic convention is essentially irrelevant. As ethnomethodology reminds us, whether or not an account is 'factually correct' is not of interest, it is how an account is understood to be 'fact' (see, for example, Smith 1978). The sense people make of visual materials depends on personal knowledge, cultural assumptions and the context in which they are presented. In addition to a literacy which we acquire (differentially) that directs what we see (Berger 1972), we are frequently directed to see particular things by the indexicality of visual image and written/verbal text. Visual images seldom appear without captions, labels, titles and other forms of language text. There are bodies of knowledge that rely on the visual aspects of texts to transform the nature of knowledge for different audiences (Law and Whittaker 1988). So there are further textual investigations required that may be important in changing our use of the visual text. However, despite our recent concerns with the way our knowledge is constituted by the text and the strategic work of their production (see, for example, Atkinson 1990; Clifford and Marcus 1986), we seem unable to consider the epistemological relevance of visual construction as routes to knowledge, even given the eclectic opportunities of post-modernism.

CONCLUSION: PRACTICALITIES AND OPPORTUNITIES

In this chapter I have attempted to demonstrate that the visual in social life offers resources and topics for sociological research outside of traditional concerns within a sociology of art or the mass media. I have paid little attention to some of the practical issues of doing visual sociology. The issues for consideration differ little from the kinds of evaluations we make of any research design or set of techniques. Some research questions will be more suited to visual techniques than others, and there will be practical considerations which will either facilitate or constrain our use of them. There are important issues of sampling, such as selecting images or time frames for collection and analysis, and decisions about observer/researcher roles in relation to the use of the visual medium, particularly the degree of intrusion/involvement. There have been concerns (Becker 1974; Wagner 1979) about the degree to which access is negotiated, and related issues of informed consent as a cornerstone of ethical practice, when this leads to both selectivity and reactivity. But the problems here may be no worse than those encountered in any field work. The presence of the camera as observer may not be able to claim to access 'naturally occuring situations', or the lives of subjects whose social worlds are other than our own, any more than the human observer is able to (Bittner 1975). I would suggest that, despite a self-consciousness among subjects that any user of a camera will have noted, there are also times when they will be less reactive or intrusive. We should take note of how much we already accept the routine camera surveillance of much of our daily lives.

In addition to visual technologies which enable us to obtain data resources about a wide range of sociological questions, I have suggested that we can make considerable use of data that are already at our disposal. We are surrounded by forms of visual display, and visual images and materials are there for us to utilise for a wide variety of purposes. Such data can act as resource and topic. Further, the use of existing materials or the creation of visual projects can be used alongside other methods of data collection, or in 'triangulated' designs such as case studies. There are no special considerations here either that differ from evaluations we make about any design or method and the purposes to which it has been put.

The realisation of the possibility of using and creating visual resources and topics in sociology is a continuing challenge, particularly because the language of words is the dominant set of symbols and form of communication in our professional culture. It is not just that 'every picture tells a story' or that a picture 'may be worth a thousand words', which warrants us giving serious consideration to visual methodologies. If the visual has been and can be used in strategies of power and control, it suggests that it has an authority which sociology is only just beginning to appreciate. We should cease to be paralysed by a heritage of claims about 'realism' in visual data and accept the challenge they offer for sociological investigation into ways our social world is constituted, reproduced and experienced, in which seeing is as important as saying and doing, and visual depiction performs social work.

REFERENCES

Akeret, R. V. (1973) *Photoanalysis.* New York: Peter Dryden.

Anders, J. F., Keener, M., Bowe, T. R. and Shoaff, B. A. (1983) 'A Longitudinal Study of Night Time Sleep-Wake Patterns in Infants from Birth to One Year', *Frontiers of Infant Psychology.* New York: Basic Books.

Atkinson, P. (1990) *The Ethnographic Imagination: Textual Constructions of Reality.* London: Routledge.

Ball, M. S. and Smith, G. (1992) *Analysing Visual Data.* London: Sage Publications.

Barthes, R. (1973) *Mythologies.* New York: Paladin.

Becker, H. (1974) 'Photography and Sociology', *Studies in the Anthropology of Visual Communication* 1: 3–26.

Becker, H. (1979) 'Do Photographs Tell the Truth?' in T. D. Cook and C. S. Reichardt (eds) *Qualitative and Quantitative Methods in Evaluation Research.* Beverly Hills: Sage Publications.

Bendelow, G. (1993) 'Using Visual Imagery to Analyse Gender Differences in the Perception of Pain', in C. Renzetti and R. Lee (eds) *Researching Sensitive Subjects.* London: Sage.

Berger, J. (1972) *Ways of Seeing.* Harmondsworth: Penguin.

Bittner, E. (1973) 'Objectivity and Realism', in G. Psathsas (ed.) *Phenomenological Sociology.* New York: Wiley.

Brooker, C. (1993) *Unplanned Interactions between Nurses and Patients' Visitors: An Observational Study in a Renal Ward,* Unpublished B.Sc Dissertation, School of Advanced Nursing, North East Surrey College of Technology.

Burgin, V. (ed.) (1982) *Thinking Photography.* London: Macmillan.

Cherrington, R., Tomlinson, D. and Watt, P. (1987) 'Pinch and Clark's Patter Merchanting and the Crisis of Sociology', *Sociology* 21: 275–80.

Clifford, J. and Marcus, E. (eds) (1986) *Writing Culture: The Poetics and Politics of Ethnography.* Berkeley: University of California Press.

Collier, J. (1967) *Visual Anthropology: Photography as a Research Method.* New York: Holt, Reinhardt and Winston.

Curry, T. J. and Clarke A. C. (1979) 'Photographic Exercises', in J. Wagner (ed.) *Images of Information: Still Photography in the Social Sciences.* Beverley Hills: Sage.

Dowrick, P. W. and Biggs, S. (eds) (1983) *Using Video: Psychological and Sociological Applications.* Chichester: Wiley.

Farran, D. (1990) 'Analysing a Photograph of Marilyn Monroe', in L. Stanley (ed.) *Feminist Praxis: Research Theory and Epistemology in Feminist Sociology.* London: Routledge.

Finch, J. (1987) 'The Vignette Technique in Survey Research', *Sociology* 21: 106–14.

Foucault, M. (1977) *Discipline and Punish.* London: Allen Lane.

Fyfe, G. and Law, J. (eds) (1988) *Picturing Power: Visual Depiction and Social Relations,* Sociological Review Monograph, 35, London: Routledge.

Goffman, E. (1976) *Gender Advertisements.* London: Macmillan.

Green, D. (1985) 'On Foucault: Disciplinary Power and Photography', *Camerawork* 32: 6–9.

Harper, D. (1986) 'Meaning and Work: A Study in Photo-elicitation', in L. Henny, (ed.) *Current Sociology* 34: 24–6.

Heath, C. (1984) 'Participation in Medical Consultation: The Co-ordination of Verbal and Nonverbal Behaviour between Doctor and Patient', *Sociology of Health and Illness* 6: 311–38.

Henny, L. M. (ed.) (1986) 'Theory and Practice of Visual Sociology', *Current Sociology* 34: 1–71.

Holsti, O. (1969) *Content Analysis*. Reading, Mass: Addison Wesley.

Krippendorf, K. (1980) *Content Analysis: An Introduction to its Methodology*. Beverley Hills: Sage.

Law, J. and Whittaker, J. (1988) 'The Art of Representation: Notes on the Politics of Visualisation', in G. Fyfe and J. Law (eds) *Picturing Power: Visual Depiction and Social Relations*. London: Routledge.

Mead, M. (1963) 'Anthropology and the Camera', in W. J. Morgan (ed.) *The Encyclopaedia of Photography* Vol. 1. New York: Greystone Press.

Musello, C. (1979) 'Family Photographs', in J. Wagner (ed.) *Images of Information: Still Photography in the Social Sciences*. Beverley Hills: Sage.

Pasveer, B. (1989) 'Knowledge of the Shadows: The Introduction of X-ray Images in Medicine', *Sociology of Health and Illness* 11: 360–81.

Petschesky, R. (1987) 'Foetal Images: The Power of Visual Culture in the Politics of Reproduction', in M. Stanworth (ed.) *Reproductive Technologies: Gender, Motherhood and Medicine*. Cambridge: Polity.

Pinch, T. and Clark, C. (1986) 'The Hard Sell: "Patter Merchanting" and the Strategic (Re)-Production and Local Management of Local Reasoning in the Sales Routines of Market Pitchers', *Sociology* 20: 169–91.

Pinch, T. and Clark, C. (1987) 'On Misunderstanding the Hard Sell', *Sociology* 21: 281–86.

Plummer, K. (1983) *Documents of Life: An Introduction to the Problems and Literature of a Humanistic Method*. London: Allen & Unwin.

Scott, J. (1988) *A Matter of Record*. Cambridge: Polity Press.

Smith, D. (1978) '"K" is Mentally Ill: The Anatomy of a Factual Account', *Sociology* 12: 23–53.

Spence, J. (1986) *Putting Myself in the Picture: A Political Personal and Photographic Autobiography*. London: The Camden Press.

Spence, J. and Martin, R. (1988) 'Phototherapy: Psychic Realism as a Healing Art', *TEN 8*, no. 30.

Spence, J. and Holland, P. (eds.) (1991) *Family Snaps: The Meanings of Domestic Photography*. London: Virago

Sontag, S. (1978) *On Photography*. London: Penguin.

Stasz, C. (1979) 'The Early History of Visual Sociology', in J. Wagner (ed.) *Images of Information: Still Photography and the Social Sciences*. Beverley Hills: Sage Publications.

Stoeckle, J. and White, G. (1985) *Plain Pictures of Plain Doctoring: Vernacular Expression in New Deal Medicine and Photography*. Cambridge Mass: The MIT Press.

Tagg, J. (1980) 'Power and Photography – A Means of Surveillance: The Photograph as Evidence in Law', *Screen Education* 36: 17–55.

Tagg, J. (1982) 'The Currency of the Photograph', in V. Burgin (ed.) *Thinking Photographically*. London: Macmillan.

Tagg, J. (1988) *The Burden of Representation*. London: Macmillan.

Wagner, J. (ed.) (1979) *Images of Information: Still Photography in the Social Sciences*. Beverley Hills: Sage Publications.

Wagner, J. (1979) 'Photography and Social Science Process,' in J. Wagner (ed.) *Images of Information; Still Photography in the Social Sciences.* Beverley Hills: Sage.

Weber, R. (1990) *Basic Content Analysis.* London: Sage.

Wetton, N. (1992) 'Primary School Children and the World of Drugs', in R. Evans and L. O'Connor (eds) *Drug Use and Misuse.* London: David Fulton.

Williamson, J. (1978) *Decoding Advertisements.* London: Marion Boyars.

Worth, S. and Adair, J. (1972) *Through Navaho Eyes: An Exploration in Film Communication and Anthropology.* Bloomington: Indiana University Press.

Ziller, R. C. (1990) *Photographing the Self: Methods for Observing Personal Orientations.* Newbury Park: Sage.

Zimmerman, D. H. and Pollner, M. (1971) 'The Everyday World as a Phenomenon', in J. D. Douglas (ed.) *Understanding Everyday Life: Toward the Reconstruction of Sociological Knowledge.* London: Routledge and Kegan Paul.

Zolberg, V. L. (1990) *Constructing a Sociology of the Arts.* Cambridge: Cambridge University Press.

6 Visual Imagery and the Iconography of the Social World: Some Considerations of History, Art and Problems for Sociological Research

Anthony Pryce

INTRODUCTION

This chapter stems from the experience of undertaking sociological research where visual images formed a principal source of data. The study, 'An Anxious Hour' (Pryce 1989), was concerned, at least as a starting point, with images of death in the nineteenth century (see Plate 1). As such it provided the challenge of selecting visual material from a huge array of sources, genres and locations. The interrogation of pictures yielded a great richness of detailed social data beyond the depth of a few millimetres of paint on the canvas, which is a screen upon which symbolic, projected representations of the social world are constructed. Indeed, as Fyfe and Law suggest, visual depictions are ... 'the apparently stabilised product of work ... the site for the construction and depiction of social difference' (1988: 1). The reading of texts through images relies on the viewer's perception to decode the stories, on the narrative configuration of forms, meanings and symbols which constitute the picture as language and discourse.

Art history has utilised the concept of 'iconography' to describe how the precise use of imagery, symbolism and subject matter has been codified, and used in visual representations to provide consistency in meaning and ideological weight, as in the use of classical allusions or Christian symbols. The most obvious of these become conventions such as the colour blue for the Virgin Mary, the lamb for Christ or the display of artefacts associated with martyrdom or signifying holiness. Such conventions provide, like sacraments, outward and visible signs of hidden symbolic universes. *The Dictionary of Art and Artists* defines iconography as 'A sign that has some of the characteristics of that which it signifies, for example, a cloth sample or portrait' (Murray and Murray 1989: 206). The term is most commonly used in the context of medieval or classical art, where the entire reading of the narrative is dependent on the viewer's recognition of a sometimes complex system of human and spiritual references, spatial relations and social meanings. This is not to say that these are immutable symbols nor, indeed, that their meanings do not change over time. Clearly some iconographic symbols are very enduring, others may be revealed (or constructed) only through the possession of esoteric knowledge or the archaeological gaze. An interesting example is given by Barbu who suggests that many depictions of Christ in the thirteenth century were of the richly clothed 'Christ in Majesty' (Pantacratos), but that this changed to that of a suffering and profoundly physical, embodied 'Christ in Passion' by the following century. He suggests that:

> extra-cultural events such as wars, plagues and natural disasters shook the confidence of late medieval man in the stability of his society, and the security of human existence in general. All this was bound to change man's perception of, and feelings about, God expressed at a cultural level in the conventional representations of Christ (1970: 20).

In other words, to 'read' the text of the picture there has to be some recognisable imagery, a vocabulary which both carries and reveals meaning, meanings which are embedded in social contexts of the artist, patron, economic and status systems. 'Art' and its products represent realities and are thereby vehicles for ideological work, of discursive practices and control.

   Art would seem to be ideal territory for the social researcher. However, relatively few sociologists seem to have engaged with the potential growth in imaginative research opportunities which the judicious use of art-historical techniques makes available. There is evidence that this may be changing with the development over recent years of cultural and media studies, together with the post-modern concern with surfaces and imagery. Nevertheless, despite this new discovery of the visual world, the use of pictures ('art' or otherwise) would seem still to generate some disquiet for some sociologists. This may be the result of inadequate or even non-existent reference to their use or value in research methods training, or perhaps a lingering anxiety about their validity and the theoretical complexities of analysis or even functional usefulness.

The use of the visual image, or indeed 'art' as a basis for sociological study is clearly problematic, particularly if the intention is for such images to be illuminative rather than simply illustrative or decorative. For the purposes of my study, 'visual imagery' was taken to mean 'art', under which generic heading is included painting, photography, graphical illustration and, on occasion, extended to include sculpture and architecture. Conventional cultural hierarchies need to distinguish the notion of 'art' from the 'decorative' or the 'commercial', which if it is an issue may generally prove to be a further problematic element in the research process, and be based more in aesthetic or value judgements than any methodological need. However, any such need to make qualitative distinctions between decorative imagery and 'art' may be thought spurious and imply an uncritical acceptance of received values of taste or economy. Similarly, as a sociologist using visual techniques, the images were utilised without reference to whether they constitute 'good' or 'bad' art. The initial difficulties in approaching visual data obviously lie with the definition and clarification of methodological purpose. In other words, what is the legitimate field of study and the methodological implications which stem from this? Second, what are the distinctions between the aims and values of such a study being rooted in sociology as opposed to art history or history?

In this chapter I intend to identify some methodological and theoretical issues which were highlighted by the experience of my study. I am not attempting here to present a sophisticated theoretical or abstract analysis of visual representation from a particular perspective. Nor am I proposing to provide a thorough overview of the 'Anxious Hour' study. This chapter is essentially a selection of both practical and conceptual vignettes which may provide some methodological stimulus for others who suspect, like me, that given the opportunity, there is much good sociology (and fun) waiting to be excavated from the use of visual representations.

I shall, therefore, briefly review the development of the 'new' art history and then consider the myopia which sociology appears to have experienced when gazing on the visual world. An example of how this may be utilised in the sociology of health, for example, will be described with reference to what could be called the 'Fallen Woman Genre', as a sample of the rich detail which may illuminate the social world(s) of the nineteenth century. I shall conclude by proposing that sociological research is strengthened by the interdisciplinary rigour of art-historical analysis. Further that, despite the potential problems, the scholarly discipline involved in this iconographic archaeology reveal data of great richness and subject to interrogation and exploration as rigorous as any in the repertoire of social research.

'NEW ART HISTORY'

It is useful, of course, to explore and give some consideration to the development of what has been called the 'new' art history which developed in the late 1970s and throughout the 1980s, and to the question of what is art history and its relationship to sociology. In Rees and Borzello's introduction to *The New Art History*, they cite Roskill's traditional view of the discipline which strongly supports the notion of art history being about: 'style, attribution, dating, authenticity, rarity, reconstruction, the detection of forgery, the rediscovery of forgotten artists and the meanings of pictures' and suggest that this demonstrates an attitude which stands out like a beacon 'illuminating the last days of art history's innocence' (1986: 2). The question of the definition of art history is obviously changing and the development of the 'new' art history increasingly challenged the formal and enclosed divisions of modern academic disciplines with their tendency to singular discursive practices. A convenient, although somewhat abbreviated, definition of this new development was given on the back cover of the book:

Q
What is the New Art History?
A

A convenient title for the impact of feminist, marxist, structuralist, psychoanalytic and socio-political ideas on a discipline notorious for its conservatism.

A more extensive exploration and thorough critique of art historical theory lies outside the scope of this paper. However, it is evident that such an (obvious) reworking of its epistemological drives, together with the strength of its methods, provides extremely interesting opportunities for research when utilised by sociology. It is helpful to mark clearly the methodological potential and firmly establish the role of the increasing interdisciplinary cross-currents between the social sciences and this new emphasis in art history.

Rees and Borzello further suggest that there are two distinct themes which are emerging in this more sociologically driven perspective. First, in the social aspects of art, and second, a strong emphasis on theory. With reference to the former issue, they suggest traditional and mainstream art history tried to place:

> art in its context, [it] began from the art and worked outwards: the new form reverses the procedure, looking from the social fabric to the art it produces. Its central interests lie in investigation of how the social order is represented and endorsed by art and in the analysis of the institutions of art, including art history itself (1986: 8).

Following this significant premise it becomes clear that the content and concerns of art can, and should, be legitimately brought into the field of wider sociological enquiry. Indeed, Rees and Borzello acknowledge that the language of the new art history betrayed its origins in the social sciences with its Marxist perspectives, and critiques of ideology, class and patriarchy. However, this also brings with it significant theoretical questions relating to structure and individual creativity, as Wolff argues:

> it is not useful to think of artistic work as essentially different from other kinds of work, and that, therefore, the issue of the practical activity, including the creative or innovative activity, of any agent arises in the same way in all areas of social and personal life (1982: 2).

This would, then, seem to provide a bridge with the other central trend in the 'new' art history, that of theory. According to Rees and Borzello (1986: 3), this would be particularly apparent after 1974 which they regard as a 'watershed year', citing Clark's *The Absolute Bourgeois* (1973a) and *The Image of the People: Gustav Courbet and the 1848 Revolution* (1973b) as harbingers of a change in art history which took account of the social world in which art is produced. This is very clearly rooted initially in traditional Marxist thought and psychoanalysis and further developed in feminist critiques of patriarchal culture (Wolff 1982: 6; Pollock 1988: 1–17). Exemplars of this new wave of predominantly feminist art historians include Nead's *Myths of Sexuality* (1988), Nochlin's *Women, Art, Power and Other Essays* (1989), and Jordanova's *Sexual Visions* (1987). These analyses have been particularly concerned with representations of women and power, but have also been influential in the formation of queer theory and the deconstruction of gay and lesbian imagery (Dyer 1993). They provide an arena which is located in time, which problematises perception and can be satisfyingly *empirical* whilst not compromising post-structural credentials.

In other words, this 'new art history' rejected the traditional constructions of cultural history, and posited a challenge to a belief in *eternal truths* being embodied in art, continuities which transcend class and time and which is 'above' society. By its close affiliation to social constructionism, again it would appear that this locates the potential study of the social history of art as the legitimate domain of sociology.

SOCIOLOGY AND THE OPTIC NERVE

Hijacking John Berger's title, it would now seem that we have less of a new sub-discipline, rather a *Ways of Seeing* (1972). Social researchers could now expand their range of both methods and perspectives without compromising the *sense of being* sociologists. At the risk of revisiting over-rehearsed arguments, the question arises of why sociologists have been reluctant to incorporate the visual into the central repertoire of research opportunities. As Giddens, for example, has defined it, sociology is: 'a social science, having as its main focus the study of the social institutions brought into being by industrial transformations of the past two or three centuries' (1986: 9). On this basis it ought to be assumed that art and its institutions should be prime targets for sociological enquiry as it was largely as a result of industrialised society that 'art' became a widespread bourgeois commodity and clearly reproduced its capitalist means of production. Indeed, it is as commodity and artefact rather than social or political statement that the visual may be engaged initially. Fischer asserts that: 'Capitalism is not essentially a social force well-disposed to art or that promotes art: in so far as the average capitalist needs art at all, he needs it as an embellishment of his private life or else as a good investment' (1959: 51). A significant example depicted by Zoffany is Dr William Hunter, who lectured at the Royal Academy (Bignamini and Postle 1991: 84)

Where, however, is sociology at this Aladdin's cave of potential riches? The American positivistic traditions particularly have been criticised for their concern with secular and social problems. Grana suggested that this was explained by their 'conventional, perhaps notorious reluctance to acknowledge art as an aspect of culture consequential to their researches' (1971: 65). Where art and sociology have been in contention, there have been extensive disputes about the value of any analysis of society through art or the attempt to establish causal relationships between art and society. It is also perhaps significant that most arguments, such as those described by Grana, may be dated prior to the emergence of the 'new' art history (Rees and Borzello 1986: 3).

Fyfe and Law forcibly argue that the visual has been marginalised throughout the development of sociology for when 'the body was deleted from mainstream classic social theory... so was the eye' (1988: 6–7). In other words, the analysis of perception was dispersed into the domain of other disciplines such as psychology or art history. As a result, they argue, 'most sociologists were blinded to the visual and social character of perception and reproduction'. They go on to suggest that sociology: 'in its aversion to visual argument... should not act as if the visual were absent in, or simply peripheral to, its objects of study'. On the surface, this claim may now seem to be a little passé with the explosion of post-modern re-reading of texts and media, and the apotheosis of the discourse of 'visible fictions' in queer theory, cultural studies, feminism and so on. However, these areas of scholarship may themselves be seen as marginal to 'mainstream' sociologists. As such, Fyfe and Law's criticism still holds.

SOCIOLOGY?

The interface of sociological and historical study has also been an arena of contention. The conventional view has held that they are concerned with distinct and often opposing perspectives in which history is essentially an idiographic discipline 'concerned with unique and particular events' and sociology is a nomothetic, generalising discipline (Goldthorpe 1984: 162–74). However, another view is that sociological explanation is, of necessity, historical. Lloyd cites Abrams's assertion that:

> All varieties of sociology stress the so-called 'two-sidedness' of the social world, presenting it as a world of which we are both the creators and the creatures, both makers and prisoners: a world in which our actions construct and a world that powerfully constrains us. The distinctive quality of the social world for the sociologist is its facticity – the way in which life is experienced by individuals as a fact-like system, external, given, coercive, even whilst individuals are busy making and remaking it through their own imagination, communication and action (1986: 23).

Lloyd goes on to suggest that this 'two-sideness' of the 'awesome paradox' referred to by Berger and Luckmann (1967: 33ff) could only be resolved historically, because whatever reality a society has, is an historical reality which is located in a temporal space. Once again, art and its institutions may be a means of engaging sociologically with how realities may have been constructed as facts in the other country that was the past.

The art historian Hauser asserted that prevailing power relationships are expressed in the world of art. This must therefore be deemed to include the artists and their patrons, the institutions of art such as colleges, galleries and museums, the buyers and dealers of the artwork market, as well as, of course, the pictures themselves. Through their subject, form, techniques, iconography and context, pictures are specifically located both culturally and historically. This is particularly true as the production of art and its markets in the nineteenth century increasingly conformed to the capitalist model, whilst it also developed the visual image as commodity. Indeed, Lowe in his analysis of perception suggests that in the bourgeois society of the period, the dominant field of perception was: 'constituted by the predominance of typographical media, the hierarchy of sensing which emphasised the primacy of sight, and the epistemic order of development-in-time' (1982: 18). In other words, he explains that: 'typography promoted the ideal that knowledge could be detached from the knower to become impartial and explicit. The primacy of sight made possible scientific verification of that knowledge.' Here is an echo of the belief system underpinning the supremacy of the nineteenth century cult of facticity exemplified by Dickens's Mr Gradgrind in *Hard Times*. Any number of examples may be used to illustrate the significance and the influence which even a single work might make within discourses, such as those surrounding the emergence of new definitions of health or sexuality, gender and respectability in the mid-nineteenth century. Certainly, within the emerging sociology of the body, it is fatuous to ignore the histories of its representations and the problematic of the nude or naked figure. Within such analysis, however, conflicts may be articulated in terms of iconography but also iconoclasm.

A French example may be helpful. Manet's *Le Dejeuner sur l'Herbe* (Plate 2) was not accepted to be exhibited at the Salon of 1863, rather it was shown at the Salon des Refusés to a storm of protest and ridicule. Initially, it might be thought that the unclothed female figure was in the acceptable tradition of Giorgione and Raphael. However, the presence of two men clothed in modern dress created a very different and threatening construction where the woman ceased to be 'nude' but 'naked'. Similarly Manet's *Olympia* (1865), whilst presenting the image in the form of morally acceptable and grand iconographic tradition, subverted the representation of Venus into a contemporary prostitute. In doing so, he enters the bourgeois discourses of moral culture, respectability, the public and private, sexuality and power. That these pictures received such a violent response clearly indicates the extent to which they challenged the existing order and articulated threats to that order. For, whilst the critics, inflamed by Manet's effrontery to the academic pantheon of artistic convention, condemned his technique and 'vulgarity', it is clear that such images were powerful engagements in the wider discourses of early modernism. Such assertions may be validated by the commentary of Zola, Baudelaire and other contemporary writers, and with reference to their political and cultural context.

MORAL TALES: A VIGNETTE

From the British perspective and the particular focus of the 'Anxious Hour', it is relevant briefly to explore the potential insights which might be provided by art in historical analyses within the sociology of health or gender. The genre which may be termed 'Fallen Women' is particularly helpful. Bound up in the construction of male and particularly female sexuality was the deviance, defined medically, of 'immoral' fallen women who, once they had embarked upon a 'life of sin', had limited life options. Immediately declassed, they might become prostitutes, and thus compound the deviance. Mort cites Acton, a doctor who was committed to 'expansionist sanitary reform', basing his argument on a norm of the asexuality of respectable women. He used this as a biological phenomenon to assert that: 'in a state of nature wild female animals will not allow the approach of the male except when in a state of rut' (1987: 79). As Mort points out, this clearly defines motherhood, marriage and domesticity as natural basic female instincts of the asexual bourgeois woman, as opposed to the 'unnatural' sexual desire and instincts of the working class prostitute. The likely cost of being 'fallen', even if it did not result in prostitution, would be in a removal from the arenas of respectable gaze, if not surveillance. In either case, disease and death were the likely consequences.

As paintings may provide potent resonances of social discourse and provide 'validating anchors' from other documentary sources, it is helpful to consider these narratives in relation to specific concerns such as the regulation of sexualities. It is illuminating to take as an example just one year, 1857. Acton's reports in 1857 were concerned with the moral, social and sanitary aspects of prostitution, with recommendations for its regulation. Also in 1857 there was a parliamentary bill to regulate the sale of obscene books, pictures, prints and other articles. In the same year, a report of commissioners appointed to inquire into the sanitary conditions of the army was published. The Matrimonial Causes Act, again of 1857, sought to enhance the 'sanctity' of the home and reinforced the double standards within marriage, the inequality in relation to divorce in particular. At the height of this moral panic, Augustus Egg's triptych,

Past and Present (1857–8) (Plates 3–5) was exhibited at the Royal Academy with a sub-title:

> August 4th. Have just heard that B- has been dead more than a fortnight, so that now his poor children have now lost both parents. I hear she was seen on Friday last near the Strand, evidently without a place to lay her head. What a fall hers has been!

This Hogarthian moral tale of the consequences of a wife's adultery is permeated with symbolism – in an iconographic representation accessible to the middle class viewer. The first picture (see Plate 3) shows an affluent middle class drawing room, apparently furnished with the latest painted furniture and a *papier maché* chair on which two small girls are building a 'House of Cards' which is just collapsing. As a foundation for the 'house', the girls are using a novel by Balzac, a metaphor for the 'dangerous' influence of French morality and vice when allowed into the sanctuary of the English home. On the wall are two pictures, one of a shipwreck, *The Abandoned*, the other of the expulsion from the Garden of Eden, *The Fall*. The large overmantle mirror reflects the new gas-light chandelier, but also the open door through which an errant wife must now pass forever; it shows nothing beyond the door. A stern husband is seated beside a table, and under his heel he crushes a miniature portrait of his wife's lover as he clutches a letter revealing her guilt. She is lying on the floor, her hands clenched in dramatic supplication, beside her a symbolic half-eaten apple, the other half being 'rotten at the core'.

The next two pictures (Plates 4 and 5) depict an evening five years later, the father has died, a fact revealed by his portrait now being in complete shade. The two girls sit by a window in a plain but comfortable bedroom, the younger kneeling and saying her prayers. The elder girl, dressed in mourning, comforts her sister and gazes out at a waning moon. The miniature portrait of the mother is shown in half-shadow. At the same moment, the mother is shown in the third picture gazing at the same moon. She is in the Adelphi arches 'the lowest of all the profound deeps of human abandonment in the metropolis' (Nead 1988: 77) and the Thames is just a few feet away. She looks ill and weary, and her 'downward' moral career is confirmed by the young baby she cradles. Behind her are posters advertising 'Pleasure Trips to Paris' analogous to the capital of sin and far for 'Victims' and 'A Cure for Love', both plays at the Haymarket Theatre. The symbolism contained here is obvious, and perhaps intended to be all the more powerful as it has penetrated the security of the familiar domestic scene, thereby emphasising the potentially very fine line defining the security of fidelity, affluence and respectability. The potent symbolism expressed in these paintings emphasised too the fragile social status of women, but also the havoc which their immorality might bring on their 'innocent' children and husbands. The stakes of respectable security were high, so clearly the intimations of the price of failure needed to be extreme: expulsion, loss and death. The iconography of this third image would suggest that suicide by drowning is the likely (inevitable) outcome for this woman. Suicide by drowning, and suicide in the Thames particularly, again represented ideological work in many of the moralising social commentaries and has been explored elsewhere (Pryce 1989). Nead (1988: 167ff), in her analysis of the representation of women in Victorian art, has outlined the influence on popular culture and mythology of Thomas Hood's poem *The Bridge of Sighs* which explores the issue of prostitution and suicide. It was suggested that suicide by drowning accounted for most of the 500 deaths per year in the Thames.

However, as with Mary Magdalene, the hope of redemption offered by the light of moral virtue was always held out. Although any such redemption was possible, even at the level of *passing* as respectable it was unlikely. The seminal image was Holman Hunt's *The Awakened Conscience* (1853), which is symbol-laden and anecdotal (see Plate 6). It clearly acts as a vehicle of moral regulation which the Athenaeum critic suggested was 'drawn from a very dark and repulsive side of domestic life' (Wood 1981: 137). The young woman's seducer sits at a piano; the music is 'Oft in the Stilly Night', whilst on the floor another manuscript has been discarded – 'Tears, Idle Tears'. The conspicuously new furniture suggests that she has been installed as a 'kept woman'. The picture was painted in Alpha Place, St John's Wood, which was well known as an area for 'maisons de convenance', the outwardly respectable and leafy suburban area highlighting the hypocrisy. As Weeks suggests: 'It is inescapably true that the familial ideology was accompanied by, and often relied on a vast underbelly of prostitution which fed on the double standard and an authoritarian moral code' (1989: 30).

The woman is rising from the man's lap as she begins to 'repent'. A mirror once again is used to reveal an open door, this time into a sunlit garden and the 'natural' order of feminine purity which she can see awaiting her. The image suggests clearly the virtue of repentance, but beneath that is the spectre of future misery and isolation when she is inevitably deserted by her seducer. For Ruskin, this picture was 'painting taking its proper place beside literature' confronting 'the moral evil of the age' (Wood 1976: 139).

Whilst the enriching potential of utilising such visual data in research is apparent, it is helpful to identify briefly the various problems and advantages of using art to help illuminate these relationships and consider whether or not it is possible for art to become a valid and reliable source of legitimate social data.

ART AND PROBLEMS OF METHODOLOGY

The social researcher approaches a picture, photograph or painting, with a certain caution for, whilst the image may present a rich source of social and historical information, it is essentially value laden. It is helpful to consider any such historical visual images in the same ways as one can analyse contemporary images, but without becoming 'unhistorical'. In other words, by exploring the 'facticity' of the image as artifact but also as symbol, it is possible to scrutinise them with the same methodological priorities, rigour and concerns as any other data and documentary evidence (Wollheim 1970; Barbu 1970).

Initially, of course, it must be acknowledged that the production of art cannot be neutral but is a highly subjective process, selective and not value-free. This underpins the analysis of a number of particular notions, especially those of both the artist and the production of art. As in the use of film or photography as documentary evidence, art must be open to scrutiny regarding whether or not it is a distortion or an accurate and representative account of experience or events. Why and how was the picture created, and with what intention? Does the subject and its interpretation result from the bias, class position or ideological perspective of the artist and/or the patron? This question, of course, raises the issues of just who is buying or commissioning the work, for what reason and who is to be its target audience? Some of these issues were addressed elsewhere, with particular reference to aspects of the social construction of art in the nineteenth century (Pryce 1989: 43ff).

Nevertheless, from a research perspective it is obvious that paintings and other art productions impose some limitations. Conventional definitions of art tend to suggest that it is 'the use of the imagination to make things of aesthetic significance, or objects made by creative artists' (*Longman's Dictionary* 1976). As one can readily see, little is clarified by such definitions. 'Aesthetic significance' is obviously a notion underlying the production and history of art itself and upon which there can be clearly no single standard or consensus. Similarly, the idea that art is reducible to the form of an 'object' which is made by 'creative artists' is again highly problematic as the role of the artist has been socially constructed and is culturally and historically located. The social status and identity of the

artist has clearly changed from the generally nameless manuscript illum-
inators of the middle ages, through to the notion of the individual creative
'genius' of nineteenth- and twentieth-century artists.

As a reliable single source of social and historical evidence art is therefore somewhat unreliable, particularly if the creative role of the artist is
identified as being rooted in the realm of the imagination, art being the
product of a solitary and transcendental Romanticism. Herbert Read
appeared to reinforce this powerful belief in 'inspiration' and individual-
ism in the production of art:

> the artist ... is a unit of a necessary social organisation and cannot even
> arrive at the threshold of his potentialities without the conditions which
> a culture provides. But having reached that threshold he must be left to
> proceed alone, as an individual. For he can cross that threshold only
> within his own self. Across the threshold is the subliminal self which is
> more than the conscious entity of the ego (1967: 80).

Clearly the message here suggests that the artist is functioning at a higher,
more intense, perhaps politically insightful, level than an artisan, and like
the reference to 'aesthetic significance', such rationales in other contexts
have been used to distinguish 'good' art and artists from 'bad', the commercial from 'fine' art. However, as Wolff suggests, the concern for sociological study in this context does not lie with the exploration of aesthetic
values, except where the associated class values may require analysis, but
rather how they are contemporarily addressed in their historical location.
The question raised, in other words, is not whether an object or painting is
'beautiful', but what it represented at the time to observers and the society
of the period. Also of importance is the reading of the image by the
modern viewer, who may or may not be aware of the contemporary discourses and sometimes hidden or obscure iconographies rich in meanings
and symbols. Ultimately, however, all these elements in the production
and reproduction of visual images/art are part of discursive practices.

An aesthetic issue with methodological implications lies in the categori-
sation of high or fine art from other contemporary forms of representation. There are clearly problems here in the relations between ideology
and aesthetics, particularly for Marxist historians (Wolff 1982). The
images explored in the 'Anxious Hour' study were not only drawn from
pictures which have been acclaimed on aesthetic grounds, indeed most
were what have been dismissively referred to as genre or social realism.
These were generally highly popular but have since been critically
denigrated by the art establishment. However, they do form what might be
called the main gallery of representations of domestic ideology.

Having suggested that there are potential methodological problems in using pictures as valid sources for sociological study, nevertheless there are several advantages in providing access to rich seams of data. In the 'Anxious Hour', a study of imagery and death in the nineteenth century, the explicit, revealed subject, the visual content, could provide a baseline located in time and space. This gives insight to the construction of the bourgeois self-idealisation, reflecting a concern with the material and social fabric of life and against which changes in the organisation of loss and death may be gauged. Historically, this may reflect changes of emphasis, but also provides visual evidence of artifacts and their location or association in terms of class, gender or time. Second, the text of these visual dramas provides a means of analysing their symbolic relations. Thus, the dynamic tension creates a juxtaposition between the signifier and the signified, the real and the imaginary, transgression and order, life and death.

That death, often used allegorically, was a common motif can be seen in the Academy Exhibition of 1876 when titles such as *The Widower*, *At Death's Door*, *Sown in Dishonour it shall be Raised in Glory*, *Fatherless* and *Whither* were exhibited (Treuherz 1987: 80). Paintings could be 'read' for their many layers of symbolism and moral injunctions, locating both the signifier and the signified within a class and therefore a moral order.

The problems of reliability may be addressed by using other cultural and official records of the period. In this paper, artworks have been regarded as varieties of artistic activities and enterprises which are repositories of cultural meaning; they can be used in the context of other documentary evidence to support what may be deduced visually from the images of the period. Within the boundaries of research using essentially secondary sources, the ideal of methodological pluralism may be rather restricted, but wherever possible given the limitations of space and the large scope of the 'Anxious Hour' study, triangulation of data was attempted. This was particularly helped by the large amount of contemporary documentary material in the form of newspaper and journal articles, novels which were often concerned with social realism, diaries, monographs, official records and statistics. Clearly, at this level, the research process utilises techniques of the social historian, but essentially treats the content of images and paintings as traceable genealogies of socially constructed realities. Art ceases to be a realm of esoteric or other knowledge.

CONCLUSION

In conclusion, what have visual representations to offer which other methods do not? There are two central benefits for the social researcher in using visual imagery. First, the visual domain allows the researcher to gain insights, sometimes blinding in their power and vivacity, to representations of social relations and codes of meaning. Following Lowe's (1982) argument in the history of perception, if the researcher is seeing, *perceiving* an historical representation, there is a process of reflexivity within an historical consciousness. Utilising a visual imagery in research is a reflexive act, and in his procedure for undertaking research in the history of perception, Lowe suggests that this provides 'the intermediate link between the content of thought and the structure of society'. The methods he suggests are to:

(1) periodise a society, in terms of its multi-level structure;
(2) within the context of the period, constitute the ongoing field of perception in terms of its culture of communications media, its hierarchy of sensing, and its epistemic order of discourse;
(3) within that perceptual field, describe the lived experience of time, space and bodily life.

Clearly, much of the nineteenth-century art explored in the study was concerned with hegemonic, moral discourses in which class and gender were developing recognisable tensions and forms. Works such as Manet's, rather more than British examples, used conventions to affront convention in what can be seen as powerful modernist statements. However, in much nineteenth century art, the use of metaphor and allegory, revealed and made accessible through sometimes complex, perhaps often risible, narrative and iconography, provides the researcher with a very rich seam of data.

Second, like conversation analysis, the interpretation of such representations demands the deconstruction of languages(s) in order to reveal meaning and knowledge. There is no reason why the use of visual techniques should be simply associated with sociology of culture. On the contrary, the utilisation of rigorous historical techniques and the systematic (pragmatic) use of secondary sources may enhance the interpretation of data. Such a research role is not inconsistent with some aspects of Denzin's (1989) description of interpretive interactionism. Whilst he is clearly more focused on the 'real-life problems' such as wife-battering, in his exemplars the use of extracts of novels and other texts provide 'thick descriptions' like that in Foucault's *Discipline and Punish* (1979). Denzin suggests that these descriptions... 'create verisimilitude' and that it 'goes beyond mere fact and surface appearances. It presents detail, context, emotion and the webs of social relationships that join persons to one another. Thick description evokes emotionality and self-feelings. It inserts history into experience' (1989: 83).

It might not at first appear that the esoteric deconstruction of visual images by sociologists is consistent with the 'individual' emotional emphasis which Denzin argues is central to the interpretive process. However, in using visual techniques, the researcher engages with the 'screen' that carries the complex construction of social representations but must also augment and validate the potential 'reading' by reference to contemporary viewers like Ruskin or Baudelaire. If further justification is needed that the iconography of the visual image may inform us of meanings and relations in the social world, Baudelaire asserted that critics must be partial, political and passionate and for him 'art was ultimately connected to social experiences, to the contingencies of actual life' (Frascina *et al.* 1993: 9). This was one of the imperatives of modernity. The skills and practices of other disciplines can be most powerful in freeing the research imagination, and if we allow it, provide a more acute gaze upon the social world.

REFERENCES

Abrams, P. (1982) *Historical Sociology*. Somerset: Open Books.
Barbu, Z. (1970) 'Sociological Perspectives in Art and Literature', in J. Creedy (ed.) *The Social Context of Art*. London: Tavistock.
Berger, J. (1972) *Ways of Seeing*. London: Penguin.
Berger, P. and Luckmann, T. (1967) *The Social Construction of Reality*. London: Penguin.
Betterton, R. (ed) (1987) *Looking On*. London: Pandora.
Bignamini, I. and Postle, M. (1991) *The Artist's Model*. Nottingham: University of Nottingham and English Heritage
Blake, N., Frascina, F. *et al.* (eds) (1993) *Modernity and Modernism*. London: The Open University Press.
Clark, T. J. (1973a) *Absolute Bourgeois: Artists and Politics in France 1948-51*. London: Thames & Hudson.
Clark, T. J. (1973b) *Image of the People*. London: Thames & Hudson.
Clark, T. J. (1974) 'The Conditions of Artistic Creation', *The Times Literary Supplement*, 2nd May: p. 562.
Collier, J. and Collier, M. (1987) *Visual Anthropology*. Albuquerque: University of New Mexico Press.
Creedy J. (1970) *The Social Context of Art*. London: Tavistock.
Denzin, N. K. (1989) *Interpretive Interactionism*. London: Sage.
Dyer, R. (1993) *The Matter of Images*. London: Routledge.
Ellis, J. (1982) *Visible Fictions*. London: Routledge.
Fischer, E. (1959) *The Necessity of Art: A Marxist Approach,* London: Peregrine.
Foucault, M. (1979) *Discipline and Punish*. Harmondsworth: Penguin.

Frascina, F. *et al.* (1993) *Modernity and Modernism.* Yale: Open University Press.
Fyfe, G. and Law, J. (1988) *Picturing Power: Visual Depiction and Social Relations.* London: Routledge.
Gallagher, C. and Laqueur, T. (eds) (1987) *The Making of the Modern Body.* Berkeley: University of California Press.
Giddens, A. (1986) *Sociology.* London: Macmillan.
Gill, M. (1989) *Image of the Body.* New York: Doubleday.
Gilman, S. L. (1988) *Disease and Representation.* Ithaca: Cornell University Press.
Goldthorpe, J. H. (1984) 'The Relevance of History to Sociology', in M. Bulmer (ed.) *Sociological Research Methods.* Second Edition. London: Macmillan.
Grana, C. (1971) *Fact and Symbol: Essays in the Sociology of Art & Literature.* New York: Oxford University Press.
Jordanova, L. (1989) *Sexual Visions.* London: Harvester Wheatsheaf.
Kuhn, A. (1985) *The Power of the Image.* London: Routledge.
Lloyd, C. (1986) *Explanation in Social History.* Oxford: Blackwell.
Lowe, D. M. (1982) *A History of Bourgeois Perception.* Sussex: Harvester Press.
Mort, F. (1987) *Dangerous Sexualities.* London: Routledge.
Murray, P. and Murray, L. (1989) *Dictionary of Art and Artists.* London: Penguin.
Nead, L. (1988) *Myths of Sexuality.* London: Blackwell.
Nochlin, L. (1989) *Women, Art and Power and other Essays.* London: Thames & Hudson.
Pollock, G. (1988) *Vision and Difference.* London: Routledge.
Pryce, M. A. (1989) 'An Anxious Hour: Visual Imagery, Death, Loss and the Domestic Ideology in the Nineteenth Century'. Unpublished MSc Thesis, University of the South Bank.
Read, H. (1967) *Art and Society.* London: Faber & Faber.
Rees, A. L. and Borzello, F. (eds) (1986) *The New Art History.* London: Camden Press.
Sprinkler, M. (1987) *Imaginary Relations.* London: Verso.
Stasz, C. (1979) 'The Early History of Visual Sociology', in J. Wagner *Images of Information.* California: Sage.
Treuherz, J. (ed.) (1987) *Hard Times.* London: Lund Humphries.
Wagner, J. (1979) *Images of Information.* California: Sage.
Weeks, J. (1989) *Sex, Politics and Society.* Second Edition. London: Routledge.
Wolff, F. and Cassin, M. (1987) *Bodylines: The Human Figure in Art.* London: National Gallery.
Wolff, J. (1982) *The Social Production of Art.* London: Macmillan.
Wollheim, R. (1970). 'Sociological Explanation of the Arts: Some Distinctions', in Albrecht *et al.* (eds) *The Sociology of Art and Literature.* London: Duckworth.
Wood, C. (1976) *Victorian Panorama: Paintings of Victorian Life.* London: Faber & Faber.
Wood, C. (1981) *The Pre-Raphaelites.* London: Weidenfeld & Nicolson.

7 Ethnography, Ethnicity and Work: Unpacking the West Midlands Clothing Industry

Monder Ram

INTRODUCTION

Workplace studies in the ethnographic tradition occupy an unusual position within the broad area of industrial relations sociology. Although they resulted in some 'classic' contributions, notably Dalton (1959), Gouldner (1954) and Roy (1954), the studies themselves have not formed the basis of mainstream research practice. The ethnographic method is far from common as a means of investigating workplace relations (Edwards 1992). This paper is based on an initial survey but, more centrally, on intensive fieldwork in three small clothing firms over a year long period. It explores particular methodological issues arising from a workplace-based study in the ethnic minority-dominated West Midlands clothing sector (Ram 1994), and argues that to explain adequately the negotiation of order in such a context, a research approach sensitive to the issues of ethnicity, family and gender is required.

The study aimed to explore some basic issues around the regulation of work, that is, the rules, procedures, customs and understandings which regulate the way in which workers' capacity to labour is translated into actual effort. This regulation is a continuous process, and it is through this process that workers and managers develop conceptions of themselves and each other (Edwards 1992: 7). Three issues were of particular concern: first, the processes involved in the negotiation of order on the shopfloor. This involved examining the bargains, calculations and negotiations involved in managing the workplace. Second, the nature of management organisation in a sector often associated with managerial autocracy was explored. The final issue of concern was the relationship between ethnicity and the labour process.

These concerns have tended to be neglected within debates on management strategy and the labour process more generally. But, more importantly

112

for the purposes of this chapter, the manner in which such issues have been studied has not often been a subject for discussion. As noted, there have been few workplace studies conducted from a primarily ethnographic framework. Rarer still has been the conduct of such a study by an 'insider', as was the case with the present example. The basis of my insider status is discussed later; the point to note is that most shopfloor studies to date have been conducted by 'outsiders'. In many of the factory-based studies within this field (Lupton 1963; Cunnison 1966; Beynon 1973; Nichols and Beynon 1977; Pollert 1981; Cavendish 1982; Westwood 1984), the researchers began as outsiders who had little understanding of the workers' situation until they engaged in their research (Burgess 1984).

My own position as an insider derived from my ethnic, familial and work background. The remainder of this chapter discusses the significance of this background in the research process. The first section explores the nature of my ethnic resources and their importance in securing access to the research site, raising points similar to those identified in feminist approaches to methodological issues (Finch 1984; Oakley 1989). In particular, the advantages of having a shared 'structural location' with participants in the research context are presented. Ethnicity figures in the second section too, but the focus shifts to its significance in managing gender relations during the research. I argue that the insider role is neither uniform nor unvarying. Finally, some issues around the theme of 'researching the familiar' are examined, focusing particularly on concerns over partiality and subjectivity which are sometimes raised in relation to research of this nature. But before this discussion, it is necessary to sketch in some of the features of the West Midlands clothing industry, for they reinforce the importance of ethnicity to the research process and the wider study in general.

THE WEST MIDLANDS CLOTHING SECTOR

The clothing industry in the West Midlands comprises a large number of relatively small manufacturers producing mainly lower volume, untailored garments. These products involve short run lengths and relatively simple production methods. This type of clothing business is thought to account for about 500 firms throughout the West Midlands; it exists alongside approximately 50 'older' firms in the region producing tailored garments and formal outerwear. Most of the 'new industry' consists of Asian-owned firms with fewer than 50 employees, the majority of whom are Asian women. In addition, many firms use homeworkers or sub-contractors to minimise costs with fluctuating levels of production. It is likely that clothing employment now surpasses 20,000 workers including some 5,000 homeworkers (West Midlands Low Pay Unit 1991).

This Asian-dominated clothing sector is a comparatively recent phenomenon. Before the 1970s, clothing was not a significant industry in the region, and what little there was tended to be dominated by larger firms manufacturing lines such as men's outerwear (Hayden 1992). Continuing economic austerity, however, precipitated the closure or relocation of these predominantly white firms. It also created high levels of unemployment within the large Asian community in the area, further restricting their opportunities within mainstream employment. These were the conditions that gave rise to the West Midlands clothing sector.

The context in which the industry emerged highlights the point that the comparatively high level of Asian involvement was more a product of racism and economic decline than of any cultural predisposition towards entrepreneurship, as is sometimes suggested (Werbner 1984). Respondents in the survey stage of the study (comprising detailed interviews with 16 employers) stressed that to become self-employed was the only way that they could hope to earn a decent living. The choice often lay between the drudgery of poorly rewarded factory work or the possibility of achieving something better through enterprise. Racism in the wider labour market prevented advancement from being achieved through mainstream employment, a point that was equally relevant in explaining minority women's employment in these firms.

The market position of most West Midlands clothing firms is characterised by intense competition and uncertainty, as well as racial constraints. Unlike the industry nationally most clothing firms in the West Midlands sell their goods through intermediaries. These intermediaries, be they wholesalers, larger manufacturers or agents, characteristically impose onerous conditions on manufacturers and display little loyalty. To compound this situation, the capacity of manufacturers to break out of this market position was impeded by what many employers perceived to be racially discriminatory attitudes of retailers and agents. This sentiment was echoed by owners in a more general study of Asian enterprise in the inner-city area of Wolverhampton (Ram 1992).

The three case study companies were broadly characteristic of firms in this sector. Company A came into being in 1979. It is one part of my family's business, the other elements being a wholesale operation (run by Bas, my younger brother) and a separate clothing manufacturing company (run by my elder brother, Sol, and a cousin). Phu (my father), who runs company A, employs around fifteen direct workers all of whom are male. There are five machinists, two cutters and a varying number of ancillary staff. The overwhelming majority of the company's production comes from outworkers and sub-contractors. They account for over 80 per cent of the firm's output. Some of these external workers are situated in premises adjacent to the proprietor's home and are supervised by the proprietor's two daughters-in-law.

Company B is run by two brothers and a cousin. The company employs around twenty-five machinists on the premises who produce the bulk of the firm's output. In addition to these on-site machinists, the company utilises a small number of outworkers and sub-contractors. As well as the machinists and the three partners (who between them share the cutting duties), the company has on its staff three packers and one supervisor. Company C is run by nine brothers and the wives of four of them. Between them, they are responsible for managing, cutting, quality control and supervision. The company employs around thirty machinists on the premises, the majority of whom have been working for the firm for over ten years. In addition to these on-site workers, the company makes use of homeworkers and sub-contractors, especially during the busy season.

THE FAMILY, THE BUSINESS AND THE STUDY

> ... full time research is not a job: it is a way of life, and so one's life becomes woven into the research just as much as research becomes part of one's life (Moore 1997: 87).

For two years, Moore 'ate, breathed and slept' Sparkbrook in order to unravel the processes of racism in an inner city area in Birmingham. I have been in and around the clothing industry for slightly longer. For most of my life I have been involved with the clothing trade. More accurately, I have been privy to a particular part of the 'rag trade'. It has not been a world of catwalks, designers, models and other such features associated with the world of high fashion. Rather, it has been an existence of hard labour in a harsh and hostile environment. For my family and, to a lesser extent, myself, long tedious hours in the factory of doing almost everything from clipping loose threads from jackets to trying to extract payment for goods from boorish wholesalers in the East End of London have been the natural order of things.

Making visible the researcher's background and position in the field is being increasingly recognised as important to the total research process

(Armstrong 1993; Roseneil 1993). And so it was in my case. The family business has been just that – a family business, with no real dividing line between the home and the factory. Every member of my family is firmly ensconced in the clothing industry. My father is the head of the whole enterprise, although most of his time is spent running company A. My mother is not 'officially' involved in any part of the business, but at an informal level her influence is considerable. She recruits machinists, mediates in disputes between workers and management and plays an active role 'behind the scenes' in managing the company's financial resources. My two elder sisters and one younger sister are 'married into' clothing families, where they work as sewing machinists and assist in the management of the in-laws' firms. My elder brother runs a clothing manufacturing business with a cousin. This business was 'created' especially for him by my father. My younger brother is in charge of the family-owned warehouse. Furthermore, beyond the immediate family, numerous relatives are engaged in varying capacities in the local clothing industry.

Yet, it was not always like this. My father came to England from India in the late 1950s leaving his wife and two young daughters behind. Like many others in his position, he did not have much in the way of possessions and had no job. Finding cramped accommodation with other newly arrived Indians, he eventually started work in a foundry. He laboured hard in order to save enough money to bring his family over, who arrived some five years later. He saved hard so that he could scrape enough money together to escape from the toil of factory work and start a business. He duly opened a grocery shop in the early 1970s. Typical of many 'corner-shops' today (Jones *et al.* 1989), family members were the main source of labour. For my brothers, sisters and me, it was school, then serving in the shop, unloading vans full of stock and making deliveries to the homes of the primarily Asian and West Indian clientele.

The shop was soon disposed of; my father formed a partnership with a few other relatives and set up a small garment manufacturing company. He hoped that rewards from clothing would be better than the meagre offerings of the food shop. From serving groceries, my brothers, sisters and I adapted to the art of manufacturing garments. My two elder sisters learned to sew, while my brothers and I laboured to varying degrees in the factory. This business survived until 1979 when the various partners decided to go their different ways. It was in 1979 that company A came into being, followed a few years later by the family warehouse and the clothing business for my elder brother.

By the early 1980s, my brothers were running various parts of the family enterprise whilst my sisters had 'married into' families also involved in the rag trade. I was the only member of the family to enter higher education, embarking on a degree in politics. But despite being a student, the balance between the family, business and education had to be maintained as it still, to certain extent, has. As a student, I recall writing essays in the shop, postponing a tutorial because I had to make a delivery of garments and ruminating over academic debates whilst engaged in delivering and collecting work from the homes of outworkers. Today, the emphasis may have shifted a touch, but the juxtaposition remains. Part of this study was written up on the premises of company A. Indeed, during the fieldwork period, my father went on holiday to India leaving my younger brother and me to run the firm.

Between 1984 and 1986, the balance of interest appeared to shift quite markedly in the direction of the 'business'. After completing my degree, I started to work full-time in company A. For the first time, I was to devote my entire working attention to the business. This prospect, however, was too daunting. I soon enrolled on a management course, ostensibly to improve my financial and accounting skills. The real reason was that it gave me a day in an environment in which I was happy. It was envisaged that I would remain in the business permanently, eventually replacing my father at the helm. During the two-year period, I was exposed to the extreme tedium of 'managing' a clothing factory. I performed a number of functions, from the actual cutting of garments to negotiating deals with customers. In my first week at the factory, I kept a diary. But the process of documenting these mundane activities and the realisation that this could be my lot for the rest of my working days was too painful to contemplate. I soon abandoned the exercise. The trials of working long hours, coping with the competing demands of wholesalers, workers, officialdom and the family finally prompted me to leave. This was an extremely difficult decision since I was effectively removing myself from a 'natural' path laid down for me by my family.

I 'escaped' into higher education to pursue a further degree, only to return to the clothing industry a year later, albeit in a different guise. In 1987 I undertook a project on behalf of Wolverhampton Council on the training needs of the clothing industry in Wolverhampton area (Wolverhampton District Council 1988; Ram 1988). The project involved interviewing over thirty manufacturers, the overwhelming majority of whom were Asian, in order to establish their training requirements. The outcome of this project was the creation of a clothing centre for the training of sewing operatives. I was the first manager of that centre and, as manager, I liaised closely with local employers as well as potential recruits to the industry. I left that post in 1989 in order to enter the world of academe, and embarked upon the current research towards the end of the year.

It was in this context, then, that the study was rooted. The experiences of growing up 'in the business', of a family 'managing to survive' against the backcloth of racism, of a very blurred dividing line between home and work, and the 'flight' to academe to avoid the drudgery of factory life, were all major issues in shaping the eventual parameters of the research. Others have commented on the significance of their background in formulating research projects (Armstrong 1993; Burgess 1984; Hobbs 1988; Roseneil 1993). Not all these backgrounds facilitated insider status. In the case of the current study, and that of Hobbs, they unequivocally did.

Researching the Current Study

Researchers' lack of success in getting into ethnic minority firms has been a feature noted generally (Marlow 1992); previous attempts at studying the West Midlands clothing industry (notably, Leigh and North 1983) have tended to rely on the accounts of a few 'key informants' in larger firms rather than the small businesses that make up most of the sector. My background was crucial in facilitating the required trust to access the sixteen companies in the initial survey and, more importantly, the three case firms.

I had to rely on my resources to establish contact with such firms. Most field research is more than simply the translation of a particular set of techniques from one social situation to another. Access issues involve questions about relationships and particular questions about trust between researcher and researched (Burgess 1984). In drawing on my own resources to get into the firms in the study, I used an 'opportunistic' approach recommended by many (Bresnen 1988; Buchannan *et al.* 1988; Crompton and Jones 1988), in which contacts, friends and relatives were used to the full. Being a member of a 'respected' family in the local Asian community was an undoubted advantage. Pettigrew (1981), a white woman married into a Sikh family, has remarked on the usefulness of family connections in eliciting information for her research into state-level politics in rural India. Being part of a prominent family allowed her access to individuals and organisations to which she would not have been privy without such connections.

In all three companies, community and familial ties were drawn upon in order to effect an entry. In the case of company B, I had known one of the partners who ran the firm for over fifteen years – he was a school-mate of my brothers. We would socialise together quite regularly. I informed him of the nature of the study and requested access into this firm. He agreed, but it was an agreement made possible by the strength of kinship ties rather than any obvious enthusiasm for the study. With company C, community ties were again drawn on in order to gain access. My father and the father of the brothers who ran company C were of the same caste and from the same village in India. They had come to this country in similar circumstances and had known each other for over thirty years. To cement this relationship even further, a cousin of mine had married one of the brothers of company C.

In the case of my family's firm, company A, gaining access was even easier. I had worked for the company, either full-time or part-time, since it came into being and, in a sense, I have never left. Despite my present occupation, I am still associated with the company. Although I have no formal or legal connection with the firm, I can sign cheques, purchase stock, make use of the firm's equipment and give instructions to the company's workers. My presence over the duration of the fieldwork was not seen as unusual. Workers were accustomed to seeing me writing, asking questions and engaging in conversation. In the past, whilst working there, I was usually involved in part-time or full-time study. Hence the sight of me writing in the office or on the shopfloor was not particularly exceptional. It was accepted that I was 'doing work for college'.

Tapping into the Shopfloor Culture

Once access had been negotiated and management in the various companies understood that I would be around for some time, there were few, if any, restrictions on my movements. At no point did they prevent me from talking to anyone or constrain my activities. However, the management's apparent sang-froid should not be overstated, since their general amenability was due to obligation rather than comfort with my presence on the shopfloor.

Although there were no formalities, rules or constraints on my movements on the shopfloor, there was, nevertheless, an informal, unspoken agreement, adherence to which permitted me considerable latitude and discretion. For example, although I did request, and was granted, formal interviews with management, I kept them to a minimum and used them mainly to extract factual information. There were two quite simple reasons for this. First, the managers were very busy people. They were continually engaged in one task or another, rarely having the opportunity for decent breaks let alone time to partake in interviews with me. Had I insisted on formal, structured interviews, it would have been doubtful whether I would have secured the required information and, more to the point, I may have quickly outstayed my welcome. Second, by far the most interesting insights came from general observations and informal conversations that I struck up with managers while engaged in their daily tasks. I would wait for the most opportune moment and then start a conversation in order to elicit the required information. The main themes of these conversations tended to be their relationships with customers, the role of the family in the firm, the payment system, the management of the machinists and generally what life was like as an Asian garment manufacturer. My reliance on informality minimised my obtrusiveness to such an extent that, after a week or so, my presence barely caused comment. Hence, the process of 'blending' into the research situation, which is often seen as integral to fieldwork methods (Burgess 1984; Adler and Adler 1987), was greatly facilitated by my position as an insider.

Despite the extreme industry of many of the managers, once they engaged in conversation with me they would often take the opportunity to vent their feelings and talk about almost anything. For example, Gel, one of the brothers who ran company C, always appeared to be busy. He would be immersed in such diverse tasks as fixing machines, creating a new design, producing a jacket sample, setting a piece-rate and dealing with customers. I had very few formal interviews with him and when we were engaged in such a process, I was careful not to detain him unduly. Yet it was not uncommon for him to strike up conversations with me in which he would talk of his general frustrations, the 'problems' with the machinists and the burden of working for the family. He often spoke of his desire to leave the 'rut' of the family business and branch out on his own, perhaps in the field of design. However, the 'pull' of the family was too great.

Rarely, if ever, did I adopt the role of a 'textbook' interviewing which exhorts the interviewer to remain aloof while seeking to extract information from the respondent. It would have been totally absurd and counter-productive if I had attempted to remain indifferent to questions from people I had known for many years. The utility of this exchange process in the field has been noted by many others who share some kind of experience or characteristic with those being researched, particularly in the case of woman-to-woman research (Finch 1984; Oakley 1981). Finch, for example, points out that in her study of clergymen's wives, the easy flow of information between researcher and researched was made possible by a shared cultural position based on gender. This shared structural and personal identification was central to the woman-to-woman interview. A further resource on which Finch was able to draw was her then position as a clergyman's wife; it was this revelation rather than her professional credentials as a sociologist that eased discussion with the women in her research. Similarly, in my case, the process of being 'placed' in terms of a shared structural location was crucial to the fieldwork.

Bulmer (1988) makes the point that language is an important part of the art of fitting into a setting. Being able to speak fluent Punjabi (the mother tongue of most managers and workers in the field) was essential in understanding people at the workplace; but of equal importance was my capacity to be conversant in the language of the particular shopfloor cultures. In order to unravel complex issues it is necessary, as Oakley claims, to 'get inside the culture'. Commenting on her own research on women and the transition to motherhood, she states that 'A feminist interviewing women is both "inside" the culture and participating in that which she is observing' (1981: 57). Hobbs, an 'East Ender' researching 'entrepreneurship' and the police in the East End of London, similarly flags up the importance of this point, 'I had come to accept that my background, and particularly my London accent were major attributes, and I became more confident of utilising aspects of style, linguistic constructs and any knowledge of the ecology and culture of the East End' (1989: 5). My background enabled me to be an 'insider'. Without this intimate knowledge of the nuances, idiosyncrasies and customs of life on the shopfloor, in the family and within an Asian community attempting to find its way in British society, the task of researching workplace relations in such settings would have been extremely difficult.

TALKING TO THE WOMEN

The focus of much of the study was management, but in order to ascertain the ways in which order was negotiated on the shopfloor, the part played by the machinists (most of whom were women) had to be brought into the picture. Despite my vantage point as an insider, researching the machinists was perhaps the most sensitive part of my remit. It was here that culture had its most obvious impact. The nature of gender relationships in Asian society was a factor that had to be taken into careful consideration in dealings with the machinists. Pettigrew, in relating her experiences of undertaking research in India, pointed out that contact between men and women in the rural settings of the Punjab was highly regulated and had important implications for the family: 'Customarily they have not been expected to talk to men except on certain prescribed occasions ... The reputation of the family depends on the behaviour and conduct of its women'

(1981: 66). Most of the women in companies B and C were from the Punjab and appeared to display a fairly strong attachment to their culture. In recognition of this, the women worked in separate rooms from the men. Given this setting, it would have been extremely foolish of me simply to engage individual machinists in conversation in the manner that I did with the men in management. Sig, a partner in company B, was only half joking when he said to me 'You can talk to the women, but not the young ones.'

An awareness of the particular nature of gender relations when talking to women machinists in this setting clearly highlights the extent to which access is not a discrete step at the start of some linear fieldwork procedure. The negotiation of access is patently not a once-for-all agreement but a continuous process of winning people's trust (Edwards 1992). Initially, I asked the supervisors to let the machinists know that I was conducting research into clothing companies. I asked them to relay the confidential nature of the study and that it had absolutely nothing to do with the Council or the Department for Social Security. After this was done, I made regular sorties into the machinists' room for a month or so. I did not interview any of the operatives during this time, being content at this stage to listen and observe. This allowed the machinists time to become accustomed to my presence on the shopfloor. Indeed, it was the machinists who asked me questions about the study, about my family and whether or not I was married. Some even recognised me; one asked me to pass on her regards to my sister (it transpired this particular machinist had gone to school with my elder sister).

Through these regular visits to the shopfloor, I gained rich material, but there was still a need for more direct and factual information. I wanted to know why these women had come to this country, why they chose this industry and this company, how often they had to switch jobs and their general thoughts about life on the shopfloor. To do this I needed to talk to them as individuals, but again it would have been unwise for me to interview them alone. Consequently, I asked a senior machinist in companies B and C to accompany me when I questioned individual operatives. These senior machinists were not necessarily acting as interpreters, for I can converse fluently in the machinists' mother tongue (Punjabi). Rather, they were there to act as a chaperone and support.

It appeared to be a fairly productive manoeuvre, for the machinists appeared to be amused rather than intimidated by the interviews. After the interviews, my presence on the shopfloor went virtually unnoticed, save for the continual offers of cups of tea on my arrival. Some of the women referred to me variously as 'son', 'our boy' or a colloquial version of my first name.

Although the data that I gained from my observations and discussions with the women were rich and contained valuable insights, it is perhaps this area that constitutes the main limitation of the study. As an Asian man operating in an environment where Asian women were obviously strongly in accord with their particular customs imported virtually intact from the Punjab, it was impossible for me to participate in the working and domestic lives in the manner that Westwood (1984) did with white women workers in StitchCo. (Whether she achieved this degree of congruence with the Asian workers, however, is debatable). It would have been impossible for me to do and extremely foolhardy to try.

However, in mitigation, two points need to be stressed. First, the focus of this study was management rather than the lot of women workers. This was not solely an ethnographic exercise in the vein of Cavendish (1982), Pollert (1981) or Westwood. Secondly, the issues raised in connection with the workforce – for example, the resources that Asian women drew upon to shape their working environment— were apparent and available for analysis. Gender relations undoubtedly mediated the research process; and it is highly probable that the finer details of the culture on the shopfloor could have been painted in more vividly by an Asian women researcher. But the general processes at play were captured.

RESEARCHING THE FAMILIAR

Managing the interaction with women machinists in this way was again based on my insider's judgement of what was possible. Although I think that this process and the overall handling of the project was sensible in the context, it does give rise to some general issues around the theme of 'researching the familiar'. The advantages of my ethnic and familial background were considerable, but like other work employing various forms of participant observation, this study potentially lays itself open to a variety of criticisms which, taken together, relate to the supposed 'subjectivity' of this approach (see Burgess 1984: 82). Jenkins for example, makes the point that '... one negotiates an identity and this identity colours the rest of the research. By its very nature, participant observation must lead to partial accounts' (1984: 161). Burgess warns of the danger of 'going native' whereby researchers play their roles so well that they are unable to gather data or record observations (1984: 81). Then there is the whole question of generalisability (Bryman 1988a: 172–9).

The concern over subjectivity echoes the controversy surrounding the saliency of quantitative and qualitative methods in research. This debate has been pursued at length elsewhere (Bryman 1988a); there is no need to rehearse it here. However, the pejorative connotations of subjectivity need to be addressed. The value of intimacy with the research site has been stressed throughout. It was an aid rather than an impediment to critical analysis, serving as it did to deepen understanding of the internal processes of the workplace. The shared structural location with participants in the field enabled issues to be broached which would probably have been difficult for an outsider to address. As such, familiarity with the setting and the social world under scrunity was extremely important to the research method. Holloway argues as much in discussing her study of gender differences, much of which involved discussions with women (and men) whom she had known over a long period of time: 'I did not feel skilful because it came so easily. It was easy because the research participants were people like me and we were continuing an activity that was a vibrant part of our subculture at the time. Now I can believe that this made for good research practice' (1989: 11).

Similar sentiments have been stressed by others researching markedly different contexts. Armstrong's (1993) study of the hooligan element who supported Sheffield United Football Club was greatly assisted by his background: he was born in Sheffield and was a United supporter. Although not a hooligan, he was able to construct and maintain a more authentic form of access than would have been available to an outsider. Had Roseneil (1993) not been a 'Greenham woman' herself she would not have been able to expedite her study of the Greenham women peace campaigners protesting at Britain's accommodation of Trident nuclear missiles. And the importance of Hobbs's East End credentials to his study have already been noted.

The merits of 'familiarity' in this sense need to be stressed and seen as a valuable resource in the production of 'quality' research. Nevertheless, the aim of the current study was not simply to report on the vagaries and idiosyncrasies of a particular workplace. It was concerned with identifying processes and patterns and making wider connections with other contexts and debates. Consequently, the dangers of undue partiality and specificity, although not to be overstated, should not be entirely ignored either. In Pearson's terms, there was a need for a bridge between 'authenticity' and 'distance' (1994: xi). Hence, there were certain features in the study that militated against excessive partiality; they included a flexible research role, the diversity of my own background, the benefits of being a researcher as well as an 'insider', and a concern for the wider implications of the study. Each will now be considered.

In terms of the actual form of participant observation, I was not a 'covert' or 'full' participant observer in the way, for instance, that Dalton

(1959) was. I did not disguise my identity or the purpose of my presence, and I was not constrained by having to assume a full-time work role. My intention was to undertake research, and those around me were aware of this. Rather than being a full participant or a pure observer, I was more a 'participant-as-observer' (Gold 1952, in Burgess 1984: 81), a role which essentially involves the researcher developing relationships with key informants. By adopting this method, I was not confined to a particular role or level within the organisation, and I had the freedom to pursue any line of inquiry I felt would be germane to my investigation.

Moreover, although the participant-as-observer role was crucial to the study, it was not the only research method used. The observational work was complemented by a wide-ranging and intensive survey of sixteen 'typical' clothing manufacturers in the West Midlands. The methodology, therefore, contained a quantitative component too. Furthermore, once on the factory floor, formal and informal discussions were held with workers and managers. Research roles, then, like the question of access, are not necessarily fixed entities. They vary over time and between respondents; and they also require negotiation and renegotiation. Using Adler and Adler's (1987) role membership framework, with male participants I occupied an 'active' membership research role, where I could participate in the core activities of respondents while not committing myself to their goals and values. However, with the women machinists 'peripheral' membership was more appropriate. I was still an 'insider' but closer involvement was foreclosed by the particular nature of gender relations as well as the remit of the study. The fluidity of the research process and the diversity of the roles occupied afforded a certain methodological heterogeneity, which guarded against the problem of partiality that is sometimes seen as a significant drawback of the pure participant observer method (Jenkins 1984: 161).

An example from the current study demonstrates the utility of having an eclectic methodology. At the survey stage, all sixteen owner-managers interviewed stated that machinists were individually respons-ible for the mistakes they made on a garment, and they were not paid for rectifying them. This was seen as non-contentious and seemed to be taken for granted. However, during the detailed case study investi-gations, it was evident that this was not the case. Machinists devised a number of ways of getting around being identified as the person respons-ible for sewing the garment, for example, by not putting their 'tag' on it. Furthermore, management would not always enforce the rectification of mistakes. It would often depend on whether they could 'get away with it', how urgent the order was and the 'hassle' it would cause if the machinist were to be confronted. Consequently, it was not uncommon to find the supervisor, who was usually paid a wage rather than piece-work, repairing the garment.

This example serves to illustrate the benefits of using a combination of research methods for data collection. A total reliance on survey evidence would not have brought out the complex and contested nature of workplace relations. However, without it, recognition of pervasiveness of the issue and the opportunity to reflect upon differences between workplaces might not have been possible.

The diversity of my personal background was a further defence against undue subjectivity. As I have pointed out, my social and familial milieu were a considerable resource and invaluable in affording insights into work relations in West Midlands clothing firms. However, an equally strong theme that has permeated much of my life has been my attachment to education. I have been in higher education as a student and lecturer (or both) since leaving school ten years ago. Even whilst working for the family business or other organisations, I was involved in part-time study or part-time lecturing. Although I could not ever (and did not wish to) let go of my attachments to some of the research participants, it was always recognised that I would return to academe. Lecturing is my job; and it has been the impact of some of the debates in my specialism that has fuelled an interest in the study as well as my background. Consequently, I could not occupy a 'complete membership role' (Adler and Adler 1987), where the researcher becomes so immersed in the field that he or she can only speak from the perspective of those being studied. There was always a balance to be struck.

The nature and importance of this balance was exemplified in the discussion of management 'rationality'. The 'rationality' or otherwise of management in this sector is an important theme of the study. For example, a seemingly popular view is that clothing manufacturers in the region survive hostile markets through the intensification and casualisation of work (Mitter 1985). This appears to be a fairly 'rational' policy on the part of management. However, on closer inspection, the nature of work organisation is demonstrated to be much more complex, uncertain and unpredictable. By actually being in a position to observe the shopfloor over a period of time, it was possible to witness the negotiations and tensions inherent in managing the workplace. Seemingly rational features, like a single-task production process, an apparently arbitrary piece-rate system, the widespread use of outworkers and the extensive use of familial and community labour were quite manifestly in evidence. But by observing them in action, it became clear that the process of operationalising such policies involved trade-offs, calculations and bargains which went against the grain of the notion of economic rationality. The method, therefore, was important in demonstrating that the task of management was more a question of balancing conflicting pressures than the simple implementation of ostensibly rational practices.

A pure 'insider's' account may have run the risk of 'telling it how it is' without sufficiently questioning the vagaries of workplace behaviour and the existing order. On the other hand, a totally detached investigation may not have fully comprehended the dynamics of the processes at play on the shopfloor and therefore the behaviour as aberrant or without logic. As Dalton points out in defence of his 'masquerading research' into the informal aspects of management organisation: 'Studying situations at a distance the investigator may be so "objective" that he misses the subject matter and cannot say what he is objective about' (1959: 283). My position, however, enabled the rationality or 'bounded rationality' of management to be explored and analysed against the context in which it operated. I hope that the 'observations together with theoretical insights [will] make seemingly irrational or paradoxical behaviour comprehensible to those within and beyond the situation that is being studied' (Burgess 1984: 79).

Finally, there is the concern about generalisability of participant observation studies and qualitative research in general. Others have pursued this debate at great length (Bryman 1988b), and it is almost a commonplace to make the point that qualitative research should be assessed along different, but no less valid, criteria to quantitative work (Bryman 1988a; Hammersley 1990). The current study addressed this issue in four ways: by adopting a flexible research approach; by making comparisons with other studies; by studying different firms; and by locating the findings within a more general framework of industrial relations.

The flexible as opposed to the fixed nature of the research process and its effectiveness in aiding analysis of the dynamics of the workplace has already been stressed. It was integral to securing the benefits of an insider approach whilst maintaining a concern for the wider implications of the study. A particular way in which these implications were addressed was by placing the study in a general framework of workplace relations in an attempt to speculate on some factors which might account for differences between workplaces. It was suggested that autocracy may be related to firm size and market competition. In very small firms, the employment relationship is likely to be characterised by diffuseness, a high degree of informality and considerations beyond the cash nexus. At the other end of the spectrum, in large firms the pattern of control is likely to be more bureaucratic/autocratic and associated with a high degree of regulation. In relatively stable market conditions, however, it is likely to be hegemonic. The framework highlighted the trend towards autocracy as firm size increased – larger companies within a competitive market setting operated in a more bureaucratic/autocratic fashion than smaller firms. In veering towards autocracy, flexibility became increasingly organised out of the employment relationship.

CONCLUSION

The research on which the chapter is based, then, adds to the somewhat limited stock of intensive workplace studies in the broad area of industrial relations/sociology. Its novelty lies not only in the subject matter, which challenges stereotypical views of small firm industrial relations and Asian enterprise, but also in the manner in which the study was conducted. It was a prime example of 'insider' research. The benefits of being an 'insider' in terms of ethnicity and proximity to the working lives of the research participants were of immense value. They were crucial in examining the processes of a hitherto neglected sector of industry. But my insider status, even in the case of my own family's business, was never complete; it did not prevent holding up the nature of this setting to the light of analytical scrutiny. Like Hobbs (1988: 18), I avoided 'going native' by going 'academic'.

Acknowledgement

I would like to thank Paul Edwards for his comments on an earlier draft of this paper.

REFERENCES

Adler, P. and Adler, P. (1987) *Membership Roles in Field Research*. London: Sage.

Armstrong, G. (1993) 'Like That Desmond Morris?', in D. Hobbs and T. May (eds) *Interpreting the Field*. Oxford: Oxford University Press.

Beynon, H. (1973) *Working for Ford*. Harmondsworth: Penguin.

Bresnen, M. (1988) 'Insights on Site: Research into Construction Project Organisations', in A. Bryman (ed.) *Doing Research in Organisations*. London: Hyman.

Bryman, A. (1988a) 'Introduction: Inside Accounts and Social Research in Organisations', in A. Bryman (ed.) *Doing Research in Organisations*. London: Routledge & Kegan Paul.

Bryman, A. (1988b) *Quantity and Quality in Social Science Research*. London: Unwin Hyman.

Buchanan, D., Boddy, D. and McCalman, J. (1988) 'Getting In, Getting On, Getting Out and Getting Back', in A. Bryman (ed.) *Doing Research in Organisations*. London: Routledge & Kegan Paul.

Bulmer, M. (1988) 'Some Reflections Upon Research in Organisations', in A. Bryman (ed.) *Doing Research in Organisations*. London: Routledge & Kegan Paul.

Burgess, R. (1984) *In the Field*. London: Unwin Hyman.

Cavendish, R. (1982) *Women on the Line*. London: Routledge & Kegan Paul.

Crompton, R. and Jones, G. (1988) 'Researching White Collar Organisations: Why Sociologists Should Not Stop Case Studies', in A. Bryman (ed.) *Doing Research in Organisations*. London: Routledge & Kegan Paul.

Cunnison, S. (1966) *Wages and Work Allocation*. London: Tavistock.

Dalton, M. (1959) *Men Who Manage*. New York: Wiley.

Edwards, P. K. (1992) 'Comparative Industrial Relations: The Contribution of the Ethnographic Tradition'. *Relations Industrielles*.

Finch, J. (1984) 'It's Great to Have Someone to Talk to: The Ethics and Politics of Interviewing Women', in C. Bell and H. Roberts (eds) *Social Researching*. London: Routledge & Kegan Paul.

Gouldner, A. (1954) *Patterns of Industrial Bureacracy*. New York: Free Press.

Hammersley, M. (1990) *Reading Ethnographic Research*. London: Longman.

Hayden, C. (1992) 'A Case Study of the Clothing Industry in the West Midlands', in D. Gillingwater and P. Totterdil (eds) *Prospects for Industrial Policy in the 1990s: The Case of Study of the British Clothing Industry*. Aldershot: Gower.

Hobbs, D. (1988) *Doing the Business: Entrepreneurship, the Working Class and Detectives in the East End of London*. Oxford: Oxford University Press.

Hoel, B. (1982) 'Contemporary Clothing Sweatshops: Asian Female Labour and Collective Organisation', in J. West (ed.) *Work, Women and the Labour Market*. London: Routledge & Kegan Paul.

Jenkins, R. (1984) 'Bringing it All Back Home: An Anthropologist in Belfast', in C. Bell and H. Roberts (eds) *Social Researching*. London: Routledge & Kegan Paul.

Jones, T. *et al.* (1989) *Ethnic Communities and Business Needs*. Report for the Commission for Racial Equality.

Leigh, R. and North, R. (1983) *The Clothing Sector in the West Midlands*. Report for West Midlands County Council.

Lupton, T. (1963) *On the Shop Floor*. London: Pergamon Press.

Marlow, S. (1992) 'Take-Up of Business Growth Training Schemes in Britain', *International Small Business Journal* 1: 7.

Mitter, S. (1985) 'Industrial Restructuring and Manufacturing Homework', *Capital and Class* 27: 37–80.

Moore, R. (1977) 'Becoming a Sociologist in Sparkbrook', in C. Bell and H. Newby (eds) *Doing Sociological Research*, London: Allen & Unwin.

Nichols, T. and Beynon, H. (1977) *Living with Capitalism*. London: Routledge & Kegan Paul.

Oakley, A. (1981) 'Interviewing Women: A Contradiction in Terms', in H. Roberts (ed.) in *Doing Feminist Research*. London: Routledge & Kegan Paul.

Patel, S. (1988) 'Insurance and Ethnic Community Business', *New Community* 15: 79–89.

Pearson, G. (1994) 'Talking a Good Fight: Authenticity and Distance in the Ethnographer's Craft', in D. Hobbs and T. May (eds) *Interpreting the Field*. Oxford: Oxford University Press.

Pettigrew, (1981) 'Reminiscence of Fieldwork among the Sikhs', in H. Roberts (ed.) *Doing Feminist Research*. London: Routledge & Kegan Paul.

Pollert, A. (1981) *Girls, Wives, Factory Lives*. London: Macmillan.

Ram, M. (1988) 'Clothing in Wolverhampton', *Local Work* 8: 5–6.

Ram, M. (1992) 'Coping with Racism – Asian Employers in the Inner-City', *Work Employment and Society* 6: 601–18.

Ram, M. (1994) *Managing to Survive – Working Lives in Small Firms*. Oxford: Blackwell.

Roseneil, S. (1993) 'Greenham Revisited: Researching Myself and My Sisters', in D. Hobbs and T. May (eds) *Interpreting the Field*. Oxford: Oxford University Press.

Roy, D. (1954) 'Efficiency and the "Fix": Informal Intergroup Relations in a Piecework Machine Shop', *American Journal of Sociology* 60: 255–66.

Werbner, P. (1984) 'Business on Trust', in R. Ward and R. Jenkins (eds) *Ethnic Communities in Business*. London: Cambridge University Press.

West Midlands Low Pay Unit (1991) *The Clothes Showdown: The Future of the West Midlands Clothing Industry*.

Westwood, S. (1984) *All Day Every Day*. London: Pluto.

Wolverhampton District Council. (1988) *The Training Needs of the Wolverhampton Clothing Industry*. Wolverhampton D. C.

8 Emotional Labour and Qualitative Research: How I Learned Not to Laugh or Cry in the Field

Karen Ramsay

INTRODUCTION

This chapter explores the difficulties encountered when attempting to use feminist methodologies in predominately male organisational environments. It explores issues of power in research relationships and the development of rapport in ethnographic research. A central concern of this essay is the emotional impact that research has on the researcher. It is argued that the management of emotions necessary for the feminist researcher in an all-male environment may create distorted field relationships and may be too high a price to pay to illustrate the patriarchal culture of academia.

The chapter is divided into four sections. The first introduces the research project, the researcher and the research subjects. The second briefly reviews some of the literature on feminist methodology and ethnographic methods in organisation studies. The third provides an overview of the types of relationships which emerged during the research and the role of emotions in shaping these relationships. The final section discusses the implications of this study for an understanding of the study of men from a feminist perspective.

THE RESEARCH, THE RESEARCHER AND THE RESEARCHED

The Research Question, Design and Methods

The research in which I have been engaged is concerned with the history, culture and values of academia. It explores the extent to which the

131

organisational culture of specified academic disciplines affects the type of equality strategies employed in the respective departments. Particular attention is given to equality in employment rather than equality in education provision. This focuses attention on the norms and values regarding assessment of newcomers, applicants for promotion, methods for integrating new members of staff, the decision-making process, expectations of behaviour, as well as the more general culture of the departments (see Becher 1989).

The project locates academic values within an organisational context. Values are not created or reproduced in a vacuum; they develop in interaction between individuals and groups in an institutional setting (Becher 1989; Smircich 1982; Thomas 1990). Two disciplines were studied, engineering and the humanities. These represent the two extremes of disciplines that are described (Becher 1989), using gendered terms, as hard, applied and quantitative and soft, pure and qualitative. The research comprises three case studies, two in a former polytechnic and one in an 'old' university.

The case studies referred to in this paper are the two engineering departments. The fieldwork took place between October 1991 and April 1992. In one department there were no female lecturers, although all the secretarial staff were female and fifteen per cent of the students were female. In the other department there was one full-time and one part-time female lecturer. All the secretarial staff and ten per cent of the students were female. Both departments were developing policies intended to increase the numbers of women students.

The Researcher

At the time of writing this essay I was a full time PhD student in my third year of study. The research was funded by a University Scholarship. I am now employed as a full-time lecturer and the PhD is nearing completion. I am white, female and carry some of the cultural capital of my middle-class background. My father was a chemical engineering lecturer and my mother a telephonist. I was considered bright but lacking in motivation at school. The school's careers adviser suggested that I try banking as a job before I marry, as it was evident that I would never get anywhere with my attitude. I left school at sixteen with 'O' levels in arts subjects and a determination never to touch education again.

I returned to education when I was twenty-six after ten years of shop work, factory work, cleaning and catering jobs and a host of other 'unskilled' and manual jobs. I never married or had children. I took a degree in organisation studies, part of which was a two-year option in women's studies. This gave me a framework to understand my life and the world I lived in. My feminism has altered over the years and has been shaped by my experiences. Generally I have moved between structural/economic feminism and cultural/ideological feminism, resting uneasily between the two. I would identify myself as a socialist-feminist, with radical feminist interests.

METHODOLOGY AND RESEARCH METHODS

Before starting the field work I prepared by reading case study reports, and advice on techniques and practice in the field. As a feminist and as an organisational sociologist I have tried to develop a strategy that combines imperatives from both areas.

Feminist Methodology and Practice

From the late 1970s, a sophisticated debate established definitions of 'feminist methodology', 'feminist research practice' and 'feminist epistemology' (see, for example, Stanley and Wise 1983). This debate influenced how I approached my work as a doctoral student. At the start of the research the most important issue for me was the rejection of distance and objectivity in the researcher-researched relationship. This approach is not exclusive to feminist research. From a social constructionist perspective not only is the world which we study as sociologists constructed through interaction and negotiation; we as researchers are involved, with our research subjects, in this process. As Steier argues: 'the research process itself must be seen as socially constructing a world, or worlds, with the researchers included in, rather than outside, the body of their own research' (1991: 2).

Sandra Harding (1987) argues that placing the researcher on the same critical plane as her/his research subjects breaks down the false distinction between 'subject' and 'object' in research. In traditional research, objectivity and distance between the subject of the researcher and the objects of research are advocated as methods for preventing bias. Feminist sociological theorists argue that all research is biased; this is similar to the position taken by earlier writers such as Becker (1971). In order to understand what these biases are and how they affect the research, the researcher must understand her/his own previous experiences, prejudices and values. These biases should be made clear so that the framework of analysis and interpretation are understood by the reader (Reinharz 1983).

Helen Roberts (1981) argues that the self-reflexivity required to identify one's own experiential and theoretical framework (bias) is a fundamental characteristic of feminist research. This has implications at all stages of the research. Liz Stanley (1990) identifies the importance of self-reflexivity in the publication stage of feminist research. The production of 'non-alienated' knowledge requires that the finished knowledge project is presented as part of an explicit academic process.

Methodology and Method in the Organisational Research

A semi-participant approach seemed most appropriate as this allowed me to explore shared meanings and values with the organisation's members in the organisational setting. Smircich, an organisational sociologist, advocates an approach which involves the researcher always seeking to comprehend the organisation from the insider perspective:

> The interpretative researcher ... aims to see the world as the organisation's members see it, to learn the meaning of actions and events for the organisation members, and to portray these accurately (1983: 164)

The goal is not to become an insider but to see the world from an insider's perspective and to represent these as clearly as possible. She refers to this as 'empathic ethnography'. This strategy appeared to be in sympathy with my decision to avoid the pretence of a research relationship based on objectivity and distance from the research subjects.

However, the research subjects were predominately men. The aim in the fieldwork was to collect data which would enable me to understand an interpretation of events which might be at odds with my interpretation as a woman and as a feminist. The problems for feminists researching men have been identified by, amongst others, Laws (1990), Smart (1984), Easterday *et al.* (1987) and McKee and O'Brien (1983). A common theme in the literature concerns the power imbalance in the researcher-researched relationship. Feminist researchers who interview women (for example, Oakley 1981) identify power as resting largely with the researcher; much feminist literature on methodology deals with redressing this imbalance. However, when the interviewer is female and the interviewee male, the balance of power is less clear. Carol Smart found that a more traditional, non-feminist interview approach was required when she interviewed men; to act as a feminist in her interviews with men in the legal profession would have endangered the research. Due to the nature of her research design, Smart was able to use a more structured approach in the interviews and this did not invalidate her data. However, in an ethnographic project the use of the more traditional method, where the researcher sets the agenda and asks people to respond to a series of questions, does not allow the respondent's interpretations to emerge.

A key issue in ethnographic research is the process of building rapport. Laws (1990) identifies the problem of rapport and empathy between different social groups (e.g. between the woman researchers and the male subjects) as one of interpretation. She suggests that it is possible for a person with average social skills to simulate rapport in an interview; the real problems come later in attempting to interpret the collected data. In this way, Laws was able to interview men, while not sharing their understanding of the world, by maintaining rapport at a superficial level. This may be possible for an interview or multi-site research strategy. However, if the organisational researcher has chosen a semi-participant research strategy based on immersion into another culture, then the question of maintaining the simulated rapport emerges not only as a problem during interpretation, but also as a problematic process in the field.

Using Smircichs's model, I aimed to immerse myself in the culture of the departments and to understand the world as the department members did. This was particularly important as I wanted to know how the men in the departments (which a few lone women were entering) understood the departments and the changes which were taking place. While these data were being analysed and interpreted from a feminist perspective, I needed to get access to the raw data in the first place. As the interpretation was rooted in the organisational context, it was necessary to have access to the departments as well as the individual men involved. Thus, rapport became an issue not only during the interview, as it had been for Laws and Smart, but something to which I had to attend everyday, all day, for ten weeks.

However, as a feminist I was aware that, as women in a patriarchal society, we spend much of our life understanding a world where masculine values are the norm and feminist values are deviant. In order to do research in a masculine setting, and maintain both access and a sense of integrity, it seemed necessary to create a 'researcher self', a role which was distinct from my self as a feminist. I wore make-up and bought new clothes; I consciously used techniques to develop and maintain rapport, rather than assuming that rapport would develop from shared experiences.

There was a tension in this solution which rested on my experiences of myself as a researcher who created a research persona in order to manage relationships in the field, and myself as a feminist researcher who located herself in the research, using the process of self-reflexivity. During the fieldwork, I moved between these two roles, maintaining the traditional researcher role while in the field and moving into the feminist role when analysing and interpreting the data, at week-ends and in the evening.

Broch-Due (1992) questions the validity of making a distinction between the researcher-as-researcher, and researcher-as-person. In terms of locating the self in the research process, this distinction is unreal; as academics we are influenced by the knowledge we draw upon and produce. As producers of knowledge we are also recreating our selves in the process. As Stanley states, feminism is a way of being in the world, it is an ontological state – I could not separate my feminism from myself, nor could I separate my behaviour in the field from my feminism. I was constantly and consciously critical of my role in the field.

Presentation of Self and the Management of Emotions

The intensity of the fieldwork process is typically accompanied by psychological anxiety resulting in a continuous presentation and management of self when in the presence of those studied (Shaffir *et al.* 1980).

From an interactionist perspective every part of our social life is played out through roles. A new or unfamiliar role draws attention to this as we have to learn how to behave in a new situation. During the case studies I was not only learning how to play my researcher role, I was also learning how to be a woman in an engineering department, a male defined and male dominated environment. To play a role we have to manage the impression we give of our selves to others.

Arlie Hochschild (1983) explores the effect that impression management has on the way that an individual understands and acts in the world. She used the term 'surface acting' to describe the management of outward appearances; it is this acting which Goffman (1959), as an interactionist, was concerned to understand. The term 'deep acting' is used by Hochschild to describe the activity of shaping one's emotions so that the observed display is spontaneous. She is concerned particularly with how organisations: 'control us not simply through their surveillance of our behaviour but through surveillance of our feelings' (1983: 218).

Central to this is that people actively work on, and manage, their emotions in order to display the required impression. From an interactionist perspective, the emotion or feeling is created in interaction with others; Hochschild takes us a step further back into the individual by using biological and psychoanalytic understandings of emotion as a: 'signal function ... it signals where we stand vis-à-vis the reality we apprehend' (1983: 441).

It was necessary for my role in the field to appear authentic and spontaneous in order to gain and maintain access. If it was apparent that I disagreed with senior academics about equal opportunity practices I felt that I was in danger of loosing access. However, I was not always able to rely on shallow acting and at times I needed to manage my emotions at a deeper level in order to maintain the impression I had started with: sympathetic, interested, organisational researcher.

IN THE FIELD – IMPRESSION MANAGEMENT AND EMOTIONS IN RESEARCH

In each case study I introduced myself as someone doing research into women in engineering education and explained that I would be interested to talk with them and hear their views. I had little problem in gaining access partly because I expressed concern with 'good practice' and because I saw that many departments were developing strategies which were not always recognised or supported by the institution. In this way I placed myself on the side of the department in the politics of the institution. This created an atmosphere of interest; I was concerned with them and what they were doing.

While I emphasised my interest in women and in gender inequality, I did not identify myself as a feminist. If asked, I explained my political and theoretical position without using the word feminism. I felt that to do so would have created suspicion and antagonism before I had even started. My experience in the departments supported this initial assessment and I collected some interesting data on men's attitudes to feminism which I would not have got if I had been one of 'those feminists'.

The self I presented in the case studies varied and was shaped by what I thought would be acceptable to the people I was with at the time. This adjustment of myself was based on the belief that people are likely to reveal more of themselves to a person who seems to share some of their beliefs and assumptions or at least unconditionally accepts them as people. When I met someone for the first time I generally asked them about how they had come into engineering, how they came to be in education, and how the institution had changed since their arrival. Through these early conversations I was able to get an idea about what mattered to them and what values might be antithetical to them.

This process resulted in different types of researcher–researched relationships. These are distinguished by my behaviour (determined by my calculated 'learner' role in the field), by the power differential between myself and the respondent, and by my status as an insider or outsider in the department. The first type of relationship was when the man set the agenda; in empathic ethnographic or feminist terms this is preferable as it allows the respondent to identify issues which are relevant to them. However, this can be tricky if there is not space to ask for clarification or confirmation and the interviewee is simply concerned to state opinions.

My experience of these types of conversation is common. I have found myself the audience of male monologues enough times to confirm feminist analyses of male/female interaction. As Dale Spender (1980) argues, in conversations between men and women, women learn to facilitate male speech. This type of conversation occurred predominately with men who were in a senior position in the department. In these situations I felt that the man was taking control because I was a woman researcher (lower status on both counts) and this mode of conversation was the norm for him. During these conversations I had to manage the desire to interrupt and insist that he listened to an alternative view. However, I was aware that interrupting men like this made me feel anxious, as if I was going against a rule which could lead to conflict. As a feminist I felt that I could not challenge the system and be accepted by it; to be a feminist was to accept conflict. However, as a researcher I felt that I needed to avoid conflict.

In one instance a man was telling me about how there were two types of women students in engineering. One type were conscious of their gender and used it to get their own way; they wore make-up and skirts. The other type looked like any other student on the course (male) and concentrated on getting on with people (men) and getting the job done. The first type were a problem while the second type were the best students. This was a lovely piece of data and I had no wish as a researcher to stop him. I listened, giving feedback in terms of head nods and indistinguishable 'umms'. However, as a feminist who did not share his assumptions about sexuality and power, I wanted to challenge him. When I left the office I was exhausted and unhappy about the interview. I had some good data but I had colluded with a powerful man in recreating understandings about women, sexuality and power.

My exhaustion was rooted partly in the conflict I experienced about my behaviour in the interview. It also derived from the emotional labour I had performed during the interview. Rather than hiding what I felt, I tried, when he was talking, to imagine why he felt as he did. I drew upon what he had told me about his experiences which led him to view as a problem women students who exploited their femininity. I did this in order to keep the conversation going and to preserve access in the future. I was in a relatively powerless position in these situations as the men I was interviewing could end the interview, refuse to talk to me again or refuse to let me back into the department if they thought I was going to misrepresent them.

Another type of relationship was one where the respondent and I had a shared interest; this could be disciplinary or occupational status, experience of doing a PhD, being a newcomer to academia or a political interest. In these relationships, an equal status was simulated through our shared interest and a series of topics were explored by common consent. An example is when I was talking to a man who spoke warmly of some women writers I knew, who told me very early in the conversation that he felt that women had a difficult time in engineering and his concern was, as a principal lecturer, to help women to create space in the department for themselves. Another example was a conversation I joined in the staff common room, where people were talking about a possible strike in the university. In these kinds of situations I found that I was worried about being too relaxed and too friendly. I was worried for two reasons. My first concern was that if I relaxed too much I would take over the conversation and would gear it too much to my own interests, not theirs, and I would not get the information I needed for the thesis. My second concern was that if I revealed any favouritism, this could fuel political game playing in the department. One man did introduce me as 'his personal adviser on equal opportunities' to another member of staff; I had not said very much, mostly listened, but this had been taken as a sign of approval and my 'approval' had been used in departmental power games.

These two types of relationships differ at a superficial, interpersonal, level; the first was a male dominated conversation which the interviewee controlled by virtue of his power as a man, while the second had some characteristics of a mutual, reciprocal relationship which most closely matched my understanding of feminist research practice. However, in both situations the male interviewee adopted a position of power in the conversation. In both situations I worked on my emotional state (anger and pleasure) in order to reproduce what I felt were the best interview conditions. In both situations I played a traditional feminine role as the facilitator of men's conversations. This clearly reflects Smart's statement (1984: 155) that interviewing is an 'intrinsically feminine' activity as the interviewer's job is to facilitate speech and not to interrupt it. Smart describes this experience as potentially oppressive and frustrating to the feminist researcher interviewing men.

Other kinds of relationships developed with the men in the departments. One type occurred when the respondent had little interest in the topics and where the conversation became one of a structured interview. At one level it might have seemed that in this situation I had the power as I set the agenda and asked questions which were meaningless to them, but to which they felt compelled to respond because the Head of Department had 'instructed' compliance. However, in these situations I felt powerless, helpless and foolish. It sometimes transpired that these people had strong opinions which they felt were not appropriate in the setting or feared I would report back to the Head of Department. This situation forced me into a traditional researcher role, where I struggled (and failed) to develop a rapport consciously using techniques of reflection and non-verbal feedback.

Another type occurred when the respondent used the interview as a means of releasing emotions, sorting out emotions or moaning about other people, sure that I would take this further. Possibly they were testing whether rumours would start from me. At times I felt that my presence was used as part of a political game. At other times I felt that as a woman I represented someone who would listen and sympathise with them. I was conscious of myself acting out the traditional, caring 'woman' vis-à-vis 'man'. The expectation of my behaviour as a woman was reflected in the data: one of the most common explanations of why a woman was needed in the department was that the woman academic could provide pastoral care. These interviews revealed some useful insights into departmental sub-cultures and politics, and into people's emotional responses to working in higher education.

What stands out for me now, reflecting on the fieldwork, is how emotionally drained and exhausted I was. All research is draining, and research which involves participant observation, where the researcher is constantly on show and being observed, is especially tiring. The amount of energy I had to put into managing my impression all day, everyday, was the aspect which I found most disturbing. In an interview situation the researcher can put energy into maintaining a rapport, as Laws (1990) argues, but once the interview is over, the researcher can relax. In participant observation this is not possible.

For much of my time in these departments I was conscious of engaging in surface and deep acting. As a researcher I was acting out a role in the departments of the interested newcomer who wanted to learn about the department. I also managed my impression at a deeper, emotional level. I did this when I was conscious of myself, as a woman and a feminist, talking to men. I felt this was necessary because to stay, as myself, in the interaction would have had repercussions: I would have laughed, walked away or challenged the speaker. This was experienced by Smart (1984) during her study of the legal profession. Like Smart, I was aware that such a response would have seriously damaged my access to the department, to the individuals and to the data I needed. In order to maintain my research persona for more than a few hours at a time, I needed to alter what I thought and how I felt about them as people. Rather than thinking about them as men who were actively reproducing gendered stereotypes, I needed to think of them as agents, enabled and constrained in their possible actions by a particular social structure. This was not only a cognitive exercise; it also involved me trying to feel differently about them as people.

DISCUSSION: EMOTIONS, ORGANISATION STUDIES AND FEMINIST METHODOLOGY

The theme explored in this chapter is the importance of emotions and emotional management in research. Many feminist and interpretivist researchers refer to the importance of emotions in research. However, the insights gathered from these studies have not been reflected in organisation studies.

According to James (1989) emotion work of any kind is undervalued because it is associated with the undervalued work carried out in the private sphere. Women are commonly employed in emotion work jobs because of the association of women with emotional caring skills. Much of the research on emotions in organisations has focused on the emotional care of others (e.g. Dent *et al.* 1991; James 1989). In attending to jobs which require emotional work there is a danger of perpetuating the image of other types of work, such as management, as rational, unemotional and task oriented. It is possible to overlook the emotional management exerted by any person who is required to appear calm and unemotional as part of their work.

This is now being recognised in organisation studies, as those by Fineman (1991), Albrow (1992), Van Maanen and Gideon (1989), Sutton (1991) and Sutton and Rafaeli (1988) indicate. These studies explore emotional management and labour as a method of managerial control, as an aspect of culture and as exploitation. It is significant that none of these writers deal with their own emotions in relation to their respondents. Emotion is dealt with in a general sense and as research data, but not as an experience which permeates and affects the research process. This may be part of the legacy of the masculinist research agenda which shaped sociology (Morgan 1981) and organisation studies.

A notable exception is Sutton and Schurman's paper (1988) on the experience of the 'death' process of the failing organisations they studied.

They refer to this as an 'emotionally hot topic'. Both the researchers and the 'informants' experienced deep emotions at this time including anger, frustration, guilt, and sadness. Sutton and Schurman offer advice to the researcher dealing with emotionally hot topics. These include anticipating the emotional temperature of the topic, developing the clinical skills required to manage the interview (that is, skills needed for emotion work) and providing social support for the researcher. This is an important paper as it addresses the effect that emotionally hot topics have on the researcher. It clearly shows that researchers are human beings with feelings who are affected by the emotional state of their respondents. However, the authors imply that it is only topics defined as emotionally 'hot' which have an emotional impact on the researcher. This overlooks the emotional management required in any research, whether the topic is 'hot' or 'cold'.

As Stanley and Wise (1983) note, emotional involvement is unavoidable in research. Whether the research is relevant to the researcher's own life, whether the data are clearly emotionally 'hot' or 'cold', and whether or not the researcher chooses to acknowledge this aspect of research, the researcher will be working on her/his emotions. The rules for emotional expression in research may be different from everyday life (particularly in a traditional research setting), but the interaction skill involves two people whose life histories will shape how they respond to one another.

The analysis of the emotions I experienced was useful to me as a correspondent in the research as they indicated where I placed myself in relation to those I studied. By attending to my feelings I was made aware of how uncomfortable I felt, especially when I was in full view and the object of the male gaze, during meetings, in the coffee room, in seminars and so on. I also became conscious of how I managed my feelings in order to maintain the persona I had adopted. My experience of emotional management affected both myself and the research.

By managing my feelings in order to do empathic ethnography, I changed the way I looked at the world and myself in the world. The effects on me outside of the field included disorientation, extreme tiredness, an inability to relax, being tearful and feeling like a sponge filled with other people's ideas and thoughts and with none of my own. For a while I lost touch with my feminist perspective and viewed social interaction as radically localised, having little relationship to the wider social structure. In the next case study I worked with many feminist women and pro-feminist men. In this case study I regained my sense of self, partly through the research interviews and conversations. These experiences have made me extremely sensitive to the impact the social environment has on my politics and my epistemological and ontological position.

By attending to emotions in research, the researcher is forced to assess the effect her/his emotional state has on the research. Steier (1991) suggests that research should be understood as not simply representing a particular social reality but as constructing the social reality which will be represented in the research report. In my fieldwork I wanted to act as a mirror to the departmental members; as in person-centred research, my aim was to allow the respondents to explore with me issues of gender in the departments, with an agenda which was set more by them than by me.

However, I was conscious that the impression I was making in the departments, and my attempts to make myself acceptable, shaped the structure and content of our conversations. People may have been more polite, more cautious or reserved with me than they would have been had I been more assertive or stated stronger opinions. The role I played was one that is often played by women in organisations (Sheppard 1989). I felt that if I was too feminine, too feminist, too assertive, I would be excluded. The pressure on women to conform to organisational sex-role stereotypes is well documented. The expression of female sexuality is frowned upon; however, the woman who rejects traditional female roles in organisations is seen as deviant.

The choice of methods used in this project was influenced by the phenomenological and feminist traditions in sociology. The aim of the project was to uncover taken for granted assumptions and everyday patterns of behaviour in the departments. Thus, an ethnographic approach seemed to be the most appropriate. As a feminist, influenced by texts on feminist methodologies, I was concerned to avoid the false subject-object dichotomy of traditional research strategies. However, I was not fully aware of the impact that gendered power relations would have on interactions in the field. What I had overlooked, when choosing participant observation and unstructured interviews, was that these methods are advocated to empower the interviewee. As a woman in a male dominated environment, I was the less powerful subject and arguably the one in need of empowerment.

Feminism is not only a rational, cognitive position, it is an emotional experience. As a feminist researching cultural values and organisational practices in a male environment, I was aware that my view of events in the department was at odds with dominant interpretations. Other studies of organisations by women researchers do report a similar experience (Easterday *et al.* 1987). However, what is not discussed in great depth is the impact that the researcher's management of self and emotions has on the interpersonal dynamics and thus the type of data collected.

Kelly, Burton and Regan (1994) evaluate the connection between feminist research and qualitative methods. Their discussion deals with the problems of using interviews to uncover very sensitive material. They suggest that while matching interviewees and interviewers in terms of age, gender, class and race can aid rapport, the impact of interactional dynamics cannot be avoided but can be reduced in survey strategies.

On reflection, as a feminist, I now feel that structured interviews or questionnaires would have been more appropriate as they would reduce the levels of tension experienced. However, some of the most valuable data came from my reactions as a woman and a feminist conducting research in an all-male environment. What I felt, and how I managed my emotions and my impression, are similar to reports of other women coping in male-dominated settings.

CONCLUSIONS

The central theme in this chapter has been the emotional difficulties faced when researching men as a feminist woman. What struck me, both in the field and later, during interpretation and analysis, was the level of emotional labour required to manage the impression I gave in order to maintain my access to the departments and the individual people. An ongoing concern has been that, because I was presenting a false self, the spontaneous rapport I believed I needed in order to collect valid qualitative data could not occur. A second concern was the impact that the research had on my emotional and physical health. I am not arguing that women cannot conduct ethnographic research in male dominated environments; rather I feel that the methods need to be carefully thought out, especially the importance of rapport and impression management in the context of unequal gender relations.

REFERENCES

Albrow, M. (1992) 'Sine Ira et Studio or Do Organizations Have Feelings?' *Organization Studies* 13: 313–29.
Becher, T. (1989) *Tribes and Territories.* Milton Keynes: Open University Press.
Becker, H. (1971) *Sociological Work.* London: Allen Lane.

Broch-Due, A-K. (1992) 'Reflections on Subjectivism in Biographical Interviewing: A Process of Change', in T. Iles (ed.) *All Sides of the Subject: Women and Biography*. New York: Teachers College Press.

Bryman, A. (1989) *Research Methods and Organization Studies*. London: Unwin Hyman.

Dent, M., Burke, W. and Green, R. (1991) 'Emotional Labour and Renal Dialysis: Nursing and the Labour Process', *Ninth Annual Conference*. University of Manchester April 1991.

Easterday, L., Papdemas, D., Schorr, L. and Valentine, C. (1987) 'The Making of a Female Researcher: Role Problems in Field Work', in M. Deegan and M. Hill (eds) *Women and Symbolic Interaction*. Winchester, MA: Allen & Unwin.

Fineman, S. (1991) 'Organising and Emotion'. *Towards a New Theory of Organisations*, 3–5 April 1991, University of Keele.

Goffman, E. (1959) *The Presentation of Self in Everyday Life*. Harmondsworth: Penguin.

Harding, S. (1987) 'Introduction: Is There a Feminist Method?' in S. Harding (ed.) *Feminism and Methodology*. Milton Keynes: Open University Press.

Hochschild, A. R. (1979) 'Emotion Work, Feeling Rules and Social Structure', *American Journal Sociology* 81: 551–75

Hochschild, A. R. (1983) *The Managed Heart: The Commercialization of Human Feelings*. Berkeley, CA: The University of California Press.

James, N. (1989) 'Emotional Labour: Skills and Work in the Social Regulation of Feelings', *The Sociological Review* 37: 15–42.

Kelly, L., Burton, S. and Regan, L. (1994) 'Researching Women's Lives or Studying Women's Oppression? Reflections on What Constitutes Feminist Research', in M. Maynard and J. Purvis (eds) *Researching Women's Lives from a Feminist Perspective*. London: Taylor & Francis.

Laws, S. (1990) *Issues of Blood: The Politics of Menstruation*. London: Macmillan.

McKee, L. and O'Brien, M. (1983) 'Interviewing Men: Taking Gender Seriously', in E. Gamarnikow *et al.* (eds) *The Public and the Private*. London: Heinemann.

Morgan, D. (1981) 'Men, Masculinity and the Process of Sociological Enquiry', in H. Roberts (ed.) *Doing Feminist Research*. London: Routledge & Kegan Paul.

Oakley, A. (1981) 'Interviewing Women: a contradiction in terms', in H. Roberts *Doing Feminist Research*. London: Routledge & Kegan Paul.

Reinharz, S. (1983) 'Experiential Analysis: A Contribution to Feminist Research', in G. Bowles and R. Duelli-Klein (eds) *Theories of Women's Studies*. London: Routledge & Kegan Paul.

Roberts, H. (1981) 'Women and Their Doctors: Power and Powerlessness in the Research Process', in H. Roberts (ed.) *Doing Feminist Research*. London: Routledge & Kegan Paul.

Shaffir, W. B., Stebbins, R. A. and Turowetz, A. (1980) *Fieldwork Experience: Qualitative Approaches to Social Research*. New York: St Martins Press.

Sheppard, D. (1989) 'Organizations, Power and Sexuality: The Image and Self-image of Women Managers', in J. Hearn *et al.* (eds) *The Sexuality of Organization*. London: Sage.

Smart, C. (1984) *The Ties That Bind: Law, Marriage and the Reproduction of Patriarchal Relations*. London: Routledge & Kegan Paul.

Smircich, L. (1983) 'Studying Organizations as Cultures', in G. Morgan (ed.) *Beyond Method: Strategies for Social Research*. Beverley Hills, California: Sage.

Spender, D. (1980) *Man Made Language*. London: Pandora Press.

Stanley, L. and Wise, S. (1983) *Breaking Out: Feminist Consciousness and Feminist Research*. London: Routledge & Kegan Paul.

Stanley, L. (1990) 'Feminist Praxis and the Academic Mode of Production: An Editorial Introduction', in L. Stanley (ed.) *Feminist Praxis*. London: Routledge.

Steier, F. (1991) 'Introduction: Research as Self-reflexivity, Self-reflexivity as Social Process', in F. Steier (ed.) *Research and Reflexivity*. London: Sage.

Sutton, R. (1991) 'Maintaining Norms about Expressed Emotions: The Case of the Bill Collectors,' *Administrative Science Quarterly* 36: 461–8.

Sutton, R. and Rafaeli, A. (1988) 'Untangling the Relationship between Displayed Emotions and Organizational Sales: The Case of Convenience Stores', *Academy of Management Journal* 31: 461–87.

Sutton, R. and Schurman, S. (1988) 'On Studying Emotionally Hot Topics: Lessons from an Investigation of Organizational Death', in D. Berg and K. Smith (eds) *The Self and Social Inquiry*. London: Sage.

Thomas, K. (1990) *Gender and Subject in Higher Education*. Buckingham: Open University Press.

Van Maanen, J. and Gideon, K. (1989) 'Real Feelings: Emotional Expression and Organizational Culture', in L. L. Cummings and B. Straw (eds) *Research in Organizational Behaviour* 11: 43–104.

9 The Research Process: Context, Autonomy and Audience[1]

Geoff Cooper and Steve Woolgar

Director of the Research Centre: Great news that we got our essay accepted for the BSA Conference volume!

Research Fellow: Yes, terrific. Although I am a bit surprised. I wasn't at all sure they would accept it.

Director: Really? Why? Remember how encouraged we were by the theme for the conference: 'Research Imaginations'. The original call for papers made a particular point of inviting alternatives to 'the traditional paper-to-audience format', suggesting we might explore some novel and innovative means of presentation.

Research Fellow: But instead, we just ended up using dialogue!

Director: Yes! Ah well. Just shows you what a tricky thing innovation is. Enormously novel, imaginative and risky formats of presentation are innovative for some people but completely old hat for others.[2]

Research Fellow: I'm still not sure whether the silence that followed our presentation meant the audience were stunned or just bored. But then again there was that nice report of the conference in *Network* which referred to our 'highly original presentation – as – duologue'.[3]

Director: So we were innovative, then!

Research Fellow: Although the same report also commented that our presentation made it impossible, in the time available, to fashion an appropriately innovative question/response before the chairperson moved on to the next presentation. So it was not, perhaps, a very productive kind of innovation.

Director: Anyway, we really need to get a move on with revising it for the conference volume. What are we going to do?

Research Fellow: Don't we just publish the same dialogue?[4]

Director: I don't think we could get away with that.[5] And we have to be careful that readers don't mistake the apparently flippant format as denoting an absence of serious argument.[6] Let's have another look at what we

147

said in our abstract. Ah yes: 'Our aim is to problematise the standard conception of the research process with sociology...' Sounds appropriately grandiloquent.

Research Fellow: What did we mean by 'the standard conception of the research process'?

Director: The idea is that the standard approach to the research process treats the techniques, methodologies and theories of research as essentially separate from its political, organisational and administrative context. In other words, there is an implicit distinction between what is construed as the technical business of research, on the one hand, and as the social and contextual circumstances, on the other.

Research Fellow: It is extraordinary that almost all sociological methods texts assume that researchers work on their own, make their own decisions and otherwise proceed in isolation of the demands of their colleagues, their institutions and discipline.

Director: Doesn't sound much like what goes on in this research centre.

Research Fellow: It's such a misleading picture of the research process, especially when you think this is what is being taught to newcomers to research!

Director: Researchers have to learn that textbook versions of research don't tell anything like the whole story.

Research Fellow: And it's curious, isn't it, that so few of those terribly sophisticated discussions in (and of) 'post-modernism' engage with the nitty-gritty of what it's like actually to do research in sociology.

Director: Yes, all those tremendously interesting questions: Can we escape totalising discourses?[7] Is the world experienced as a mere simulation of itself?[8] What are the consequences of eroding the social?[9] And so on. But hardly anyone bothers to bring these concerns to bear on the institutional realities of day-to-day research practice.[10]

Research Fellow: It's as if all those discussions of post-modernism take place in a social vacuum.

Director: They claim the important impact of post-modernism on knowledge generation but don't look to see how this might affect the actual working practices of sociologists.

Research Fellow: Of course, there has been some criticism of the distinction between 'research' and its 'social and cultural context' which has alluded to the empirical circumstances of research practice. For example, sociologists of science, technology and knowledge have long argued that the technical content of research (whether in the natural or social sciences) cannot be considered in isolation from its social and cultural context.

Director: But the problem is that this is far too general a way of putting it. What does it mean to talk about 'understanding the research process in its social and cultural context'?

Research Fellow: It is a bit bland, isn't it?

Director: Yes. 'Understanding the research process in its social and cultural context' suggests we just need to juxtapose a description of researchers at work with another description of the prevailing social circumstances. The important point is that by placing a description of the technical details of research *alongside* a description of social circumstances, you still imply that the two domains are basically discrete; that the realm of the technical is separate from, even if in some way connected to, social context.

Research Fellow: Yes, the danger is that you can end up merely talking about parallels between research and its social context, as if they were separate domains, rather than exploring more profound senses in which research is social.

Director: Exactly. The challenge is to find a way of demonstrating how aspects of 'context' permeate and sustain the practice of research, the practical activities of research, the arguments, the interactions and actual talk between researchers and so on. For example, it would be really good if we could focus on one particular aspect of 'context' – say the ways in which researchers relate to, and think of, themselves and others – and show its importance for the way research is done.

Research Fellow: And we need to demonstrate the important – but often unnoticed – effects of researchers' conceptions of audience, without merely offering a description of the research as separate from a description of the social relations involved.

Director: That's good. There must be a better way of conveying that aspect of the research process, of getting across its essential dependence upon locally attributed, contingent conceptions and assessments of audience. Anyway, perhaps we can generate some ideas for the chapter for the BSA volume if we discuss where we've got to in our empirical research project. How are things in the field?

Research Fellow: What field?[11] Oh that, well same as ever, you know, nothing particularly dramatic this week … although there have been some interesting developments in the Software Quality Programme I've been following.

Director: Yeah?

Research Fellow: Yeah. In fact I've decided to make that into the main focus of my presentation to our research centre's Industrial Advisory

Panel next week. Could we talk about that before we talk about the paper for the BSA volume? I've done some notes. Maybe we could discuss them?

Director: Good idea.

Research Fellow: I thought I'd start by reminding them that the project is called 'A Sociological Study of Changing Research Culture', and that the main aim is to assess the effects of changes in research organisation upon the practice of research. I'll mention that we are especially interested in the effects on research of increasing demands for 'accountability', 'relevance' and 'policy orientation'. (Pause). Do you think that's sufficient by way of introduction? I don't have a very clear sense of what sort of presentation you're expecting us to give to the Advisory Panel. Who's going to be on the Panel? Any sociologists?

Director: No.

Research Fellow: Any academics at all?

Director: Probably not. Let me see. We have a senior civil servant, a consultant specialising in IT, an insurance company manager, and someone from marketing. I think what's required are snappy, upbeat presentations with nothing too technical. The important thing to get across is that we are a lively research centre with lots of ideas and a coherent identity.

Research Fellow: So it's very much a PR event. Suits and overheads?

Director: Yes. And I think we'll get the overheads made up on the desktop publisher so that they're all in the same style and have the Centre logo on them. We have to look professional.

Research Fellow: Maybe you should look at this document I came across during my field-work that gives guidelines for presenters at one of the sessions in the annual ESPRIT IT conference. It's amazing how finely regulated their presentations are – hang on I've got it here somewhere – yes, presenters are advised to use a maximum of six lines per slide, six words per line, and to change their overheads once a minute! It even suggest that 'Consideration may be given in advance to typical questions which would help to highlight some of the key points of the presentation; arrangements could be made to ensure that such questions are raised from the audience in the absence of other questions'. It's like show business! You put a plant in the audience. It's just stimulating the exchange of ideas. I think it's a really depressing trend: research evolving into marketing.

Plant in the Audience:[12] But isn't that a very archaic view of research? Surely the recent work in the sociology of scientific knowledge (SSK), especially by authors like Latour and Woolgar, has shown that science is precisely about competing in the market place, the translation of interests, the enrolment of allies and so on.[13]

Director: I agree. And as for simulating the exchange of ideas, you could ask whether the so-called 'pure' forms of academic discourse ever achieve more than simulation.

Research Fellow: Well, all right, maybe I should be more critical of the distinction: but if anything, saying that work in SSK 'has shown that science is precisely about competing in the market place' supports my point.

Director: Why?

Research Fellow: SSK is a historically specific enterprise: if it's using these kinds of terms, it simply exemplifies the 'marketisation of public discourse' that I'm talking about.[14]

Director: Look, the point is that our meeting with the Industrial Advisory Panel *is* a marketing occasion: these people can be very useful for us, both in offering advice and suggesting leads, and we really need to explore other sources of funding with our main source of ESRC support coming to an end.

Research Fellow: I know, but don't you ever worry about the increasing frequency of these kinds of events?

Director: Well, you're right. It *is* happening more and more. But not just with us. I'm sure that many other research teams and centres – both within and beyond sociology – are being asked to make their work more accessible to non-sociologists and to non-academics. It's all part of what Howard Newby calls 'Sociology Coming In From The Cold'.[15] Other places may not exactly have an Industrial Advisory panel, like we do, but I know a lot of them are under pressure to strike up relations with business, industry and commerce.[16]

Research Fellow: But it seems such a distraction from the *real* work. And having to make these bland little presentations every other month has an effect on your academic work, quite apart from the valuable research time that it wastes.[17]

Director: Ah! But what do you mean by 'bland'? Bland for whom? I wonder if you are using a rather inflexible conception of audience here. Surely these presentations will only seem 'bland' from the point of view of one narrowly defined group of peers. Don't you want to branch out? Isn't the point to see how many and different audiences we can interest? After all, recent work in the sociology of scientific knowledge makes it very clear that the impact and achievement of science comes about as the result of going well beyond one's own research community! Isn't it precisely by reaching out and converting more and different and unexpected new audiences that success is achieved?!

Research Fellow: Ah, but what do you mean by 'success'? Success for whom? It may be important for directors of research centres to reach new audiences: but my first priority, as a contract researcher, is to make an impression on conventional academic audiences.

Director: Well, of course, but there's no conflict there: it's important to the Centre that you keep up a healthy rate of publication in academic journals.

Research Fellow: Yes, but having to summarise key findings at a ridiculously early stage for these kind of events has effects on the development of the research itself. I'm not sure you can keep the marketing and the academic content separate: the one contaminates the other.

Director: It is a different and additional task to research as traditionally defined. But why should we want uncritically to accept the traditional definition of research? It's precisely the myth of the unsullied scholar that we need to challenge.

Research Fellow: Yes, but isn't there a danger that challenging the myth of pure scholarship might turn out to be just an excuse for a form of research which embraces the ideology of the market, commercial utility, relevance and so on? I found this great quote from Heidegger which makes a similar point about the drift towards purely performative criteria:

> The scholar disappears. He is replaced by the research man who is engaged in research projects. These, rather than the cultivation of erudition, lend to his work its atmosphere of incisiveness [...] The research worker necessarily presses forward of himself into the sphere characteristic of the technologist ...[18]

Director: Well, if Heidegger says it, it must be right, I suppose. But you have to admit it's a staggeringly unreflexive view of things (not to mention a bit sexist). Here we have the chance to make the relation between academic and commercial discourses the object of study. More than that, we can actually experiment with these discourses as we research them.

Research Fellow: But to call it an 'experiment' makes it sound as though we're completely in control of these discourses and can keep them separate. I'm not sure we can. They're continually merging.[19]

Director: I'm not suggesting that we're in control of these discourses; on the contrary, the point is precisely that we now have a topic which at last acknowledges and makes explicit, rather than concealing, the fact of our embroilment in the tension between academia and industry. So what you might think of as new constraints on research actually provide an exciting intellectual opportunity. And I do feel that it is highly suspect just to accept the idea that academic research occupies a separate and unsullied space. It's also very unsociological.[20] Anyway let's carry on.

Research Fellow: Okay, well after outlining the rationale for the Changing Research Culture project, I thought I'd explain that the main part of the empirical work is an ethnographic study in a prominent computer science department. And I would then explain that the idea is to focus on the computer scientists' participation in a software quality research programme. Incidentally, I'm never quite sure how to deal with the question 'why a computer science department?' It seems a bit lame to say it's because of a series of funding contingencies and then pass it over to you.

Director: We could maybe emphasise the strategic significance of computer science; the point that since computer science is relatively close to industry, it is perhaps the last place where you might expect evidence of adverse effects upon research culture of the demands for utility, accountability, relevance and so on. So computer science research represents a kind of hardest case for the general thesis about the effects of these demands upon research in general.

Research Fellow: Yes, but computer scientists don't necessarily see it that way; in some settings they are rather keen to distinguish between (pure) computer 'science' and IT.

Director: H'mm. You're right. And some of them get quite upset, don't they, by the suggestion that they spend most of their time on fat consultancies.

Research Fellow: Perhaps it would be better to say what actually happened. I mean I'd heard that since the ESRC wouldn't fund this kind of research into one of its own social science research programmes, you were forced to reframe your original proposal in terms of going out to observe a computer science research programme.

Director: Is that what really happened? I'd rather think of computer science as offering an especially appropriate location for tackling the more general question.

Research Fellow: But we really shouldn't lose sight of the very real constraints on the choice of research site. We should point out the reflexive significance of this constraint for understanding the way research is done.

Director: Well, I wouldn't use words like 'reflexive significance' with the Advisory Panel. Better stick to the hard case story. You might also mention that computer science fits in with our Centre's general interest in studying social aspects of computers and IT.

Research Fellow: Right. So then I'll move on to talking about the software quality stuff more specifically. I'll describe how I've been able to follow the early stages of the programme from the preliminary meeting at the DTI, through the process of bidding for the feasibility or scoping study contract, and most recently at the presentation of the final report to the DTI. Then I'll just highlight some points of interest. How long will I have?

Director: Ten minutes.

Research Fellow: Okay. In that case I'll just concentrate upon the way the research programme was set up. A number of participants felt that the way the DTI went about determining the scope of the intended programme was unnecessarily elaborate. They reckoned all this activity had less to do with the stated purpose of addressing the vast technical problems of software quality and much more to do with enhancing the credibility of the programme.[21] Some thought that its real purpose was to demonstrate that those setting up the programme had consulted widely within the software engineering and software user communities.

Director: That's great! In other words, those setting up the programme drew upon a conception of relevant audience which, from what you're saying, led to a complaint that the technical issues were being neglected, that they were ignoring the content of the actual research that was going on.

Research Fellow: Yes. It was said that those setting up the programme didn't even consult adequately, and that the academic community was under-represented.

Director: Okay, so a competing conception of relevant audience -- the community which it was said *should* have been consulted – was used to fashion the complaint about inadequate attention to the 'actual' technical core of the research. The academics used competing conceptions of relevant audience to sustain the idea that 'the real stuff' existed independently of what any user community required. This shows again that the distinction between technical and social is not given. It is instead a distinction achieved and displayed through claims about the differential relevance of various communities.[22]

Research Fellow: Exactly. But do you think the Advisory Panel are going to understand it in those terms?

Director: H'mm. The distinction between technical and social is 'achieved and displayed through claims about the differential relevance of various communities'. I see what you mean. We don't want them to think we are just talking jargon.[23] Perhaps it'd be better just to say that 'technical' meant different things to different people.

Research Fellow: Okay. Anyway, the same thing came up again in the tension between the technical problems – i.e. of defining a framework for the measurement of software quality – and the frequently invoked 'needs of the user'.

Director: How do you mean?

Research Fellow: Well, for example, one issue that was raised repeatedly was whether 'quality' was susceptible to definition at all. But these doubts (or more generally what one participant described as the 'vast philosophical problems' associated with the enterprise) were often countered by appeal to the practical importance of responding to the user community's urgent need for a way of measuring software quality.

Director: So prospective users were rhetorically configured to justify the research process?

Research Fellow: I suppose so.

Director: Now that's a nice point for the Advisory Panel. You could tie that in with my introduction about how all the work in our Centre is focused on producer-consumer relations.

Research Fellow: Oh, are you doing that again?

Director: Yes, Why?

Research Fellow: Well, it's just, er, well, I wonder if that doesn't have more to do with the perceived need for our Centre to have a corporate identity than with the content of the actual research that's going on here. I know it's important in *your* work but ...

Director: No, no, I think that's far too cynical a view! It's not just a question of corporate identity, it's also a crucial intellectual issue with largely unexplored significance for social science; we need to think through how we, as producers of sociology, relate to our consumers, how we sociologists configure our users.

Research Fellow: I'm not saying you couldn't draw some parallels; but you're uncritically adopting a commercial market discourse to talk about social science. How can sociology preserve any critical distance if its first move is to collapse into the discourse of what it sets out to describe?[24]

Director: Would you be happier if, instead of producers and consumers, we talked about the relation between academics and non-academics, social scientists and non-social scientists, insiders and outsiders? It's a general problem, you see, of communication across social organisational boundaries: how your computer scientists relate to industrialists is in principle the same problem as how academic sociologists relate to non-academics.

Research Fellow: How do you mean?

Director: Well, for example, in my work with the computer system developers it became clear that the relation between the company and its users turned on close tutoring about the future of computers. The users were taught what to want.[25] And they were taught this from a very early stage in the development of the product. By contrast, it seems to me that much sociology deploys a supermarket model: results which emerge from the academic research process are dressed up and put on display in the (sometimes desperate) hope that passers-by will find them attractive. In this version of sociology, dissemination is something that only occurs after the work has been done. Indeed, the very idea of 'dissemination' connotes the conceptual separation of the two communities: production precedes consumption; producers are a distinct social community from consumers. So what I'm asking is: Is there anything about the social organisation of sociological research which prevents us acting like computer manufacturers? Can't we sociologist teach our users what to want? What scope is there for changing the way in which we relate to our outsiders?

Research Fellow: But why would we want to model ourselves on computer manufacturers?

Director: That's not the point. This is all part of our ethnographic strategy; the idea is to force what seem unlikely parallels between (apparently) different domains of social activity and then see where they stand or fall. By forcing the parallel, I reckon we will be able to understand much more about the (apparent) differences between, say, computer systems developers and social science researchers.

Research Fellow: But 'forcing the parallel' is the problem. Doesn't that mean that you're more likely to end up asserting the identity, or at least the similarity, of the two domains. Differences, if they get a look in, get reduced to participants' attributions. Why shouldn't we 'force the differences'?[26]

Director: That wouldn't get us very far though, would it? The more you emphasise difference, the more you feed the myth of pure scholarship. And it's just that myth which we're trying to interrogate.

Research Fellow: I'm not convinced. But anyway the other thing I wanted to mention was the importance attached to dissemination. When I spoke to the leader of the feasibility study, he suggested that the real challenge was not to devise technical solutions (difficult though they were), but to have an impact on industrial practice. Others complained that the stress on dissemination had contributed to the further neglect of technical content.

Director: So here you have another tension, this time between the technical content and the desire for 'impact'. And, once again, you can see how this tension arises from competing views about which is the more relevant audience.

Research Fellow: Yes, you're right. The leader of the feasibility study saw the need to combat inertia as a central problem. His portrayal of that particular audience suggested that there's quite a lot of resistance in industry to quality assurance certification and standards.[27]

Director: You mean this is all about quality assurance procedures and standards? God, they're getting everywhere.[28] Anyway, look I've got a meeting in a minute, what's your last point?

Research Fellow: A meeting?

Director: Yes, the Dean has some hare-brained scheme about selling MAs to Woolworths. He thinks we should divert yet more precious research time to making our work seem attractive to retail managers! It's outrageous! I'm going to have to protest.

Research Fellow: Well, anyway, I just had some final comments on the question of who should define the problems. I spoke to a systems manager who suggested it would be good for university researchers if the programme was funded and directed by industry: otherwise, he said, the academics wouldn't know what to research! On the other hand, one leading academic felt that this led to the neglect of crucial theoretical questions about measurement and the identification of attributes of quality. He felt that the academic community was under-represented.

Director: The point is, can you make the distinction between academics and industrialists any more?

Research Fellow: Maybe you never could. Wasn't it Kant who defined the university as 'a public means for treating the sum of knowledge .... in a quasi *industrial* manner'?[29] Perhaps the very difficulty of making this kind of distinction is a defining feature of what has been called 'post-modern post-science', that is, 'scientific practices come to be inserted in other, more pervasive, economies and discourses'.[30]

Director: I should steer clear of 'post-modernism' and 'discourse' for the Advisory Panel if I were you.

Research Fellow: I suppose you're right.

Director: We can get back to the real stuff for the chapter in the BSA volume.

Research Fellow: Okay. So what's the answer? I mean, as far as the chapter for the BSA is concerned?

Director: Our major point is that more awareness of the research process is crucial for coming to terms with the tension between being scholarly and being useful ...

Research Fellow: But it's not just a question of 'coming to terms' with it, is it?

Director: Slip of the tongue, I meant 'interrogating' the tension between being scholarly and being useful.

Research Fellow: Do you think, in any case, there is a single, identifiable, 'major point' to our argument? I mean, look at all the important differences in emphasis, not to mention disagreements that run through this text.

Director: You mean disagreements between the characters?

Research Fellow: I'm not sure. Are we characters or caricatures? After all we've both been given some rather odd lines to speak. In places you come across as a burlesque of managerial proclivities within sociology, and I'm a parody of critical tendencies within sociology.

Director: So you mean disagreements between *caricatures*?

Research Fellow: Well, perhaps it's more that the caricatures are *constituted* by tensions that are endemic to the topic under discussion.[31]

Director: Look, what is the problem here? You seem to be slipping into academic pedantry again.

Research Fellow: The problem is not to lose, in a unitary conclusion, the commitment to heterogeneity and the dialogic that was an important part of, and indeed rationale for, the way we organised the text. I mean the purpose of dialogue is an attempt to maintain some autonomy, to preserve the possibility of some form of criticism in the face of the changed circumstances in which sociology is practised.[32]

Director: 'In the face of'? For God's sake it's not a siege. The point is we need to stress the importance of maintaining reflexive awareness of the research process and, crucially, of the ways in which conceptions of audience are constructed, displayed and reaffirmed throughout research interactions. In particular, we have to emphasise the effects of these conceptions of audience, especially the various tensions in research interaction.

Research Fellow: How are we going to convey that?

Director: I'm not sure. Obviously, we need to make the point that, as you mentioned at the start of our discussion, researchers are often completely unaware just how much their talk is permeated by conceptions of audience ...

Research Fellow: Did I say that? I thought you had all the 'conceptions of audience' lines. But come to think of it, I do remember starting our discussion by saying I was surprised *they* had accepted our paper.

Director: ... And that researchers often have no notion about the effects of such conceptions on the way they plan their presentations and so on ...

Research Fellow: And didn't you start on about how certain forms of presentation are innovative for *some people* but not for *others*?

Director: ... Certainly we need an alternative to the standard presentational format: we need to find a way of demonstrating the point rather than just asserting it ...[33]

Research Fellow: ... All our talk about what the *Advisory Panel* would want ... ?

Director: What? Yes, anyway, we really need some way of *exemplifying* the importance of the ways in which research practice performs – that is, defines and constitutes – audience, rather than just offering a disengaged analysis of the phenomenon.[34]

Research Fellow: We can't use dialogue again.[35]

Director: Absolutely not. They would never wear it.[36]

Research Fellow: That's not what I meant. Look, there's nothing very radical about dialogues in themselves, especially if they finish with a safe, monologic, totalising conclusion to the effect that the whole exercise is just a device to exemplify the importance of conceptions of audience. I wonder if, in the end, you're just pandering to the Advisory Panel?

Director: Look, there's nothing very safe about dialogues which finish by undermining themselves with a conclusion to the effect that all this is just to pander to the Advisory Panel. As for 'radical' ... 'monologic' ... 'totalising' ... I wonder if, in the end, you're just pandering to social theory?[37]

Research Fellow: Do we really want to end by implying that this whole debate can be settled by an appeal to symmetry?

NOTES

1. Earlier versions of this chapter were presented to the British Sociological Association Annual Conference, *Research Imaginations*, University of Essex, 5–8 April, 1993 (under the title: 'The Research Process and Organisational Change: The Importance of Conceptions of Audience in Research Practice'), the PICT 1993 National Conference, Kenilworth, Warwickshire, 19–21 May 1993, and to the CRICT Advisory Panel, 4 November 1993. Our thanks to participants at these occasions for their comments, especially to colleagues in CRICT, to Brian Oakley and Bob Malcolm; and to Frank Webster, Rod Coombs and Christine Hine for being 'plants' in the audience. We acknowledge the support of the ESRC in funding the research reported here (ESRC grant no R000232385).

2. This tired old point has been made several times elsewhere, for example, by Woolgar and Ashmore (1988). Notice here how these interlocuters establish and display to each other their familiarity with dialogic form. *They* are not

to be hoodwinked by claims that it is innovative; it is only innovative for some others.

3. The Newsletter of the British Sociological Association, No. 56, May 1993, p. 9.
4. Is it the same dialogue? Could it be?(cf Borges 1970). From their subsequent exchanges it is reasonable to suppose that both parties would insist that the form and sense of their dialogue are constantly evolving.
5. Have they got away with it? It depends, in part of course, on whether it really is the same dialogue. See note 4.
6. In an attempt to avert this danger, participants adopt the strategy of providing extensive footnotes. For example, they are keen to refer to the cogent arguments which advocate a form of 'serious unseriousness' (Ashmore 1989).
7. cf Lyotard (1984).
8. Baudrillard (1983).
9. Lash and Urry (1986).
10. One exception being Law (1994).
11. This poor joke signals the participants' (incipient) recognition of the important resonance between the ostensive topic of their discussion and the nature of the discussion itself. Their discussion is about the project entitled 'Changing Research Culture' and about their own experience of the changing nature of research culture. Given the general, that is, a-disciplinary character of some of these changes, the interactions and institutional arrangements at the 'home' institution can be considered as germane as those being studied 'abroad' (in a computer science department). Consequently, whilst the empirical materials discussed are not incidental to our argument, neither do they constitute the sole 'findings', as will become apparent. A more extensive discussion would of course require greater attention to disciplinary specificities (see Shinn 1982).
12. The Plant in the Audience is, of course, a figment of these interlocuters' (combined) imagination and is premised on the gratuitous assumption that their discussion has an audience at all.
13. See, for example, Latour and Woolgar (1986); Latour (1987); Cooper and Woolgar (1995).
14. Fairclough (1993).
15. Professor Howard Newby was Chairman of the ESRC until 1994. For his discussion of this point see, for example, Newby (1991).
16. The Director and the Research Fellow of this Centre seem remarkably unaware of the extent to which many areas of 'applied' sociology have long been subject to the demands of their sponsors. The particular interest of their exchange, however, is the extent to which they feel their predilection for (what they would think of as) theoretical and epistemologically oriented sociology is threatened by recent institutional and cultural changes.
17. 'Dear Research Professional, No matter what your speciality, one thing is certain; without up-to-date, reliable information *you risk falling behind.* You need to know what your colleagues are doing. And you need to know about it now' (extract from an undated mailshot from the Institute for Scientific Information for 'Current Contents/Social and Behavioural Sciences'). See also note 21.

18. Heidegger (1977: 125).
19. The question here is how far it is possible, in Laclau's (1977) terms, to re-articulate academic and commercial discourses, given the extent to which equivalences have been established between them.
20. There is also a problem of social and political élitism. Heidegger, for example, goes on to lament that 'The research man no longer needs a library at home' (1977: 125)! We suggest that even critical sociologies of the left risk this kind of élitism if the distinction between pure scholarship and commercial utility is not itself interrogated. Fairclough's (1993) critique of market discourse within universities provides some examples of this kind of lapse, particularly in relation to his discussion of the role of 'new universities' in the process of 'marketization'.
21. Cf Heidegger ... 'because research is, in essence, ongoing activity, the industrious activity of mere 'busyness', which is always possible, gives the impression of a higher reality behind which the burrowing activity proper to research work is accomplished' (1977: 138).
22. Cf Low and Woolgar (1993).
23. This recurrent concern about language can be read in terms of an anxiety to balance the apparently conflicting demands of being intelligible to a new audience with the preservation of identity and cultural capital which academic discourse confers within the 'university market' (Bourdieu 1988: 11). Note, however, that Bourdieu's use of the market metaphor itself poses further problems for attempts to separate academic and market discourse.
24. Whether or not this 'collapse' is misguided, it seems to represent an unusual inversion of the more usual problem of sociological description in which the language of the domain studied is inadvertently transposed into a sociological frame of reference (Smith 1990).
25. Woolgar (1991).
26. The Research Fellow's attempt to preserve, via the assertion of difference, some critical distance for contemporary sociology is fraught with difficulty if recent conceptualisations of the character of post-modernity are taken seriously. Lash, for example, suggests that cultural post-modernization is to be understood precisely as a process of 'de-differentiation' (Lash 1990: 11); while Bauman suggests that the very theorisation of post-modernity is the unconscious articulation by intellectuals of their own changing – that is diminishing – status and thus, we may infer, difference (Bauman 1992: chapter 4). Such a change is highly germane to both participants' concerns. If criticism based on distance and separation seems untenable, then the reflexive exploration and interrogation of the embeddedness of intellectual work within wider discourses becomes a necessary development of a critical sociology, and not, as it is frequently caricatured, a form of mere navel-gazing.
27. See for example 'Red Tape Nightmare of BS5750'. *Daily Telegraph* 5 February 1992, p. 12. For a discussion of the political context of the 'immense fashionableness' of 'quality', see Pollitt (1991).
28. 'Quality' in Higher Education was the subject of extensive discussion in *The Times Higher Education Supplement* throughout 1993.
29. Cited in Derrida (1992: 4), original emphasis.
30. Crook *et al.* (1992: 217).

31. The participants would probably want to warn against any simplistic inference of correspondence between the two characters in the dialogue and the two authors of this paper. Interestingly, it often turned out to be easier for them each to concoct caricatured utterances for the 'other party' rather than for the character ostensibly closest to their own persona.

32. Bauman sees the shift form monologic to dialogic discourse as crucial for sustaining and renewing critical thought (1992: chapter 3). However, he employs a less literal sense of 'dialogue' than is used here.

33. For an attempt to both assert and demonstrate the point see Cooper and Woolgar (1994).

34. For an attempt to find a way of exemplifying this point rather than just offering a disengaged analysis see Cooper and Woolgar (1995).

35. Dialogues are too old hat.

36. Dialogues are too radical.

37. An interesting further twist to the tale arises from the authors' experience in deciding from whom to elicit comments on the draft of this chapter. For example, in agonising over whether or not certain parts might be (mis)read as offensive to certain parties, and in trying to decide whether and how to invite comments from members of the CRICT Advisory Panel, they discovered the strength of their own unexplicated (and mostly incorrect) preconceptions about the likely reactions of readers of this piece.

REFERENCES

Ashmore, M. (1989) *The Reflexive Thesis: Wrighting the Sociology of Scientific Knowledge*. Chicago: Chicago University Press.

Baudrillard, J. (1983) *Simulations*. New York: Semiotext(e).

Bauman, Z. (1992) *Intimations of Postmodernity*. London: Routledge.

Borges, J. L. (1970) 'Pierre Menard, author of the Quixote', in *Labyrinths*. Penguin: Harmondsworth.

Bourdieu, P. (1988) *Homo Academicus*. Cambridge: Polity.

Cooper, G. and Woolgar, S. (1994) 'Software Quality as Community Performance' in R. Mansell (ed.) *Information, Control and Technical Change*. London: Aslib.

Cooper, G. and Woolgar, S. (1995) 'The Research Process: Context, Autonomy and Audience', in S. Lyon and J. Busfield (eds) *Methodological Imaginations*. London: Macmillan.

Crook, S., Pakulski, J. and Waters, M. (1992) *Postmodernization: Change in Advanced Society*. London: Sage.

Derrida, J. (1992) 'Mochlos; or, the conflict of the faculties', in R. Rand (ed.) *Logomachia*. Lincoln and London: University of Nebraska Press.

Fairclough, N. (1993) 'Critical Discourse Analysis and the Marketization of Public Discourse', *Discourse and Society* 4, 2, 133–68.

Heidegger, M. (1977) *The Question Concerning Technology and Other Essays*. New York: Harper and Row.

Laclau, E. (1977) *Politics and Ideology in Marxist Theory*. London: Verso.

Lash, S. (1990) *Sociology of Postmodernism*. London: Routledge.

Lash, S. and Urry, J. (1986) 'The Dissolution of the Social?' in M. L. Wardell and S. P. Turner (eds) *Sociological Theory in Transition*. Boston: Allen and Unwin.

Latour, B. (1987) *Science in Action: How to Follow Scientists and Engineers through Society*. Milton Keynes: Open University Press.

Latour, B. and Woolgar, S. (1986) *Laboratory Life: The Construction of Scientific Facts*. Princeton, NJ: Princeton University Press.

Law, J. (1994) *Organizing Modernity*. Oxford: Blackwell.

Low, J. and Woolgar, S. (1993) 'Managing the Social-Technical Divide: Some Aspects of the Discursive Structure of Information Systems Development', in P. Quintas (ed.) *Social Dimensions of Systems Engineering*. Chichester: Ellis Horwood.

Lyotard, J. F. (1984) *The Postmodern Condition: A Report on Knowledge*. Minneapolis: University of Minnesota Press.

Newby, H. (1991) 'Sociology Comes in from the Cold', *The Times,* Tuesday 26 March.

Pollitt, C. (1991) 'The Politics of Quality: Managers, Professionals and Consumers in the Public Services'. Centre for Political Studies, Royal Holloway and Bedford New College.

Shinn, T. (1982) 'Scientific Disciplines and Organizational Specificity: The Social and Cognitive Configuration of Laboratory Activities', in N. Elias, H. Martins, R. Whitley (eds) *Scientific Establishment and Hierarchies. Sociology of the Sciences Yearbook, Vol IV*. Dordrecht: Reidel. 162   163

Smith, D (1990) 'On Sociological Description: A Method from Marx', in *Texts, Facts and Femininity: Exploring the Relations of Ruling*. Routledge: London.

Woolgar, S. (1991) 'Configuring the User', in J. Law (ed.) *A Sociology of Monsters: Essays on Power, Technology and Domination*. London: Routledge.

Woolgar, S. and Ashmore, M. (1988) 'The Next Step: An Introduction to the Reflexive Project', in S. Woolgar (ed.) *Knowledge and Reflexivity: New Frontiers in the Sociology of Knowledge*. London: Sage.

10 Gender, Power and Epistemology: Can Men Know Feminist Truths?

A. Mark Liddle

INTRODUCTION

Although the question of whether men can 'know feminist truths' is a relative newcomer in the social sciences, it is one of a whole family of questions concerning men, feminism and sexual politics that have arisen with increasing frequency in recent literature and academic debate. Questions such as 'Can men write like women, or write from women's perspectives?' 'Can men do feminist research?' and more generally, 'Can men be feminists?' have now arisen in a number of fields, and have also provided themes for recent conferences and collections of papers (see, for example, Jardine and Smith 1987; Hearn and Morgan 1990). While questions of this kind have been asked before, a number of developments both in social theory and other fields during the same period have perhaps given them a new significance. Post-modernist and deconstructionist work has problematised a variety of concepts that informed much previous work on gender, for example, and work on radical realism and developments in the philosophy of the social sciences have raised some fundamental questions about epistemology and social structure. There has also been a renewed focus within sociology on areas such as the body, intimacy, and the 'social structure of emotion', and issues arising in such work have, to some extent, also informed recent feminist writing, which has itself become increasingly diverse in its focus and methods. Perhaps more significantly, there has been a virtual outpouring of new books and articles dealing with men and masculinity (especially since the late 1980s), and in some areas there have also been related institutional developments, with the advent of new 'men's studies' journals and even new university departments having similar titles. While some of the theoretical developments referred to have greatly enriched a number of fields and led to some productive debates, developments of the latter sort have also lent a particular salience to questions about connections between men and feminism, and have, perhaps, also generated some new tensions within feminism itself.[1]

General developments of this kind are referred to occasionally throughout the discussion that follows, but the aim here is to focus more specifically on the question raised in the title, after clarifying some of the conceptual building blocks that an appropriate response seems to require. An investigation of the question 'Can men know feminist truths?' in any case involves reference to many of the same epistemological, political and ethical issues which arguably lie at the heart of some of these recent debates.

The discussion itself involves several stages: first, a selection of comments offered by a variety of contributors to these debates is canvassed, and an effort is made to abstract a number of recurring relevant themes from them. The literature in this area is now vast, and while the work referred to is intended to highlight the relevant theoretical landscape for the discussion at hand, the sample is by no means exhaustive even of possible 'schools of thought', let alone of writers who might be identified with one or more of the positions outlined.[2] A number of definitional matters are then discussed in order to try and clarify or disentangle some of the key concepts involved, and the main themes abstracted from the literature are considered against this background. Finally, it is argued that although 'feminist knowledge' can in some senses be acquired by men, their routes to such knowledge are radically different from women's; the gender structure of power tends to insulate men, at the level of direct experience, from forms of consciousness generated out of ongoing encounters with everyday routines in which subordination is reproduced.

GENDER, POWER AND KNOWLEDGE – SOME RECURRING THEMES

Many of the earlier feminist accounts of connections between gender, power and knowledge were offered either as part of a critique of specific academic disciplines for their sexism, or as part of a more general discussion of the 'distortions' and 'omissions' of knowledge within patriarchal societies. In an early work on the subject titled *The Prism of Sex* (Sherman and Beck 1979), for example, a number of writers argue that knowledge has been distorted by having been filtered through a 'male prism'. Bernard notes, for example, that:

> knowledge has been overwhelmingly male in subject matter, in assumptions, in methods, in interpretations; that a disproportionate share of human knowledge in all the disciplines has dealt with a world viewed

through a male prism; that not only equity but also the human legacy calls for a correction of this situation in order that lacunae be filled and distortions corrected (1979: 268).

The 'male prism through which the world has been viewed has resulted in severe inadequacies' (1979: 268) in a variety of academic disciplines, she argues, and the 'correction' of these inadequacies and distortions apparently requires the *augmentation* of existing knowledge, by knowledge that has been generated through, or by, the 'female prism' (1979: 271). Bernard also employs the notion of 'male ideology' here, which she describes as being 'an elaborate rationale of the male position in society', and regards this ideology as being inexorably determined – 'it could be no other', she claims, 'It was impossible for male social thinkers to perceive or to think in other than male terms. The value premises of their research must inevitably reflect their male point of view'. Lastly, Bernard appears to invoke a notion of false consciousness, when she argues that 'many women have been co-opted; that is, they have been trained to pursue knowledge in the male style, to study subjects approved of by men, to view the world through the male prism' (1979: 268–70, passim).

In the same volume, Dorothy Smith observes that 'forms of thought' are generated by ruling élites, and she refers to Millett's (1971) view that historically, these forms of thought, 'the means of expression, which we had available to us to formulate our experience were made or controlled by men' (Smith 1979: 137). Men occupy most positions in the ruling structure, and similarity of location within this structure leads to the generation of particular 'views of the world', and to the production of (predominantly 'male') ideologies. More generally, ideology:

> builds the internal social organization of the ruling class as well as its domination over others. Its overall character, however, depends upon, and takes for granted, the social relations that organize and enforce the silences of those who do not participate in this process, who are outside it (Smith 1979: 142–3).

It is largely *women* who have been left silenced 'outside', as Smith argues in an earlier paper – since 'the loci of ideological production are largely controlled by men' (1975: 362), women inherit 'forms of thought, images, modes of expression, in which [they are] constrained to treat [themselves] as looked at from outside, as other' (1979: 138), or 'as object' (1975: 366). In the 'ideological formations which establish the hegemony of male consciousness' (1975: 367), women are not afforded the appropriate tools, as it were, to address the 'imperialism' (1979: 144) of rationality over personal experience. Women are in a sense left epistemologically stranded, and 'are confronted virtually with the problem of reinventing the world of knowledge, of thought, of symbols and images' (1975: 367).

This connection between knowledge and the gender structure of power is similarly described by MacKinnon, who argues that 'the feminist theory of knowledge is inextricable from the feminist critique of power because the male point of view forces itself upon the world as its way of apprehending it' (1983: 636). This 'male perspective' is 'systemic and hegemonic', and is adhered to by most men ('nonconsciously'), because it both 'makes sense of their experience (the male experience)' (ibid: 636), and furthers male *interests*. Eichler also echoes this view by noting that 'knowledge has been, so far, constructed by some men for the benefit of men' (1985: 630), that the 'dominant ideology ... bolster[s] and maintain[s] patriarchy', and that 'social science in general has ... been the handmaiden of sexism'. Sexism itself is 'deeply ingrained in the structure of our thoughts and procedures', and for that reason is 'difficult ... to detect', according to Eichler. Knowledge benefits men even where women *do* participate in its construction, since female scholars 'have been educated in a male-dominated educational system and have adopted questions, methods, procedures, concepts, priorities, and answers generated by male scholars' (Eichler, 1985: 630–4 passim).

General remarks of this kind continue to be offered in some of the more recent literature on feminist epistemology and research; claims such as Bernard's (1979) concerning the 'co-option' of women academics are also made by Elizabeth Gross (1987), for example, who refers to certain liberal writers and others as 'conservative feminists', who 'have come to act as female guardians of male theoretical terms' (1987: 477). Gross suggests that such women 'dutifully serve their masters, using the work of their masters to chastise wayward women for going beyond the acceptable limits of their various disciplines' (ibid.: 477), and she goes on to refer to feminist theory itself as 'sexually specific theory' (ibid.: 480).[3]

Earlier claims involving notions such as the 'female prism' have now given way to more elaborate accounts offered by feminist standpoint theorists, however, and these accounts have been articulated most clearly in the literature on feminist research. Feminist standpoint theories differ from one another in some important ways, but they usually rest on epistemological considerations of the sort focused on within the sociology of knowledge.[4] More specifically, they seek to link knowledge to its own contexts of production, and to the social location of actors who are involved in processes of knowledge production. Standpoint theorists also sometimes incorporate a Marxian style 'dominant ideology' or 'ruling ideas' perspective (as in the embryonic account contained in the above quotations from Dorothy Smith's earlier work), in which it is claimed that men's dominance and control of both ruling structures and the means of ideological production afford them greater control over the form and content of knowledge stocks, and that those in subordinate positions must struggle to find the means to give voice to their own perception of social asymmetry. More importantly for our purposes, though, is the view that, while subordinate groups must struggle to give voice to their own vision of social reality, their subordination itself affords them a 'double consciousness', or an awareness both of social reality as presented by ruling groups (men, in this case) and of social reality as they experience it directly in their position as oppressed persons. Some feminists have argued in these general terms that, because of their subordination, women are in a favoured position from which to understand social reality; their inferior position affords them a 'keener insight' into the way that society functions.[5]

A position of this general kind concerning the achievement of women's 'double consciousness' is argued by Saarinen, for example, who suggests that:

> We must be able to show how the subordinated groups or classes, in spite of (or perhaps because of?) their situation, have created something that has *intrinsic human value*, something that for structural reasons has remained beyond the reach of the rulers (1988: 37, her emphasis).

She goes on to note more specifically:

> The thesis is that women's experience differs to such an extent from that of men that their way of perceiving reality must also be different ... hegemonic epistemology is said to reflect the rulers' profoundly alienated relationship to reality – both to themselves and to nature and human life in society in general (1988: 47).

Cook and Fonow offer similar remarks, in a much-cited paper on epistemology and methodology in feminist research:

> As an outcome of being in society but not of society, feminist scholars inhabit the world with a 'double vision of reality' which is part of their feminist consciousness.... Because women and other exploited groups are forced, out of self-preservation, to know the motives of their oppressors as well as how oppression and exploitation feel to the victims, they are better equipped to comprehend and interpret women's experiences (1986: 6–7).

Sandra Harding also makes reference to the gap 'between women's experience and the dominant conceptual schemes from which both so many issues of the women's movement as well as the most important feminist research in social science and biology have emerged' (1989: 278–9), and she echoes the view developed in Dorothy Smith's (1987) later work that:

> the 'bifurcated consciousness' of the alienated woman sociologist is a great resource for the radical transformation of sociology ... [and] ... the conceptual world of male sociologists is an impoverished resource with which to try to explain *critically* our social order (1989: 279; her emphasis).

Harding goes on to note, however, that while this 'bifurcated consciousness' is a potential resource, it is neither utilised automatically by women, nor is it beyond the reach of men in particular circumstances. It is not the case, she claims, 'that only women can look at the world from the perspective of women's activities'. Even though it is true:

> that powerful critical theories *can be developed* out of the gap between the half of human experience that is assigned to women and the conceptual schemes grounded only in masculine experience ... I think that men, too, can speak from the perspective of women's activities.... But men can do so only after women have articulated what that experience is, and after men, too, have engaged in ... political struggles (1989: 279; her emphasis).[6]

Finally, Harding concludes that:

> Feminist struggle is a fundamental part of gaining knowledge – of science. People, men as well as women, who do not engage in it, who do not risk in their daily activities offending or threatening the legitimacy of male dominance, in important ways cannot *know* how the social and natural worlds are organised (1989: 280; her emphasis).[7]

While the remarks quoted above have been drawn from a wide (and as noted earlier, a highly selective) range of written work, a number of representative themes can be readily abstracted from them. First of all, the view is expressed in much of this work that knowledge is, or has been, shaped largely by male perceptions and interest. Knowledge is therefore described as standing in need of either a purging of contaminants – if the 'shaping' in question is felt to involve a *distorted* representation of social reality (i.e. one riddled with false content) – or *augmentation*, if this shaping is thought to involve some kind of misrepresentation by omission (i.e. if knowledge has become somehow lopsided or partial through the exclusion of women's perspectives). Second, it is claimed that this connection between knowledge and 'male interests' – which are themselves a reflection of men's dominant position in the social (or ruling) structure – is underpinned by a network of beliefs often summarised by the term 'male ideology', which serves to justify (or explain away) this dominance. Opinion varies concerning whether male interests themselves have a *determining* influence on men's beliefs (and the use of terms such as 'non-consciously' suggest this interpretation), or whether 'male control' over knowledge production should be understood in strategic, instrumental terms.

Third, the view is offered that male dominance in the social/political world is matched by a 'male hegemony' in consciousness itself, and that since women have been left standing 'outside' the sphere of knowledge production, they are left with the option either of non-participation, or of embracing forms of participation which require them to employ male categories or forms of consciousness (and the latter option, in turn, involves women acting against their own interests, or embracing some kind of false consciousness). Fourth, a recurring claim in the remarks quoted above is that women's generally less favourable location in the gender structure of power grants them a form of epistemic privilege, and that this privilege (usually described in terms of 'double consciousness') affords women a greater resource for accurate description and critical theorising of social reality. 'Male consciousness' supplies an impoverished resource, by contrast, since it cannot see its own historical specificity (which masquerades as universality), and its material determinants tend to leave it insulated from alternative perspectives which could allow for greater accuracy in social description. Finally, and related to the latter remarks, a linkage is drawn (especially in some of the later work referred to) between knowledge and the *political* struggles which are said to be involved in its production.

These themes are of obvious relevance to the general question of how men might be positioned with respect to 'routes to feminist knowledge', but in order to facilitate consideration of these connections, it is necessary to digress slightly to discuss a number of key concepts that an answer seems to require. More specifically, epistemic categories such as 'knowledge' and 'belief' (or knowledge and that which *passes* for knowledge) are not always clearly distinguished in the literature referred to; an effort will therefore be made to clarify and disentangle some of these notions in the following section.

KNOWLEDGE, BELIEF, AND 'S KNOWS THAT *p*' EPISTEMOLOGIES

Terms such as 'knowledge' or 'know' are, of course, used in a variety of ways in everyday language – we speak of knowing how to perform tasks, knowing other people, knowing that such and such is the case, and so on – but the initial focus in this section will be on propositional knowledge, or knowledge construed as 'knowing that'. Other characterisations of 'feminist knowledge' will be referred to later in the discussion; I simply note here that in the realm of social theory (and within the subject matter of the sociology of knowledge), knowledge is most plausibly construed in propositional terms; sociological theorising can itself be regarded to some extent as being an exercise in elaborating and synthesising various kinds of social and other evidence into propositional form, which can then form the basis of explanations, arguments, strategies for intervention and so on.

Again, the subject of propositional knowledge has generated a great deal of writing over the last two decades alone, but accounts referred to by Code (1993) as 'S knows that *p*' epistemologies provide a useful preliminary framework for discussing epistemic categories such as 'knowledge' and 'belief'. Within traditional 'S knows that *p*' epistemologies, there are three conditions which must be satisfied before it can accurately be claimed that a particular subject 'knows that *p*' (where '*p*' is shorthand for any proposition): the subject must believe that *p*, *p* must be true, and the subject must be justified in believing that *p*.

The first condition is probably the least controversial, since it accords both with current language practice, and with most of our intuitions about the meaning of the relevant terms; one would usually be met with looks of incredulity if one claimed both to know some proposition *p*, and not to believe that *p*. There are of, course, some familiar cases which appear to contradict this account, but these apparent counter-examples also disappear under closer analysis. A person might claim, for example, 'I know that I have just won the lottery, but I don't believe it', or 'I know that Mary is gone, but I refuse to believe it', but utterances of this kind usually reflect a 'lack of fit' between a state of affairs and an individual's emotional state, rather than genuine disbelief that the proposition in question is true. If pressed, those who make such claims usually end up claiming that they are simply having difficulty in aligning their own subjective state with the reality of what has occurred.

The second condition is more problematic, not least because the nature of 'truth' itself continues to be the subject of long-standing controversy.

However construed, though, it would seem that truth is surely a minimum requirement for knowledge, and *false* beliefs, no matter how they are arrived at, simply cannot qualify as knowledge at all. Hence, while I could, for example, *claim* to know that triangles have five sides I would be claiming something false, since the proposition in question (i.e. that there are five-sided triangles) is itself necessarily false. Notions such as 'distorted knowledge' are therefore either misleading (if they are meant to refer to incomplete knowledge-stocks, for instance), or self-inconsistent – to the extent that a particular belief is distorted, it cannot be said to count as knowledge (that is, if the distortion referred to consists in an *erroneous* representation of 'reality', or 'the facts'). None of this implies that false beliefs never *pass* for knowledge, of course, and history is replete with examples where false beliefs of one sort or another have been incorporated into the prevailing 'knowledge-base'.

The third condition is perhaps as controversial as the second, but there are plausible grounds for arguing that particular beliefs must also be *justified* in order to count as knowledge. If I have a true belief that it is raining outside, which is based on the fact that I recently stepped on a spider, then I will (rightly) be regarded as making a false claim if I claim to know that it is raining outside. If I make such a claim while I am looking out the window, however, then my true belief that it is raining will also be regarded as a justified one, and my claim to know that it is raining will be uncontroversial. What counts as justification is not always as straightforward as in this simple example, of course, and forms of justification themselves are dependent upon what sort of belief is being considered. The central distinction here is between non-contingent and contingent propositions, where the first refers to propositions whose truth or falsity is necessary, and the second refers to propositions whose truth-value (i.e. their truth or falsity) could have been different if other counter-factual conditions had obtained. As this distinction should suggest, the routes that one might take to know each type of proposition are usually different; the non-contingent proposition that all red cars are coloured (or that there are no five-sided triangles) can be known independently of experience, for example, by anyone who understands the language and the logical connections between the concepts employed. Propositions of this sort can be known ratiocinatively, and potential knowers in this case are more or less on the same footing, whether they are anarchists, feminists, Marxists or Thatcherites. The contingent proposition that copper conducts electricity, on the other hand, can *only* be known experientially, although there are numerous experiential routes that can be taken to know it – one could discover the connection through direct experimentation, for example, or, more commonly, one could learn about the connection 'second-hand', through studying the work of others. It is worth pointing out that the routes that one might take to know this proposition are circumscribed by the structure of power itself – people with access to education are more likely to know such propositions than those without it, for example.[8] I will return to this issue below, but again simply note here that the subject matter of sociology can be construed almost entirely in terms of contingent propositions knowable experientially (e.g. 'unemployment causes crime', 'religion is functional for pre-state societies', 'government hiring practices are discriminatory', and so on).

Of course, philosophical opinion remains divided on most of the issues raised here, and some writers vehemently reject the idea that knowledge can appropriately be construed in terms such as justified true belief; Richard Rorty, for example (along with certain other philosophers of a radical 'pragmatic' bent), argues that 'knowledge is, like "truth", simply a compliment paid to the beliefs which *we* think so well justified that, for the moment, further justification is not needed' (1985: 7; his emphasis). Rorty's critics would ask, in turn, whether claims such as the latter are true or not; if they are, then some account of what their 'truth' consists in should surely be offered, and if not, then it is quite unclear why we should be convinced by them.

Traditional 'S knows that *p*' epistemological accounts are also eschewed by many feminists, since these accounts are thought to rest on some traditional 'dualisms' such as that between the knowing subject and the 'object' known, and it has also been argued recently that propositions about red cars, triangles or ceiling wax should never have been regarded as being paradigmatic forms of knowledge in the first place. Code (1993) regards 'S knows that *p*' epistemologies as being far too narrow, for example, and she argues instead for the paradigmatic status of 'knowing other people'. Nelson (1993) offers a rather different critique of traditional epistemology, claiming instead that while the latter consistently focuses on knowers as individuals, a focus on 'epistemological communities' would provide wider scope for answering questions concerning connections between gender and knowledge. Whether the forms of knowledge referred to in traditional accounts should be regarded as being paradigmatic or not, however, it should at least be clear that some of the claims already referred to concerning *knowledge in general* must be false. The claims that *all* knowledge comes from trying to change the social order, for example, or that all knowledge is political, simply ignores a whole class of knowledge types which are political neither in their production nor their content. Knowledge *can* be produced in the manner suggested in claims of this kind, of course, but an epistemology having general scope cannot be elaborated if the possible range of knowledge types is nowhere specified.

CENTRAL THEMES REVISITED

Distinctions such as those elaborated in the previous section (though contested) provide a useful grid for reconsidering some of the themes summarised above. First of all, it seems clear that some of the difficulties encountered in trying to interpret these claims arise directly from the failure of some writers to draw any distinctions at all between the truth or falsity of belief. The notion of 'truth' in sociological work on knowledge is often ignored, or referred to only implicitly; implicit references to some account of truth are contained in descriptions of false consciousness, for example, where it is claimed that individuals might retain distorted views of social reality, as a result of the intellectual imperialism of dominant groups or ruling élites. To apply the label 'false consciousness' to this limited mental state, however, is obviously to invite comparison with some 'truer' kind of consciousness. A person afflicted with false consciousness is described as not being apprised of all the facts, as it were – in other words, there must be some number of true propositions about social reality, such that if the falsely conscious person believed them, she would then no longer retain her distorted world view. In short, the falsely conscious person's stock of beliefs about social reality does not compose an accurate or veridical account of the social world, since such a person does not (yet) believe some number of true propositions about that reality, whether because her position in the social structure somehow dulls her mental capacities, or whether the dominant forms or categories render these propositions less accessible to her consciousness.

Implicit references to truth are also reflected in arguments which ascribe special status or epistemic privilege to the beliefs of particular social groups or classes (as in Eichler's references to women's 'keener insight'), although such references are also difficult to square with the notion of false consciousness, since the latter phenomenon is also felt to be linked to position in the social matrix. That is, the *dominated* person is supposed to be subject to certain hegemonic (male) forms of consciousness which disallow or discourage accurate perception of social reality, and yet inferior position is also described as allowing for the dominated person to enjoy 'keener insight' into the inner workings of society. These two views may not be logically inconsistent though, since it is arguable (as will be seen below) that certain kinds of truths will be more readily accessible to dominated groups than to those who occupy superior positions in the ruling structure. We can imagine that unemployed black people in some Western countries might respond with greater cynicism to political rhetoric about moves toward racial equality than will middle-class whites, for example, and it seems plausible to claim that such cynicism would arise from a tension between the rhetoric of equality and direct experience of disadvantage. In other words, a black person in this case may be said to have a keener insight into the fact of his or her own exploitation, than that possessed by most middle-class whites. The scope of this keener insight may be sharply circumscribed, however, and in the case of women as a dominated group, its precise nature and limitations obviously need clearer specification.[9]

As hinted above, the idea that women are in a privileged position from which to assess the truth-value of propositions about social reality, is also difficult to fit in with the view that 'male beliefs' are *determined* by interests. The use of terms such as 'inevitable' in causal accounts of male belief (as in Bernard's version, quoted above), besides leading to a fairly straightforward reductionism, suggests that men's position in society effectively and completely locks 'male thought' into particular forms mediated by interests. Men therefore lack the capacity to think in terms other than those which reflect male interests; but if women are possessed of keener insight then their beliefs must to some extent be exempt from this kind of determination by interests. If this is so, then some account needs to be given that will explain why the causal mechanism which is operative in regard to male beliefs does not extend to the beliefs of women.[10]

Identifying the interests of classes or social groups can in any case present intractable difficulties. In the case of classes, for example, judgements concerning interests invoke particular standards whose application to collectivities may be controversial, and whose selection from a slate of alternative candidates may seem arbitrary. Marx argued that the capitalist mode of production ultimately operates against working-class interests, for example, and he supported his claim by reference to conditions of alienation which obtain under capitalism. If capitalism is characterised by a cluster of impediments to creative self-expression and fully human social activity, and if radical transformation of society's economic base can rid it of the conditions which give rise to these alienating impediments, then it is in the interests of the working class to rise up and engage in revolutionary practice. Moreover, such practice is in the interests of the working class whether or not individuals in that class are even consciously *aware* of it. Under this account, then, reference to a historical process and a (possible) future social structure are thought to provide adequate grounds for denying the validity or accuracy of *individual* (i.e. personal) accounts of interest. A similar kind of discounting results from the claim that women academics have been 'co-opted' into acting as 'guardians of male theory', where this co-option is regarded as being counter to the interests of women in general. Such judgements involve the view that the individuals who occupy a certain social position are, to some extent, precluded from knowing their own real interests. Once again, the application of a particular kind of analysis here is felt to bestow the requisite credentials for correctly assessing the real interests of a specific social group or class. Needless to say, however, these kinds of analysis are not the only ones which could have been applied.

Again, many of these objections are themselves rooted in a number of philosophical distinctions which may be thought irrelevant or inapplicable by writers such as those quoted above, since some have claimed that traditional epistemology itself has amounted to nothing more than *male* epistemology. Similarly, 'truth' may be described as being simply translatable as 'male truth', and objections such as those above which make reference to these (and other) traditional categories may be judged to be question-begging. But if these categories are to be jettisoned and replaced with other, supposedly more accurate conceptions which involve reference to male domination, then some alternative conceptual stock needs to be offered which will allow us to distinguish between 'varieties of truth'. If there is 'female knowledge' or 'female truth', then surely some criteria for recognising these things can be provided, and some means offered for distinguishing them from their 'male' counterparts; and furthermore, if 'truth' is translated to read 'truth-for-men' or 'truth-for-women', then the status of assertions such as those offered by some of the writers quoted above seems unclear. That knowledge has been constructed by men for the benefit of men, for example, is asserted as being true in *some* sense or other, but the sense of truth intended is often left quite unspecified. If such propositions are felt to be true *simpliciter* (i.e. universally, or 'in general'), then some account must be given in which the place of 'male truth' is described (if the latter is felt to be of a different sort). If such propositions are thought to be true in some other, special sense (e.g. as 'true-for-women', perhaps), then some kind of relativistic thesis is being invoked which needs more detailed elaboration and defence. Instead of clarifying matters of this kind, however, some feminist researchers have chosen to allow key theoretical concepts such as knowledge or truth to be defined in whatever way particular groups of women choose to define them as based on their own experience. Practices of this kind may, of course, be quite defensible on other (e.g. ethical or political) grounds, but they rest uneasily with simultaneous efforts to convince particular audiences that other ('malestream' or non-feminist) social theorists have 'got it wrong'. It is perhaps an essential feature of theoretical critiques that they offer arguments or reasons which are meant to convince an audience that an alternative position may be preferable to its competitors, but this task is made more difficult if the available analytical tools are jettisoned as part of the critique itself.

MEN AND ROUTES TO FEMINIST KNOWLEDGE

The issue of 'double consciousness' and the centrality of women's experience to feminist knowledge production are obviously key to the question of whether routes to feminist knowledge are accessible to men, and this issue can provide a focus for drawing together some of the above discussion. As suggested in many of the above quotations (and also as confirmed in a great deal of feminist and other research), experience of social life varies widely according to an individual's position in the gender structure of power. A wealth of data concerning employment, education, participation in state activities, rates of offending and victimisation, and so on, now provide an extremely detailed picture of how males and females are differentially positioned within structures of labour and power. In addition to 'macro' data of this kind, however, there is also a rich accumulation of information yielded by feminist research concerning the micro details of gender-as-lived, and the way in which everyday routines are experienced by women. It is experience of the latter sort (although it needs to be understood against this wider background of facts about gender oppression and inequality) which has provided not only a resource for feminist politicisation and consciousness-raising, but a resource for generating knowledge about the nature and functioning of society itself. In other words, this experience carries a potential for radicalisation and social change, on the one hand (and mobilisation of this resource is usually high on the feminist agenda), and on the other hand, provides a litmus test for the accuracy and coverage of 'malestream' theories about social reality.

Men's generally more favourable location in structures of labour and power does not provide this same sort of experiential substratum, however; and while many men no doubt find current social arrangements to be oppressive or distasteful for a variety of reasons, at a *structural* level they are afforded a degree of insulation from gender oppression in everyday routines. In short, experience of gender-as-lived provides a compelling *potential* route to feminism for women, which it simply cannot supply for men in the same way.

In order to illustrate some of the latter claims, we might consider a proposition such as the following: 'Sexual harassment and violence against women in Western industrial societies is pervasive and systemic'. I take this proposition to be both true and well documented, even though a variety of forms of violence and harassment are fairly invisible in some of the recorded statistics. Claims of this sort are often received differently by women than by men, however, since it is not unusual for such claims to resonate with long-standing and even routine personal experience for women. Such claims may be received against a background of experience of being the brunt of sexist jokes in the office or lewd remarks in public, for example, being propositioned or 'touched up' on public transport, being interrupted by male colleagues during conversation, and so on. The drawing of connections across networks of experience of this kind can provide strong justification for giving assent to propositions of the sort referred to. The routes that men might take to know this proposition, however, although they are also experiential routes, usually involve incorporation of evidence provided by women's articulation of their own experience of harassment and oppression.

The notion of justification, referred to earlier, is therefore also relevant in this context. With regard to the proposition that violence against women is pervasive and systemic, for example, it would seem that justificatory schemes available to men might make their claims to know this proposition dubious. Suppose Ronald Reagan had claimed to know this proposition while he was in office, for example; presumably, some feminists would have regarded the claim with suspicion, not because they think that the proposition in question is false, but because they would have doubted that *Reagan* was justified in claiming to know that it is true (especially in the light of his other policy positions). In other words, we can imagine that Reagan in this case would have had a true belief which was not justified, and hence, was not knowledge.[11] Some feminists want to claim this of men generally, that they cannot know feminist truths (whether they call them by this name or not), because men have been (and continue to be) insulated from the kinds of experiences which generate this form of knowledge as noted above – that is, men are insulated from the kinds of experiences which are felt to make belief in true propositions about gender oppression justified. For some writers, however, one kind of experience which can lead a person to know such propositions, is the experience of trying to 'change the social order', since it is in this kind of experience that one comes up against the solidity and resilience of structures which perpetuate women's subordination. Some who adopt this view also note that one can be a woman and not know such propositions, if one has not engaged in the sort of radicalising activity which generates an awareness of the forms and resilience of gender oppression. Hence, some might argue that Margaret Thatcher cannot truly claim to know feminist 'truths', for example, and for the same reasons.

Knowledge of the social world need not be propositional, of course; women and men will both have a great deal of knowledge of social interaction at the level of practical consciousness, for instance, in the sense that they 'know how to get on' in the social world. As noted earlier, however, feminist theorising about such experience in some sense involves making it accessible in discursive form, and 'accurate descriptions' themselves can be plausibly regarded as networks of propositions about the object or phenomenon being described. In order to illustrate the latter point, we might consider Marilyn Frye's (1983) extended metaphor about lesbian existence, for example, which is discussed in Stanley and Wise (1990). Frye likens the experience of lesbianism in heterosexual society to a stage performance in which women are involved in support work backstage, while men monopolise the performance itself; lesbians make up the audience, which foregrounds the women and views the performance as background. Frye's description is obviously much more detailed than this, but it is an attempt to convey the flavour of a certain type of experience – that is, she appears to be making an effort to describe certain facts of oppression as drawn from her own experience. She is not claiming that her description is idiosyncratic and only relevant to her as an individual, or that it bears no relation to social reality in general – on the contrary, she regards her description as capturing in an accurate fashion what it is like to be a lesbian in a certain type of society, and the result appears to be a fairly effective discursive vehicle for conveying this kind of knowledge. Feminist work has bequeathed a rich repository of accounts of this general sort, which serve not just to make a range of gender experiences more accessible, but to provide a resource for critical theorising about the nature of social reality. And in this sphere, there seem to be no *a priori* grounds for denying the possibility that men could come to know 'feminist truths' suggested by such accounts, although men's engagement with such material will always depend upon such prior articulation of women's experience, as Harding suggests.

The latter point leads to consideration of another sense in which 'feminist knowledge' has sometimes been construed in the literature, however, where the notion is understood more in terms of a 'feminist vision of social reality', for want of a better phrase. The term 'vision'

seems to involve reference to much more than just a collection of propositions about social relations, etc., and it also conveys a sort of emotional
and/or political background of commitment in which such propositions
might be lodged. When viewed in this way, the question of whether men
could acquire a 'feminist vision' seems rather different, and the answer
less clear. Gelsthorpe and Morris note with regard to the latter that 'there
is a strong argument for encouraging men to consider and make use of
feminist perspectives' (1988: 235), but they go on to suggest that there is
'a distinction between feminism (and the emotional and political commitment which this entails) and feminist perspectives', and they suggest that
'Men may not be able to be truly involved in the former, but can share the
latter' (ibid.: 235). Hence, to claim that men can acquire feminist knowledge (in the sense of propositional or theoretical knowledge about social
reality) is only to claim that there are no *a priori* grounds (whether
construed in epistemological, biological or other terms) for ruling out the
possibility that men could do so. For writers such as Gelsthorpe and
Morris it is seen to be quite another thing for men to be infused by a
'feminist vision' as referred to earlier, and this brings the discussion back
to some of the issues raised in the introduction, about ownership of the
term 'feminist'.

Even though it has perhaps been plausibly demonstrated that men and
women do not occupy the same ontological or epistemological space, and
that knowledge-production and research do not begin from the same structural location for men and women, it has not been established by any of
the writers mentioned above that a 'feminist standpoint' is, in principle,
barred to men. Even in the works which argue most clearly and explicitly
for the impossibility of men being involved in feminist research or knowledge production, the arguments mustered to establish the claim seem to
reduce either to bald assertion (men cannot possible understand women's
experience because they occupy superordinate positions), or to rather
weaker claims about perceived predispositions (men do not have the
integrity to generate this kind of knowledge). Perhaps feminist opposition
to men's involvement in feminism is most persuasive when it takes the
form of a passionate stand against ceding any hard-won territory, and
against the possible abuse that men's involvement in feminism might
engender. As Kremer summarises the latter concern:

> It is women who will suffer the mistakes and false knowledges
> produced, as feminist men experiment with their processes ... If the
> issue of feminism is transcendence for women, the right to freely define
> the world through women's knowledge of it, then the consideration of

what it is for women must be left to women. And if, having made these deliberations, feminists then hand ready made projects to men, what have we achieved except the building of a bridge – again called my back – for men to walk over? (1990: 465)

If men's generally more favourable location in the gender structure of power makes their assent to feminist propositions seem dubious in many cases – since this 'location' has *experiential* implications which tend to disallow some of the more compelling routes to a feminist vision of social reality – then it might also provide grounds for the kind of scepticism Kremer expresses.

NOTES

1. These tensions are quite apparent in collections of papers such as those presented in Jardine and Smith (1987), for example; while some feminist writers appear to welcome men's positive engagement with feminism, others remain fairly sceptical about both the underlying motivations for such engagement, and about the likelihood that men's involvement will have any benefits for women. Sceptical remarks to the latter effect are in some cases supplemented by references to the very real negative impact that such involvement can have for women in terms of employment, careers, and research funding; for a thoughtful discussion of the latter sort, see Canaan and Griffin (1990).

2. There are now a number of useful bibliographies covering this area; an extensive list of references and extended bibliography is included in Stanley and Wise (1990), and also in the second edition of Stanley and Wise's *Breaking Out* (1993). For an extensive 'Bibliography of Feminist Epistemologies' see Alcoff and Potter (1993).

3. In a separate paper, Gross also makes reference to the 'sexual specificity' of feminist *knowledge*: 'in occupying the position of subject, feminists do not continue to produce knowledge as if they were men, as if knowledge were sexually indifferent' (1986: 194).

4. As detailed, for example, in Harding (1987, 1993); see also the discussions in Stanley and Wise (1993).

5. The term is Eichler's (1985: 630); for a more recent discussion of feminist epistemology and epistemic privilege, see Bar On (1993).

6. Maureen Cain (1986, 1990) also argues for the possibility that men can do feminist research or adopt a feminist standpoint; she suggests that a standpoint *for* women requires that organic links be established with women, and that 'both men and women can and have to do this' (1990: 132). A standpoint, she continues, 'is a relational concept which, so far from being essentialist, uniquely explains how a man can work from a feminist stand-

point. A standpoint is constituted by politics, theory, theoretical reflexivity and choice (of site), not biology' (ibid.: 133–4).

7. Theoretical linkages of this kind between political struggle and forms of knowledge are sometimes expressed in much more universal terms in the literature; Ramazanoglu notes that 'knowledge is intrinsically political' (1992: 210), for example, and Hearn also concludes that 'knowledge comes from attempting to change the world' (1989: 3).

8. Epistemological accounts of this kind are well-summarised in Bradley and Swartz (1979); there is a further condition which has been elaborated in response to Edmund Gettier's (1963) now famous counter-examples to the traditional characterisation of knowledge as justified true belief, referred to as the 'indefeasibility' condition. Discussion of this condition is beyond the scope of this paper, but references can be found in Bradley and Swartz (1979).

9. Bar On (1993) argues against the claim that the attribution of epistemic privilege to marginalised groups can be sustained, and she also notes some fundamental difficulties in drawing parallels between 'feminist consciousness' and the notion of proletarian consciousness as developed in Marx's work. Cain (1990) has also noted, with regard to claims about women's social position affording them a 'double vision', that one might draw the conclusion that women will lose this epistemologically privileged vision if they cease to be subordinate.

10. The notion of 'male interests' unfortunately inherits most of the difficulties of each of its constituent terms; for a more general criticism of interest-based, instrumental accounts of 'male behaviour', see Liddle (1989) on violence against women, and (1993) on child sexual abuse.

11. Of course, 'suspicion' here could also be rooted in a perception that Reagan might simply be *lying* if he made such a claim; in this case, Reagan's claim to know this proposition would be false not because the proposition is false, but because he in fact did not believe it. In terms of the 'S knows that *p*' account outlined in the above section, the first condition would not be satisfied in this case, and the third (justification) would be largely irrelevant.

REFERENCES

Alcoff, L. and Potter, E. (eds) (1993) *Feminist Epistemologies*. London: Routledge.

Bar On, B. (1993) 'Marginality and Epistemic Privilege', in L. Alcoff and E. Potter (eds) (1993) *Feminist Epistemologies*. London: Routledge.

Bernard, J. (1979) 'Afterword', in J. Sherman and E. T. Beck (eds) (1979). op. cit.

Bradley, R. and Swartz, N. (1979) *Possible Worlds: An Introduction to Logic and its Philosophy*. Oxford: Basil Blackwell.

Cain, M. (1986) 'Realism, Feminism, Methodology and Law', *International Journal of the Sociology of Law* 14: 255–67.

Cain, M. (1990) 'Realist Philosophy and Standpoint Epistemologies or Feminist Criminology as a Successor Science', in L. Gelsthorpe and A. Morris (eds) (1990). op. cit.

Canaan, J. and Griffin, C. (1990) 'The New Men's Studies: Part of the Problem or Part of the Solution?', in J. Hearn and D. Morgan (eds) (1990). op. cit.

Code, L. (1993) 'Taking Subjectivity into Account', in L. Alcoff and E. Potter (eds) (1993). op. cit.

Cook, J. and Fonow, M. (1986) 'Knowledge and Women's Interests: Issues of Epistemology and Methodology in Feminist Sociological Research', Sociological Enquiry 56: 2–29.

Eichler, M. (1985) 'And the Work Never Ends: Feminist Contributions', Canadian Review of Sociology and Anthropology 22: 619–45.

Frye, M. (1983) The Politics of Reality: Essays in Feminist Theory. New York: Crossing Press.

Gelsthorpe, L. and Morris, A. (1988) 'Feminism and Criminology in Britain', British Journal of Criminology 28: 223–40.

Gelsthorpe, L. and Morris, A. (eds) (1990) Feminist Perspectives in Criminology. Milton Keynes: Open University Press.

Gettier, E. (1963) 'Is Justified True Belief Knowledge?', Analysis 23: 121–36.

Gross, E. (1986) 'What is Feminist Theory?', in C. Pateman and E. Gross (eds) Feminist Challenges: Social and Political Theory. Sydney: Allen & Unwin.

Gross, E. (1987) 'Feminist Theory and the Challenge to Knowledges', Women's Studies International Forum 10: 475–80.

Harding, S. (ed.) (1987) Feminism and Methodology: Social Science Issues. Milton Keynes: Open University Press.

Harding, S. (1989) 'How the Women's Movement Benefits Science: Two Views', Women's Studies International Forum 12: 271–83.

Harding, S. (1993) 'Rethinking Standpoint Epistemology: "What is Strong Objectivity?"', in L. Alcoff and E. Potter (eds) op. cit.

Hartsock, N. (1987) 'The Feminist Standpoint: Developing the Ground for a Specifically Feminist Historical Materialism', in S. Harding (ed.) (1987) op. cit.

Hearn, J. (1989) 'Some Sociological Issues in Researching Men and Masculinities', University of Manchester, Working Paper No. 2. Manchester.

Hearn, J. and Morgan, D. (eds) (1990) Men, Masculinities and Social Theory. London: Unwin Hyman.

Jardine, A. and Smith, P. (eds) (1987) Men in Feminism. London: Routledge.

Kremer, B. (1990) "Learning to Say No: Keeping Feminist Research to Ourselves', Women's Studies International Forum 13: 463–7.

Liddle, A. M. (1989) 'Feminist Contributions to an Understanding of Violence against Women: Three Steps Forward, Two Steps Back', Canadian Review of Sociology and Anthropology 26: 759–75.

Liddle, A. M. (1993) 'Gender, Desire and Child Sexual Abuse: Accounting for the Male Majority', Theory, Culture and Society 10: 103–26.

MacKinnon, C. (1983) 'Feminism, Marxism, Method, and the State: Toward Feminist Jurisprudence', Signs 8: 635–58.

Millett, K. (1971) Sexual Politics. New York: Avon Books.

Nelson, L. H. (1993) 'Epistemological Communities', in L. Alcoff and E. Potter (eds) (1993) op. cit.

Ramazanoglu, C. (1992) 'On Feminist Methodology: Male Reason Versus Female Empowerment', *Sociology* 26: 207–12.

Rorty, R. (1985) 'Solidarity or Singularity?', in J. Rajchman and C. West (eds) *Post-Analytic Philosophy*. New York: Columbia University Press.

Saarinen, A. (1988) 'Feminist Research: In Search of a New Paradigm?' *Acta Sociologica* 31: 35–51.

Sherman, J. and Beck, E. T. (eds) (1979) *The Prism of Sex*. Madison: The University of Wisconsin Press.

Smith, D. E. (1975) 'An Analysis of Ideological Structures and How Women are Excluded: Considerations for Academic Women', *Canadian Review of Sociology and Anthropology* 12: 353–69.

Smith, D. E. (1979) 'A Sociology for Women', in J. Sherman and E. T. Beck (eds), (1979). op. cit.

Smith, D. E. (1987) *The Everyday World as Problematic*. Milton Keynes: Open University Press.

Stanley, L. (ed.) (1990) *Feminist Praxis*. London: Routledge.

Stanley, L. and Wise, S. (1990) 'Method, Methodology and Epistemology in Feminist Research Process', in L. Stanley (ed.) (1990). op. cit.

Stanley, L. and Wise, S. (1993) *Breaking Out Again*. London: Routledge.

11 Doing What Comes Naturally? Standpoint Epistemology, Critical Social Research and the Politics of Identity

Paul Connolly

INTRODUCTION

> We see an emphasis on research by women as absolutely fundamental to feminist research. We reject the idea that men can be feminists because we argue that what is essential to 'being feminist' is the possession of feminist consciousness, and we see feminist consciousness as rooted in the concrete, practical and everyday experiences of being treated as a woman
>
> Stanley and Wise (1983: 18)

> black researchers will be able to bring to the research the lived experiences of racism, a qualitative contribution to producing good academic 'race' research. For many white researchers in the field, researching and confronting racism is simply an academic exercise, which they can leave at their ivory towers when they close their front doors at the end of the day
>
> Brar (1992: 195)

In this chapter I want to address a fundamental concern that has derived out of my own engagement with, and commitment to, doing critical social research. It is a concern that arises most directly from feminist standpoint epistemology and, in essence, is related to the belief that men cannot do meaningful and critical research on women. Men, it is argued, neither have the experience nor the understanding of what it is like to be a woman in a patriarchal society and will, therefore, inevitably offer biased and distorted research accounts. Whilst this is an approach that is also found, albeit to a much lesser extent, within the literature on 'race' and racism, there also remains a strong emphasis within this work, as alluded to by Brar (1992) above, on 'experience'. This emphasis on, and reification of, 'experience' within anti-racist research and feminist research more generally, continues to strongly influence methodological debates. It is against this background that I have had to reassess my own role, as a white male, doing an ethnographic study of an inner-city, multi-ethnic primary school, where I have attempted to draw upon feminist and anti-racist theories in researching the construction of racialised and gendered cultural identities amongst young children (Connolly, forthcoming).

This chapter is, therefore, the product of my ongoing engagement with these issues and the ways in which I have come to define a role for myself within the tradition of critical social research against the background of these standpoint epistemological concerns. I begin by offering a brief overview of the nature of standpoint epistemology and some of the reasons for its emergence, before going on to offer a critical assessment of its underlying arguments and practical consequences. I contend that, whilst these arguments have played an important role in challenging the very claims to knowledge underlying mainstream research, and have provided the impetus for the emergence of a renewed and vibrant critical research tradition, they continue to rely upon a number of crudely essentialist notions of identity and experience which are not only theoretically inconsistent but, more importantly, have a number of adverse consequences for contemporary critical social research and political action.

INVISIBLE, PATHOLOGISED AND CONTROLLED

The origins of standpoint epistemology lie within the critical theory tradition and its recognition that *all* research is inherently political (see, for instance, Lukacs 1971; Mills 1973; Habermas 1972; Gouldner 1971).[1] What has influenced the later feminist and anti-racist methodological debates most directly is critical theory's emphasis on problematising the view of the researcher as objective and value-free. The very act of choosing something to study implies that value-judgements have been made. As Harding emphasises: 'there is no such thing as a problem without a person (or groups of them) who have a problem: a problem is always a problem *for* someone or other' (1987: 7). The dominance of academia by white, middle-class and/or male researchers has therefore often meant that their political values and commitments have come ultimately to inform large sections of social enquiry, and social science generally has historically had a marked tendency to be Eurocentric, bourgeois and patriarchal in its focus (Lawrence 1981, 1982; Joseph *et al.* 1990; Fee 1983; Mies 1983). What has counted as important, or worthy of study, has often ignored the experiences and realities of those who do not share the political commitments or perspectives of the dominant group(s). It was against this context of women being rendered invisible by social research, for instance, that feminist methodology developed with the distinct aim to do research both 'on' and 'for' women; to place their experiences on to the agenda in their own right and to use them to generate new research questions and problematics (Duelli Klein 1983; Oakley 1981; Du Bois 1983; Harding 1987).

However, not all subordinate groups have simply been rendered 'invisible'. The agenda for anti-racist researchers has been less concerned with increasing the visibility of black people and more with challenging the distorted and pathological depictions of the black community.[2] For many anti-racist writers, the main problem relating to mainstream research is the problematic status it has assigned to the black community and the sense in which their mere presence, coupled together with 'deviation' from the dominant 'norm', has been regarded as a threat to social cohesion and control. A significant proportion of social research has therefore excessively focused upon black people and the working class more generally (Bourne and Sivanandan 1980; Gilroy 1980; Lawrence 1981, 1982). Similarly, where women do provide the focus of research, it is within an agenda set by, and developed for, the dominant groups in society – from their perspective (Smith 1987; Fee 1983). As Harding contends, for instance: 'the questions about women that men have wanted answered have all too often arisen from desires to pacify, control, exploit, or manipulate women' (1987: 8). The questions asked, and the differing realities and perspectives within which they are framed between dominant and oppressed groups, are thus often contradictory, if not diametrically opposed. As Harding goes on to argue:

> While employers have often commissioned studies of how to make workers happy with less power and pay, workers have rarely been in a position to undertake or commission studies of anything at all, let alone how to make employers happy with less power and profit. Similarly, psychiatrists have endlessly studied what they regard as women's peculiar mental and behavioural characteristics, but women have only recently begun to study the bizarre mental and behavioural characteristics of psychiatrists (1987: 8).

Moreover, many feminist and anti-racist writers have argued that not only are the research questions asked set firmly within the dominant groups' needs to subordinate and control, but the data collected from the studies themselves are validated against those same dominant groups' own characteristics and world-view. This ability of certain groups both to set the agenda for research methodology, and also to provide the epistemological criteria against which knowledge is to be validated, can be illustrated in the area of research on 'race'. As a number of academics writing in the earlier 1980s have argued, what had characterised a large section of mainstream research on 'race' relations had been a focus on the black community as the 'problem' rather than white racism (Bourne and Sivanandan 1980; Lawrence 1981, 1982; Gilroy 1980; Parmar 1981). Thus, rather than offering explanations of racial inequality in terms of the racist nature and structure of the social system, researchers tended to direct their focus, instead, upon the black community and offered explanations, via comparison with the white middle-class 'norm', in terms of their 'deviant' family structures and 'ways of life' (Troyna 1988). Young black people, for instance, were thus seen as being 'caught between two cultures' – the freedom of the 'host' society and the traditional, authoritarian nature of their parents' culture.[3] It was, therefore, not surprising that, when confronted with the 'freedoms' that British society offered, they would either find it hard to cope or use the space created by them to rebel against their authoritarian family circumstances at home (Lawrence 1982).

Racism had, therefore, been either largely ignored or redefined in such a way as to lose sight of the fundamental issue of power and consequently been replaced by a liberal, equal opportunities paradigm that left unquestioned the existing social system and was intent, instead, on simply 'integrating' black people more fully into it (Bourne and Sivanandan 1980; Gilroy 1980). Within this context, where social research was perceived as not only fundamentally distorting black people's experiences and reality, but also as gathering and collating information in order to maintain and reinforce their subordination, it was not surprising to find that some academics, such as Robin Jenkins (1971), 'warned blacks not to submit themselves to the scrutiny of white researchers who, in effect, act as spies for the government. They should, he said, be told to "fuck off"' (Bourne and Sivanandan 1980: 338).

'POLITICISING' THE RESEARCH PROCESS

It is this systematic de-politicisation of the research process that enabled powerful groups to 'universalise' their own world-view (Ben-Tovim *et al.*

1986; Duelli Klein 1983; Mies 1983; Smith 1987). The requirement that social research be 'objective' and 'value-free' has had the effect of shifting the spotlight away from the researchers themselves and their own subjective and value-laden perspectives and has focused it, instead, exclusively upon the adequacy and accuracy of the methods used by the researcher; from the 'context of discovery', as Harding terms it, to the 'context of justification' (1987: 7). The central, agenda-setting role of researchers in their ability to decide what is, and is not, worthy of research has thus been largely ignored and defined away as an issue. Concepts such as 'objectivity' and 'value-neutrality' provided the necessary ideological apparatus to ensure that not only is such a patriarchal, bourgeois and racist agenda unchallengeable but also, if an alternative perspective was offered – whether anti-racist or feminist, for instance – then it could be simply dismissed as politically biased, subjective and thus, ultimately, unscientific.

If all research is inherently political by nature then, it has been argued, this needs to be fully acknowledged by researchers who should place their own subjectivity and value assumptions, as Harding contends, in the 'same critical plane as the overt subject matter' so as to recover the 'entire research process for scrutiny in the results of the research' (1987: 9). Questions about what to research need to be problematised and critically assessed before dealing with how to go about the research and what methods to use (Duelli Klein 1983). Most fundamentally there is a need, it was argued, for the researcher to be critically reflex, to locate their own experiences and concerns centrally within the research problematic and to assess the implications of these in the development of the methodology they employ (see Connolly 1992).

STANDPOINT EPISTEMOLOGY AND THE POLITICS OF IDENTITY

A number of writers within the feminist standpoint tradition have argued that once it is accepted that all research is a reflection of the researcher's own value-judgements and political commitments, then there is a need to ensure that such commitments relate, in some fundamental way, to the values and politics of the oppressed groups themselves (Mies 1987; Smith 1987; Harding 1987; Harstock 1987). The central thread to such work is the need to place women's experiences centre-stage within the research process, using them both to generate research questions and against which to validate the data gathered and theories developed. It is impossible to eliminate the male-dominated or androcentric biases from social research simply by the use of scientific methods, especially when, as Harding maintains, 'androcentrism arrives in the inquiry process through the identification and definition of research problems' (1987: 184). The only way forward in such circumstances is to root this process of identification and definition in women's experiences. Moreover, it is argued that this privileging of women's experiences over men's should not be regarded as a move towards relativism. Men's and women's experiences do not provide equal bases for developing scientific problems. This is because the activities of men, as Harding explains, 'shape the horizons of their knowledge and support interests in ignorance of the misery generated by the domination of women' (1987: 186). For women, however, this has meant that they develop a 'double consciousness' (Du Bois 1983: 111); not only are they acutely aware of their own experiences of subordination but they are also, by their location, aware of the complex processes by which they are dominated (Mies 1983). The use of women's experiences thus provides a more full, less partial and biased, basis from which to both raise research problems and validate the knowledge that is consequently produced.

Very similar arguments privileging the experiences and epistemological standpoint of black people have also been put forward by writers within the anti-racist tradition (Parmar 1981; Lawrence 1981, 1982; Brar 1992). However, within this it is important to point to the difference of emphasis between feminist and anti-racist methodology. It is a difference that can be understood in the different ways in which women and black people have been treated within the research process: the former, as I have noted, largely being rendered invisible, the latter being rendered problematic. As Neal (1994) points out, whilst anti-racist writers have therefore been largely concerned with challenging the dominant agenda of 'race' research, feminist writers have been more concerned with rendering women visible – with developing a research programme both on and for women. Not surprisingly, therefore, whilst anti-racists have been raising questions more about *what is* being researched and *why*, a number of feminist writers have been more concerned with *who* should be doing the research. Consequently, a number of feminist writers have argued that, considering the wide gulf that exists between women and men in terms of their everyday life experiences, then men are simply unable to do meaningful research in the area of gender since they do not have the necessary experiences and perceptions of reality from which either to ask the right questions or to interpret the data that are collected in a meaningful way (Stanley and Wise 1983; Mies 1983; Kremer 1990).

The importance of this work in challenging the very claims to knowledge that academia has used to subordinate certain groups and their differing realities cannot be underestimated. Indeed, the fact that they have raised a number of central epistemological questions has, in turn, made essays like this one possible. However, such arguments raise a number of important and fundamental problems. The first relates to the simple division between women and men and the essentialist notion of women's shared experience. The problems emerging from this can be illustrated through the use of a rather simple question as an example: who would be best able to research black women – a white woman or a black man? Presumably Stanley and Wise (1983), for instance, would opt for the white woman because of their shared experiences *as women*; but surely the black woman's experiences may be influenced equally, if not more so (Davis 1981; Hooks 1982; Carby 1982), by racism and, thus, the black male researcher has an equal, if not greater, ability to gain a more substantial understanding of her experiences.

Admittedly there are problems with this example if taken much further. Surely, it could be argued, all this will depend upon what the researcher is focusing on? Thus, if her/his focus is upon how the black woman is experiencing the realities of bringing up two pre-school children then, it could be argued, the white woman is better placed to understand this. However, the research participant's experiences as a *black* mother will obviously be racialised both in terms of the differing ways that the state – whether in terms of claiming the benefits she is entitled to, contact with midwife, health visitors, social workers and so on – deals with her and also, at another level, how the local community treats her and her children. It may well be the case, for instance, that she is afraid to let her children play outside on their own in case they are racially attacked; this was certainly a reality for some of the (mostly Asian) mothers in my own research.

The white woman's prior insight and shared experiences can, therefore, only ever be partial. The logical conclusion left within this agenda is that a black woman would obviously be the best person to do the research (Kremer 1990). The problems with this, however, are: first, on a practical level, the goal of 'symmetry' between researcher and participants will, by default, render large areas of research impossible – including my own. Within the school where my own research is based there are a number of oppressed groups: obviously the working-class children themselves but, within this, their experiences are inherently contradictory being fundamentally mediated, as they are, by issues of gender and 'race'; and there are then the teachers themselves who occupy a contradictory position also

– being both oppressors *as teachers*, and oppressed *as workers, as women* etc. (Ball 1991). If, in accepting the agenda, it is felt that the ability to gain an insight into the oppressive structures of the school and thus 'ask the right questions' is linked simply to the researcher's physical identity then no researcher would be able to do this adequately and/or comprehensively. How could black women researchers, for instance, understand the experiences of white working-class boys or of white teachers (male and female)?

One answer to this is that different researchers should adopt different roles. As regards 'race', white researchers have been encouraged to study the structures of white racism rather than the black community (Bourne and Sivanandan 1980; Gilroy 1980; Lawrence 1981, 1982; Brar 1992). However, I would maintain that it is virtually impossible to understand racism and the nature of its structures and processes without acknowledging the active role that black people have played in challenging and resisting them. As Back and Solomos have argued:

> for researchers to speak rhetorically about their mission to study white racism and institutions contains a subtle sleight of hand. While superficially this seems more credible other important issues emerge. On one occasion Les Back offered an account of our 'studying the speaking position of the powerful' to a long established black activist. He reminded Les that to do so would be comparable to studying slavery by only speaking to the slave masters. It was within this kind of context that the rhetoric of our position broke down (1992: 13, quoted in Neal 1994: 11).

This convenient 'sleight of hand' is also to be found in the work of Hearn (1987) and Hearn and Morgan (1990), who have argued that men should focus on masculinity and, whilst they should support and ensure that their work is informed by feminist theory, they are neither in a position to, nor should, be critical of, or engage with, feminist theory. In a recent book review, for instance, Hearn is critical of a male author writing about feminism and points to: 'a few personal-political-theoretical problems ... to say the least, for a man writing in relation to feminism' (1994: 633). This general approach, however, raises more problems than it solves. First, it makes little sense to study masculinity without reference to women. Masculinity, by definition, is a binary concept intelligible only in relation to femininity. Central to masculine identities, therefore, is the construction of what it means to be feminine and the ways in which men should relate to women. Masculine identities and cultural forms are, therefore, determined as much by the actions of women in struggling against and actively resisting the roles prescribed for them as it is by the actions of men. My own study of infant children, for instance, is littered with examples of boys having to re-negotiate and transform their masculine identities as a result of the subversive actions and strategies of the girls. To avoid any focus on women in the study of men and masculinities is to construct a wholly distorted and demeaning view of women generally as passively and uncritically accepting definitions of masculine and feminine roles.

Second, there is an inherent contradiction within the logic that men should support feminist theory and ensure it informs their work whilst not critically engaging with it. Are Hearn and Morgan really arguing that all the work on men and masculinities can contribute nothing to feminist theory? More importantly, what do they mean by 'feminist theory'? Feminism is a term that covers a wide range of competing and, at times incompatible, critical thought. To 'support feminist theory' therefore requires that a value-judgement is made as to which strand of feminist thought is to be supported. This in turn, however, demands a critical engagement with feminism. Furthermore, can Hearn and Morgan seriously maintain that black men, for instance, should not be able to comment on certain strands of feminist theory even if they believe it is racist?

At the heart of all these problems, therefore, are the essentialist notions of men's and women's experiences and the inability to recognise the ways in which gender is experienced through the complex articulation of class, 'race', ethnicity, age, sexuality and disability. A woman's 'experience' and political commitments cannot simply be read off from her sex. Not only are the broad and competing strands of feminist theories a testimony to this, but also the female (and, for that matter black) writers who have published work which has reproduced sexist (and racist) ideas (for a critical discussion of some of this work see Ball 1991; Brar 1992; Harding 1987).

SO WHAT COUNTS AS 'EXPERIENCE'?

There are, therefore, a number of inherent problems not only with the advocacy of symmetry within the research process as discussed above, but also, more fundamentally, with attempts to delineate exactly what it is that counts as the 'experience' by which research questions are generated and data are validated. In this sense a number of central and practical problems are posed for the whole standpoint epistemological approach. Not only do experiences vary from one woman to the next and their experiences of patriarchy thus being only ever partial, but they are quite possibly also seriously distorted in terms of the constraining and inhibiting effects of dominant hegemonic ideas and values.

It is in this sense that other feminist writers advocating a standpoint epistemology argue that there needs to be a more focused and systematic understanding of what counts as 'experience', and have moved towards the anti-racist focus on the *what* and *why* of research rather than simply the *who*. For such writers it is the experience gained through political struggle that counts, since it is through such collective struggles that individuals are able to translate their own experiences into a more comprehensive understanding through the ability to share, and generalise from, other people's diverse experiences (see Harding 1987, for instance). Such an approach does, at the very least, offer a way out of some of the more constraining aspects of the essentialism within the 'politics of identity' outlined above. The most important of these is the way in which it successfully moves away from a focus upon the need for 'symmetry' and towards the political commitment of the researcher. It creates the space where men can do critical research on gender, conditional not upon their physical appearance but their ability to identify with, and get involved in, political struggle.

However, such an approach ultimately suffers from the same problems outlined earlier in terms of what exactly, within this, counts as 'experience'. There are a number of diverse and often disparate political struggles that each claim the term 'feminism': liberal, socialist, radical and black feminism to name a few. The same is also true with regards to 'race' with black groups ranging, in their politics, from an equal opportunities paradigm to black militancy and black separatism. The problem we are left with then, as before, is which political struggles to use, within the standpoint tradition, as a basis from which to generate research questions and validate the data? Given the number and range of perspectives to choose from, it would appear that virtually any political position that the researcher wishes to adopt can be validated.

Moreover, all political struggles need to be regarded as historically specific; they are obviously a response to specific circumstances and should thus, in this sense, be seen as only ever partial, and often contradictory, in the practical insights they offer. Thus, anti-racism, for instance, is never simply an abstract, removed struggle in itself, but is always focused and specific, ranging from campaigns against racist murders or deportation cases to campaigns for equal opportunities in employment or equality of treatment for black children in schools. It is in this respect that anti-racism as a broader project is only ever the sum of these constituent parts and should be seen, ultimately, as an evolving struggle which ideally (if not always in practice) learns from the specific struggles that went before, and develops a more coherent ideological and strategic framework from which to apply to existing and future struggles. It is this specificity of the various struggles involved, however, that often mitigates against broader links being made and lessons learned – not only from past anti-racist struggles, but also from struggles related to gender and class – and which, ultimately, renders such specific struggles often limited, if not contradictory. As a result, the experiences gained from such political struggles are not always the most comprehensive and logically coherent basis against which truth claims (with relation to the requirements of a standpoint epistemology) can be made.

SO WHAT ARE WE LEFT WITH?

It should be apparent from the foregoing discussion that standpoint epistemology has played a central role in challenging the value-neutrality of social research and its associated claims to rationality and truth. In many ways it was an essential and inevitable consequence of the exclusionary and distorted nature of mainstream social research that, at the time, critical researchers within the feminist and anti-racist tradition posited an alternative reality and experience to challenge the dominant and pre-existing agenda. The problem now is not so much that there is an absence of feminist and anti-racist writing but how people like myself relate to this growing body of critical knowledge. In this chapter I have illustrated some of the more central problems inherent in continuing to subscribe to some form of standpoint epistemology and how attempts to negotiate a role for men and/or white researchers within this inevitably raise more problems than they solve. To argue that white people should focus exclusively on white institutions and men on masculinity is ultimately no more than a convenient avoidance of addressing the more fundamental problems underlying the standpoint approach.

There is no doubt that a researcher's social identity will affect the way in which people relate to her or him in the field. On a practical level, therefore, it is no more than a simple truism that certain social settings are more accessible to certain researchers than others. The calls by writers such as Brar (1992), for instance, for white people to focus on white institutions where they have more likelihood of gaining access than black people and, conversely and for similar reasons, for black people to focus on the black community makes a certain amount of sense. Similarly Jenkins (1983), in his study of working-class youth in Belfast, wrote of the problems he had in 'accessing' female youth culture with its emphasis on personal and private small friendship groups. This, however, is not the issue at hand. The issue is not about the practical difficulties concerning gaining access faced by researchers but whether men and/or white people should engage in critical social research in the areas of gender and 'race' at all. Considering that we are all conscious beings capable of empathy and critical reflexivity then we are all able to, or at least have the potential to be able to, learn from and incorporate the experiences and position of others in our own work. Against the background of the discussion above concerning the ability to define and delineate what exactly counts as experience, then this leads on to the simple conclusion that it is far more important to be concerned with what a researcher is doing and why than with who they are. In essence, it is their actions rather than social identity that is of most importance.

This shift in focus raises a number of other questions that are beyond the scope of this chapter but will also, ultimately, need to be addressed. For a focus on the actions of researchers and, specifically, on encouraging them to think about what they are researching and why, inevitably requires an engagement with feminist and anti-racist theories. However, as pointed out earlier, this will necessarily involve making value-judgements, as male researchers, for instance, choose between a vast and rich array of competing feminist theories in order to inform and influence their own work. Presumably the work they do, in taking on board and contributing to certain feminist perspectives, should then be of use in developing and reassessing those perspectives. If this is successful, then the question must be asked concerning exactly what is the difference between this and feminist research other than that it has been conducted by a man. And, of course, when this is asked we are ultimately left with the question about whether, if men can do feminist research, then what is it that prevents them from being called 'feminists'?

CONCLUSIONS

This chapter has had a very limited focus. It has derived from the practical and theoretical problems I have faced, as a white male researcher, wishing to conduct critical social research in the area of 'race' and gender. It has been concerned with addressing the fundamental problem posed by those within the standpoint epistemological tradition concerning the ability of white/male researchers to do meaningful research on 'race'/gender. In doing so I have attempted to make sense of my own research in terms of engaging with the feminist and anti-racist literature and creating a role for myself within the tradition of critical social research. In highlighting the inherent problems of trying to define and delineate the concept of 'experience', which lies at the heart of the standpoint approach, I have argued that, in the last analysis, it is not a person's social identity that counts but what they actually do. I fully accept that this merely provides the starting point of any analysis of the ethics and politics of research and leaves a whole host of questions concerning my own conduct within the field, the relationships developed with those researched, the collection and interpretation of the data and the dissemination of my findings, amongst others, unanswered. These are issues explored in detail elsewhere (Connolly, forthcoming). However, as standpoint epistemology still enjoys an influential hold on methodological debates concerning critical social research, then the question of who should be able to do the research is an important one that needs to be addressed.

Acknowledgements

I would like to thank a number of people who have provided some very useful comments on earlier drafts of this chapter: Simon Hallsworth, Martyn Hammersley, Máirtín Mac an Ghaill, Julia O'Connell-Davidson, Barry Troyna, Sallie Westwood and Karen Winter. Earlier versions of this essay have also been presented at a Staff Seminar in the Sociology Department, Leicester University, and at the BSA Annual Conference (Connolly 1993). I would like to thank all those present for their valuable and insightful comments.

NOTES

1. See Harvey (1990) and Fay (1987) for useful overviews of this tradition.
2. 'Black' here refers to people of Asian and/or African/Caribbean descent.
3. Parmar (1981) illustrates this tendency to pathologise black communities most graphically when looking at what she describes as the 'plethora of ethnographies' which tried to situate the experiences of Asian youth generally, and Asian girls particularly, within this culturalist paradigm. The titles, listed by Parmar, of some of the main studies are indicative: 'The Half-Way Generation ... The Second Generation – Punjabi or English? ... Culture, Conflict and Young Asians in Britain ... In Search of Identity ... Daughters of Tradition: Adolescent Asian Girls and Their Accommodation To Life In British Society' (1981: 24–5).

REFERENCES

Back, L. and Solomos, J. (1992) 'Doing Research, Writing Politics: The Dilemmas of Political Intervention in Research on Racism'. Paper presented to the *Politics of Racism Workshop*, Birbeck College, University of London.

Ball, W. (1991) 'The Ethics and Politics of Doing Antiracist Research in Education: Key Debates and Dilemmas', *European Journal of Intercultural Studies* 2: 35–49.

Ben-Tovim, G., Gabriel, J., Law, I. and Stredder, K. (1986) *The Local Politics of Race*. London: Macmillan.

Bourne, J. and Sivanandan, A. (1980) 'Cheerleaders and Ombudsmen: The Sociology of Race Relations in Britain', *Race and Class* 21: 331–52.

Brar, H. S. (1992) 'Unasked Questions, Impossible Answers: The Ethical Problems of Researching Race and Education', in M. Leicester and M. Taylor (eds) *Ethics, Ethnicity and Education*. London: Kogan Page.

Carby, H. (1982) 'White Woman Listen! Black Feminism and the Boundaries of Sisterhood', in CCCS, *The Empire Strikes Back: Race and Racism in 70s Britain*. London: Hutchinson.

Connolly, P. (1992) 'Playing It by the Rules: The Politics of Research in "Race" and Education', *British Educational Research Journal* 18: 133–48.

Connolly, P. (1993) 'Doing Feminist and Anti-racist Research as a White Male – A Contradiction in Terms?' Paper presented to British Sociological Association Annual Conference, 5–8 April, University of Essex.

Connolly, P. (forthcoming) *Negotiating Childhood: Racialised Identities, Cultural Forms and Young Children*, Unpublished Thesis, University of Leicester.

Davis, A. (1981) *Women, Race and Class*. London: The Women's Press.

Du Bois, B. (1983) 'Passionate Scholarship: Notes on Values, Knowing and Method in Feminist Social Science', in G. Bowles and R. Duelli-Klein (eds) *Theories of Women's Studies*. London: Routledge & Kegan Paul.

Duelli-Klein, R. (1983) 'How to Do What We Want to Do: Thoughts about Feminist Methodology', in G. Bowles and R. Duelli-Klein (eds) *Theories of Women's Studies*. London: Routledge & Kegan Paul.

Fay, B. (1987) *Critical Social Science: Liberation and its Limits*. London: Allen & Unwin.

Fee, E. (1983) 'Women's Nature and Scientific Objectivity', in M. Lowe and R. Hubbard (eds) *Woman's Nature: Rationalizations of Inequality*. Oxford: Pergamon Press.

Gilroy, P. (1980) 'Managing the "Underclass": A Further Note on the Sociology of Race Relations in Britain', *Race and Class* 22: 47–62.

Habermas, J. (1972) *Knowledge and Human Interests*. London: Heinemann.

Harding, S. (ed.) (1987) *Feminism and Methodology: Social Science Issues*. Milton Keynes: Open University Press.

Harstock, N. (1987) 'The Feminist Standpoint: Developing the Ground for a Specially Feminist Historical Materialism', in S. Harding (ed.) *Feminism and Methodology*. Milton Keynes: Open University Press.

Harvey, L. (1990) *Critical Social Research*. London: Unwin Hyman.

Hearn, J. (1987) *The Gender of Oppression: Men, Masculinity and the Critique of Marxism*. Brighton: Wheatsheaf.

Hearn, J. (1994) Review of J. W. Messerschmidt 'Masculinities and Crime', *Sociology* 28: 632–4.

Hearn, J. and Morgan, D. (eds) (1990) *Men, Masculinities and Social Theory*. London: Unwin Hyman.

Hooks, B. (1982) *Ain't I A Woman? Black Women and Feminism*. London: Pluto Press.

Jenkins, R. (1971) 'The Production of Knowledge in the Institute of Race Relations'. Paper presented to the British Sociological Association Annual Conference.

Jenkins, R. (1983) *Lads, Citizens and Ordinary Kids: Working-Class Youth Lifestyles in Belfast*. London: Routledge & Kegan Paul.

Joseph, G., Reddy V. and Searle-Chatterjee, M. (1990) 'Eurocentrism in the Social Sciences', *Race and Class* 31: 1–26.

Kremer, B. (1990) 'Learning to Say No: Keeping Feminist Research for Ourselves', *Women's Studies International Forum* 13: 463–7.

Lawrence, E. (1981) 'White Sociology, Black Struggle', *Multiracial Education* 9: 3–17.

Lawrence, E. (1982) 'In the Abundance of Water the Fool is Thirsty: Sociology and Black "Pathology"', in CCCS, *The Empire Strikes Back: Race and Racism in 70s Britain*. London: Hutchinson.

Lukács, G. (1971) [1923] *History and Class Consciousness: Studies in Marxist Dialectics*. London: Merlin.

Mies, M. (1983) 'Towards a Methodology for Feminist Research', in G. Bowles and R. Duelli Klein (eds) *Theories of Women's Studies*. London: Routledge & Kegan Paul.

Mills, C. W. (1973) [1959] *The Sociological Imagination*. Harmondsworth: Penguin.

Neal, S. (1994) 'Researching Powerful People from Feminist and Anti-racist Perspectives: A Note on Marginality, Gender and Collusion', Paper presented to British Sociological Association Annual Conference, University of Central Lancashire.

Oakley, A. (1981) 'Interviewing Women: A Contradiction in Terms', in H. Roberts (ed.) *Doing Feminist Research*. London: Routledge.

Parmar, P. (1981) 'Young Asian Women: A Critique of the Pathological Approach', *Multiracial Education* 9: 19–29.

Smith, D. E. (1987) 'Women's Perspective as a Radical Critique of Sociology', in S. Harding (ed.) *Feminism and Methodology*. Milton Keynes: The Open University Press.

Stanley, L. and Wise, S. (1983) *Breaking Out: Feminist Consciousness and Feminist Research*. London: Routledge & Kegan Paul.

Troyna, B. (1988) 'Paradigm Regained: A Critique of "Cultural Deficit" Perspectives in Contemporary Educational Research', *Comparative Education* 24: 273–83.

Index